UNEARTHLY
POWERS

UNEARTHLY POWERS

A Christian's Handbook on Primal and Folk Religions

DAVID BURNETT

A Division of Thomas Nelson Publishers
Nashville

This edition issued by special arrangement with Monarch Publications, 1 St. Anne's Road, Eastbourne, East Sussex, BN21 3UN, England. Original title: UNEARTHLY POWERS.

Published in Nashville, Tennessee, by Oliver-Nelson Books, a division of Thomas Nelson, Inc., Publishers, and distributed in Canada by Lawson Falle, Ltd., Cambridge, Ontario.

The illustration in chapter 11 appears by courtesy of the trustees of the British Museum.

The Bible version used in this publication is the HOLY BIBLE: NEW INTERNATIONAL VERSION. Copyright © 1973, 1978, 1984 by the International Bible Society. Used by permission of Zondervan Bible Publishers.

Printed in the United States of America.

Library of Congress Cataloging-in-Publication Data

Burnett, David, 1943–
    Unearthly powers / David Burnett.
        p.   cm.
    Includes bibliographical references and indexes.
    ISBN 0-8407-9612-9
    1. Christianity and other religions—Primitive.   2. Religion, Primitive.   3. Missions—Theory.   I. Title.
    BR128.P75B87   1992
    261.2—dc20   91-35684
                                                                              CIP

1 2 3 4 5 6 — 97 96 95 94 93 92

Contents

Foreword

As a teacher of world religions at London Bible College, I welcome most warmly this book on primal religions. Until now we have lacked a general textbook. The Lion Handbook helpfully considers no less than twelve different forms of animism from widely scattered groups. John V. Taylor's *The Primal Vision* (SCM, 1963) was most helpful on the primal religions of Africa. But we have needed something comprehensive that at the same time analyzed the basic elements common within many different cultures. Let me then make the following comments.

First, the usefulness of this volume is not limited to those readers actually working among tribal groups where primal religions are practiced. Almost universally we find systems of primal belief masquerading as folk Islam, folk Buddhism, and sometimes even, I am afraid, folk Christianity.

Second, the biblical approach adopted here is much more helpful than a scornful rejection of such primal religion as superstition, seen from the standpoint of the Western scientific worldview. From the opening section where the writer describes his doubts and puzzlement when the rainmaking ceremonies actually produced rain, we are forced to try to think biblically, realizing that Elijah was also involved in praying for rain. We may have scarcely given a thought to relevant biblical material like the divining cup that Joseph hid in his brothers' sack (Gen. 44:5, 15); the testing of the unfaithful wife (Num. 5:16–28); or the divining of omens by the king of Babylon (Ezek. 21:21–23). We shall find material in this book that may make us better expositors of Scripture.

Third, so many presentations of other religions given in the popular media are limited to a description of the customs, festivals, and other external mores that are *seen* by the spectator. What we really need to have explained to us are the belief system and the worldview that lie behind the outward trappings. Understanding of the beliefs of others is essential.

Fourth, many of us as Christians are extremely vague about our own beliefs. We probably have never even considered whether there is such a thing as a biblical doctrine of ancestors, for example. (I believe there is, and that this should be positively taught in the appropriate cultural context. We should not be merely scornful and negative about indigenous views.) Even when we have thought about, say, the nature of human personality in biblical teaching, we may be confused about what we believe ourselves and not very helpful to those who believe in "multiple personality." Many Christians hang on to a Greek tripartite view of human personality without realizing that the Bible far more often uses a Hebrew view. Certainly many embrace what the late Professor Donald MacKay amusingly referred to as "ejector seat theology," in which the human "soul" is imagined to shoot out from the human body crashing to its death! And if that *is* what you believe, then as well as reading this book, you had better read some more Christian doctrine, too!

Fifth, we shall realize that it may sometimes be our own "civilized" view that is simplistic rather than the indigenous attitude, as in the priceless exchange between the tribesman and the white doctor described on page 109:

TRIBESMAN: This man is sick because someone worked sorcery against him.
WHITE DOCTOR: This man is sick from malaria because he was bitten by an infected mosquito!
TRIBESMAN: Yes, he was bitten by a mosquito—but *who* sent the mosquito?

Finally, all this ought to convince us that it is just not true that any thick, muscular Christian is suitable for work among those we regard as "primitive" and "simple" tribesmen: such work demands not only linguistic ability but a profound theological and biblical understanding, not to mention an ability to handle some fairly sophisticated philosophy!

Michael Griffiths

Preface

Strange customs, wild exotic dances, and primitive idols are some of the images that tend to come to the minds of Europeans when one speaks of tribal religions. These are often regarded as "primitive" and worthy only of scorn. However, this attitude fails to appreciate the person and character of those who practice primal religions and consequently builds a barrier to the meaningful communication of the gospel.

The discovery of the sea routes around Africa and Latin America by the Europeans was to prove one of the most important events in world history. This not only encouraged world trade, but it brought the European Christianized cultures in contact with numerous tribal societies. At first, during the period of slave trading, the Europeans questioned whether black people even had souls. However, with the growing missionary movement of the eighteenth and nineteenth centuries, Europeans began to realize that tribal people were indeed human beings like themselves. They regarded them as people who had been left behind in the process of human evolution and so were more like the remains of primitive human societies. Europeans regarded their own culture as inherently superior, and many, including missionaries, perceived their task to be one of civilizing the "black man" and freeing him from his "pagan" and "primitive" ways.

Subsequently, as both anthropologists and missionaries have studied tribal societies in greater detail, they have come to appreciate that these societies are not simple or childish, but complex and mature. At the same time missionaries have witnessed an amazing response to the gospel by such people. Literally thousands of people from these ethnic groups have

9

become Christian, at least in name. With the numbers of such primal societies decreasing in proportion to the total world population, it may seem right to ask whether it is even necessary to study the religion of what may seem to be a disappearing age.

In answer to this it is necessary to state first that many hundreds of ethnic groups still remain outside the influence of the church. If one is to accept the Great Commission of our Lord with any seriousness, it becomes obvious that the message of the gospel should be taken to every such group. How this message should be communicated becomes a primary question. The initial stage in answering this is to gain a more comprehensive understanding of and insight into the people themselves.

The second reason why this study needs to be made is that many of those peoples who have become Christian have often faced real difficulties in adapting to their new way of life. We need to ask what lessons can be learned from the religions of primal societies that will help today's missionary communicate the gospel more effectively to such people. New religious movements that are occurring within Christianized societies raise many new and challenging questions. It seems as though the Western form of Christianity has not met the felt-needs of the primal peoples, and in order to do so adequately, it is necessary to consider more closely the traditional religions of these people. Perhaps in doing so we may even come to appreciate some things concerning our own culture and worldview that will help us to a more biblical Christianity.

Third, many tribal peoples are being converted and absorbed into the major world religions. However, long-held beliefs do not merely disappear overnight but often become incorporated within the newly adopted religion. The study of primal religions enables one to perceive the background from which today's Muslim, Hindu, Buddhist, or even Christian has come. It may even provide clues to why a particular primal society chose Islam, for example, rather than Christianity and reveal some of the issues these people are facing as they confront the modern world. In this current text, the presence of traditional beliefs within the general context of a world religion will be called "folk religion" to distinguish it from beliefs that are not distinct major world religions.

Fourth, the study of primal religions allows one to better

understand "folk Christianity," which is still very much part of Western society. Father Christmas, fairies, horoscopes, and unlucky numbers are all part of the heritage of European culture. Added to this have been the resurgence of witchcraft and occult practices and numerous new religious movements. How is it that this neo-paganism is growing in what were the heartlands of Christianity?

This book aims not to provide a discussion of the latest anthropological theories but to help the ordinary missionary, evangelist, and Christian to understand more about the nature of primal religions. One of the aims is to show that there is a definite pattern of logic within the complexity of rituals and symbols, and that these make sense to the people themselves. This is what the anthropologist would call "functionalism" and has been an accepted part of anthropology, in one form or another, from the time of Malinowski.[1]

One of the basic principles of anthropology is a recognition that cultures are integrated, and that to remove one item for study in isolation can lead to a gross misunderstanding of its true meaning in context. For this reason anthropologists today have preferred to study just one society and draw inferences from this that could apply more widely. However, in this text another form of cross-cultural comparison has been used that considers the central questions asked by a people; the arrangement of all the data here reflects the answers obtained. Thus the material has been grouped in terms of meaning and function rather than merely about the cultural forms. Nevertheless, I should like to stress the danger of taking random items from any culture, and it is done here only to serve to illustrate common themes and to help the reader perceive similar features in other societies. For this reason I have to a large extent used examples of which I have firsthand experience.

Note

1. Edmund Leach, *Social Anthropology* (Fontana: London, 1982), p. 232.

1

Stranger than Fiction

I carefully maneuvered the Land Rover between the sharp thorn bushes and drove to the outskirts of the village. As I jumped out of the cab the old headman, named Lotieng, came to greet me with a warm smile. From his colorful headgear I could see that today was to be a special day. Lotieng held out his hand and gave me a warm African handshake. "Welcome," he said, "it is good that you have come to visit us." My interpreter quickly started talking with the people and turned to me with great excitement. "We have come on a good day," he said. "Today they are going to have a rainmaking ceremony. The headman wants to know, have you brought your camera to film the ritual?"

Although I was not able to understand all the discussions that were going on around me, I could sense the excitement and the anticipation. It was going to be a great day. Then I looked up to the sky. It was now about 9:00 A.M., and the sun was climbing into a clear blue sky. There were only a few wisps of a cloud visible, and it had all the indications of being another hot, dry day in Karamoja. This remote area of northeastern Uganda had suffered from a long drought like much of Africa. I looked on somewhat incredulously as the little group of some hundred people who made up the homestead prepared for the ritual. Did they honestly think that by offering a sacrifice they would cause rain to fall?

The little group of men began to lead the black bull into the open area just outside the village. The bull had to be black, I was informed, because that was symbolic of the black clouds that would come from the west. I looked vainly in that direction for any sign of clouds, but there were none. The animal was carefully positioned so that it faced to the west, and then with a quick stab of his spear one of the warriors pierced the bull into its heart. The animal fell over onto its left side to the general satisfaction of all. The old men were then given the honor of cutting up the carcass while the others started a cooking fire to one side of the area. Lotieng was at the center of the group giving orders about the correct way to cut the meat.

The women and children now began to make their appearance and sat in a large circle around the animal. They sat according to their clans in order of seniority. The people talked happily as they watched what was going on in the middle of the circle. Eventually one of the old men stood near the remains of the carcass and began to shout his prayers to God: "Akuj, send rain on your people." The people in the circle echoed the refrain. All the old men took their place, and in turn led the people in the prayers while the meat was being cooked on the fire.

Suddenly the cooked meat was being offered around, and the people began to jump up and dance. I scarcely noticed that the thin clouds had thickened, and from the west the sky slowly began to darken. The dance continued into the afternoon, and the air of anticipation grew. Finally, at about 3:00 P.M. a few spots of rain fell, and then suddenly the rain began to fall so heavily that everyone had to run for shelter. I jumped into the Land Rover as the rain pelted down onto the roof of the vehicle. It was clear to all that the rain was going to stay for some time, and the best that I could do was to drive back to base as quickly as possible. I waved to Lotieng who was sheltering in his hut, put the vehicle into second gear, and started back.

As I drove back I puzzled over why it had suddenly started to rain. How did they know it would rain today? Could the rituals that I had just witnessed and photographed have caused the rains to come? I would never have asked Lotieng that question because he would only have laughed and would have pointed out that this was the obvious conclusion. Even so, my scientific training would not let me accept such a view. "There must be an explanation," I said to myself. I smiled as I recognized that I was every bit as much a part of my cultural background as Lotieng was of his.

The Closed Universe

It was E. B. Tylor who first attempted to understand the difference in thinking between Europeans and other peoples. Writing at the end of the last century, he coined the term *animism* from the Latin word *anima* for "soul." He writes, "I propose here, under the name Animism, to investigate the deep-lying doctrine of Spiritual Beings, which embodies the very essence of Spiritualistic as opposed to Materialistic philosophy."[1] Tylor was an evolutionist, as were many of his colleagues of that time. He believed that humankind was in a process of development from primitive to civilized; from a belief in magic and religion to an understanding of science.

Max Weber, in the last century, wrote that Western society was becoming "demystified."[2] This was a consequence, he argued, of the relentless pursuit of rationality in all areas of life that had made modern industrial society unique in world history. As the advances in science began to expand our knowledge of the world and influence every part of our lives, the inevitable consequence was the loss of the sense of the supernatural that had previously permeated all societies in one way or another.

From the time of Weber's analysis of Western society the process of demystification has continued unabated. Science has explored the mysteries of space with radio telescopes probing to the edges of the universe. Electron microscopes have helped us to examine molecular structure, the very building blocks of the world in which we live. Not even the human reproductive process has been free from the probing of scientific investigation. As science has expanded, it has also drawn a line between what it regards as "real," or what we shall call empirical, and what is regarded as the "supernatural" (see Figure 1.1).

One early attempt to reconcile the tension between science and theology was the philosophy of Deism, which saw the universe as being some elaborate mechanical creation of God, while God Himself stood outside that creation. A line was here drawn between the Creator and the creation; the universe was being closed. God may have been the "first cause," but He was no longer concerned with the affairs of humankind. Thus, revelation from the divine was no longer regarded as a possibil-

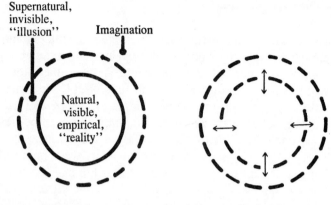

Supernatural,
invisible,
"illusion"   Imagination

Natural,
visible,
empirical,
"reality"

Secular Worldview
Distinction between natural and
supernatural. Divided appreciation
of human experiences.

Primal Worldview
No meaningful distinction between
natural and supernatural. Holistic
appreciation of human experiences.

Figure 1.1. Two contrasting worldviews: secular and primal

ity, and God was no longer One who loves and cares for His
creation.

It was only a short step from the philosophy of Deism to that
of materialism. This is indeed what happened in the eighteenth
century, and this came to its full expression in the nineteenth.
Here the line between the Creator and the creation was drawn as
a rigid boundary between the material world and the illusory.
The material world, or the world of matter (whatever we can
see, hear, and touch), is the only "real" world. Materialism
denies the existence of any divine or supernatural forces in the
universe. Man's thinking and consciousness, it would be argued, are the products not of a soul but simply of a material
bodily organ, the brain. Karl Marx was much influenced by this
particular strand of philosophy, and it has become an essential
component of Marxist philosophy. However, the philosophy of
materialism has had a much wider influence than just within
Marxism and has radically influenced much of what we may
regard as modern Western thought.

Materialism, however, has never been an intellectually satisfying worldview. As Francis Schaeffer has shown, it fails to answer some of the basic questions of life.[3] Why am I here? What happens after death? How should I live? The general response of materialism has been to ignore such questions and to encourage the enjoyment of the material world now. Another response has been that of the Marxist in assuming some progressive force at work within the world, leading to the gradual evolution and betterment of humankind. In this system of thought, humankind is the lord of the universe and so able to reach for the stars. However, for many, these responses were inadequate. They seemed to cover over the basic questions without providing any answer. Could it be, in fact, that there is no answer? For those who could not be satisfied with the enjoyment of the "closed universe," the next step was nihilism—the acceptance that there is no meaning to life. However, few could live with such a worldview.

In practice most Western people have remained satisfied with the materialistic worldview, and only a few have explored the impasse of nihilism. Nihilism is hard to translate in terms acceptable to Western man, and those who have tried to do so have followed the route of existentialism. Here one must take a "leap in the dark" and assume the existence of some meaning.[4] In this way humankind has tried to leap beyond the "closed universe." From the 1960s onward there have been those of the younger generation who have explored paths other than that of existentialism. Many Western people are fascinated by events that seem to fall outside scientific explanation, such as flying saucers. Some have sought the path of Eastern mysticism and have looked for new "saints" to follow. Others have tried the way of drugs, and yet others have tried that of the occult and sought to look for meaning in the old religions and witchcraft. Os Guinness in his book *The Dust of Death* has given an excellent analysis of this progression.[5]

The Primal Worldview

In contrast to the closed system of Western society, most of humankind has assumed a direct and discernible interaction between what Western society would call the "natural" and the "supernatural." People look for causes not just from within the empirical world but from what is beyond. At a funeral, the question that will often be asked is, "Who killed him?" The culprit is just as likely to be a spirit or ghost as to be a person. In the story told earlier, the interaction between the rainmaking ritual of the Karimojong and the coming of rain was seen as one. It is this sort of thinking that Tylor attempted to describe by his expression *animism* and in so doing to make a contrast with materialistic philosophy.

E. B. Tylor was an evolutionist and sought to identify a development of religions. In the study of comparative religions, therefore, animism indicated primitive religion, from which developed higher religions such as Hinduism, Buddhism, Islam, and Christianity. Thus in popular usage the term *animism* has come to mean all those religious practices that are not an orthodox part of the major world religions. To avoid confusion, some writers have proposed other terms such as *primitive religions* or *primal religions*. H. W. Turner advocates the use of the term *primal,* meaning that "these religions both anteceded the great historic religions and continue to reveal many of the basic or primary features of religion."[6]

The term *primal religions* is one that will frequently be used in this text. The addition of the plural *s* is deliberate because they cannot be regarded as just one religion. The term relates to particular societies, the members of which have a deep sense of shared identity. They are adherents of their own religion because they are members of their particular tribe. This was the case for most of the tribes of Africa before the coming of Islam and Christianity. The religion of the Karimojong was particularly for the Karimojong. Similarly, the Yoruba of Nigeria had their own religious beliefs, as did the Azande of Zaire and the Ashanti of Ghana. In general, no tribe would think of seeking to convert members of other tribes to its own religion. Mission is not part of the belief system of primal religions.

The subject of terminology will continue to be a major issue within this text because so many words that are commonly used have such strong connotations. Terms such as *pagan, heathen,* and *primitive* all carry strong negative feelings and fail to allow one to appreciate that one is here dealing with rational adults who have ideas that seem as logical to them as our ideas do to us. In the study of human societies, the greatest handicap is that we are, ourselves, products of a particular society. We have acquired from the society in which we have grown up particular ideas and concepts. We feel that people who see things differently from ourselves are ignorant or prejudiced. This attitude is referred to as *ethnocentricity*. In relating to primal societies one must beware the innate tendency to look down upon those societies whose technology is less developed than ours. In the areas of human relationships and the relationship to the balance of nature, we may have much to learn from them.

The basic difference between Western peoples and primal societies is that they start from a different set of assumptions about the nature of humankind and the universe. Although the worldview varies from one society to another, one can identify certain common traits in those societies we call "primal." It is useful at this point to compare some of these common themes with those of the secular worldview.

First, in primal religions, the universe is not closed—the border between the "natural" and the "supernatural" is blurred. The natural and the supernatural merge into each other, rocks and trees may have supernatural powers, and spirits take on human forms. Primal worldviews tend to provide a more integrated view of the world than the analytical thinking of secular Western societies (see Figure 1.1).

Second, the material world is therefore conceived of as being greatly influenced by immaterial forces. The universe is seen as the product of personal agents such as gods and spirits. In contrast, the secular worldview looks for an explanation of the formation of the universe in the impersonal terms of the big bang theory.

Third, primal worldviews assume that various phenomena may be controlled by means of signs and rituals. Sir James G. Frazer used the term *magic* for such beliefs and practices and contrasted them with religion.[7] Magic, he argued, is the use of particular rituals to control various forces to answer some of the practical problems of everyday life and so supplement the technical knowledge of the people. A farmer, for example, knows that he needs to prepare the soil in a certain way, sow the seed, weed the field, and care for the growing crop. He also knows that using the best of his abilities, he is not able to guarantee rain or protect the crop from pests or thieves. He will then turn to magic and set up an idol in order to draw upon unseen forces to protect his crop. In religion, Frazer pointed out, the person approaches the supernatural in an attitude of supplication and subordination to the spiritual beings. By means of worship and prayer the person seeks to communicate with the spiritual beings and gain assistance from them. These supernatural beings have personalities very much like man himself.

The distinction between magic and religion has been based on several criteria.

Magic	*Religion*
Manipulative technique	Supplication
Concerns power	Concerns personal relationships
Specific goals	General aims
Individual desires	Group desires
Impersonal	Personal and emotional
Good or bad	Consistently good as far as local society is concerned

In practice the distinction between magic and religion is not as clear as may first be thought. These two terms appear to overlap in various ways, and many anthropologists tend to regard them as two ends of a continuum. As Sir Raymond Firth writes,

> In so far as a distinction can be drawn on broad lines it is in describing certain acts, and the situations in which they take place, as primarily magical at one end of the scale, and primarily religious at the other. In between lies a sphere in which the elements are so closely combined that the institutions may be termed magico-religious or religio-magical. In practice such intermediate types are commonly found.[8]

This fact needs to be appreciated even though we do make the distinction between magic and religion. According to the secular worldview, however, nature cannot be controlled indirectly through rituals.

Fourth, humankind is seen as being essentially a part of the universe as a whole. As such, human beings must live in harmony with their environment and avoid disturbing the balance of forces occurring in the world around them. For this reason primal religions are generally based upon traditions and taboos. On the other hand, the secular worldview sees humankind as dominant over nature, using it for its own well-being by the application of scientific principles.

The Bible in Cultural Context

What answer does Christianity have for the people who believe in the reality of powerful spirits? Two main options lie before us. Either we can seek to answer the questions from our Western worldview with its underlying secular philosophy, or we can present Christ within their own cultural context as the One who is able to meet their felt-needs. It is the author's opinion that the gospel can most effectively be communicated within the cultural framework of the people themselves, and consequently it is necessary to explore something of the basic assumptions they hold.

As we approach this exploration, our study will show some surprising parallels between religious practices of primal societies and some practices described in the Bible. This may cause some Christians to feel their Christian faith is threatened in some way. This is because we have usually assumed discontinuity and antagonism between Christianity and "paganism." However, in order to fully understand the significance of these similarities, it is necessary to examine various principles by which we interpret biblical narrative.

First, it needs to be stressed that the Bible contains the revelation of God to human beings and in this sense is absolute truth. The revelation that is given by a supracultural God is constant and unchanging.

Second, this divine revelation has been given within a particular historical and cultural context. God chose to employ human language and culture as the means of His communication with people. He usually chose to reveal Himself in such a way that members of various cultures could focus in upon those aspects of God's nature that would be most meaningful for their cultural context. The apparent differences between various parts of the Bible are therefore not theological but mainly cultural. As

Charles Kraft has written, "The Bible focuses at different times on quite different cultural understandings of God's constant message and its implications, each of which is Spirit-guided."[9]

Third, the Old Testament is a record of God taking a people and molding their worldview so that it would be capable of conveying the divine message to humankind. God starts where people are in their own historical, cultural, and personal context in order to reveal Himself to them in a way that is particularly comprehensible and meaningful. For example, the concepts of God, sin, and sacrifice initially held by Abraham were enriched and reformed by the revelations of God to him and later to Moses and the prophets. In this way God took many of the traditional practices that had animistic connotations and poured new meaning into them. This accounts for many of the parallels that one finds between narratives in the Bible and other religions.

Throughout the different cultural periods of the history of Israel, there is an accumulation of revealed information until, in the fullness of time, the Jewish culture was an adequate vehicle for communicating God's ultimate self-revelation in the person of Jesus Christ. An example of this is seen in the concept of sacrifice. Archaeology reveals that sacrifice was a common practice in Ur before the time of Abraham, but God accepted such worship that was offered to Him by Abraham. In time God gave to Moses a more elaborate system of sacrifices, which were later to prove suitable idioms and concepts to convey the saving ministry of our Lord.

Fourth, our own reading and understanding of the Bible are shaped by our particular historical and cultural context. Western readers, for example, are often oblivious to certain portions of the Bible merely because they are irrelevant to their own life experiences. Within this book, mention will be made of various illustrations that may take on new meaning as we gain greater understanding of primal religions. On the other hand, people from primal societies would already find these passages particularly relevant. The wonders of sacrifice and healing as opposed to the dangers of witchcraft and sorcery are just a few of the issues that speak strongly to primal societies. The Bible is a multicultural text with something to appeal to every society.

Finally, it is also necessary to recognize that within the history of Israel are found both truth and error. False prophets are found alongside the true, and within the context of righteous laws are found forbidden practices. The Bible often warns of counterfeits to the work of God. Throughout the history of Israel, one finds the continuing influence of Baal worship, which clouded the distinctiveness that God was seeking to bring into the culture and life of Israel. We should not, therefore, be surprised to read that in the world today there are Hindu sadhus who claim to perform miracles, shamans who exorcise evil spirits, and Sufi mystics who claim visions. The Christian must have discernment to recognize the true and the counterfeit within his own as well as primal societies.

Notes

1. E. B. Tylor, *Primitive Culture* (John Murray: London, 1871), 1:425.
2. Max Weber, *The Protestant Ethic and the Spirit of Capitalism* (Allen & Unwin: London, 1930).
3. Francis A. Schaeffer, *Escape from Reason* (IVP: London, 1968).
4. Ibid., p. 91.
5. Os Guinness, *The Dust of Death* (IVP: London, 1973).
6. Harold W. Turner, *Living Tribal Religions* (Ward Lock Educational: London, 1974), p. 7.
7. Sir James G. Frazer, *The Gold Bough* (Macmillan: London, 1978).
8. Sir Raymond Firth, *Human Types* (Abacus: London, 1975), p. 142.
9. Charles H. Kraft, *Christianity in Culture* (Orbis Books: Maryknoll, New York, 1981), p. 236.

2

Unearthly Powers

Power may be understood in many ways: physical, political, economic, social, and religious. The secular worldview tends to regard all power as originating from within the material world. Even those powers that many would regard as being religious in nature are described in psychological terms. In contrast, primal worldviews see such powers not only as being real within the empirical world but as having their primary origin outside the visible world. This concept of the existence of unseen powers that influence human life is one of the basic assumptions in all primal worldviews and is perhaps the greatest difference from the secular view.

Although, according to primal worldviews, these powers cannot be directly perceived, they are considered to permeate the whole of daily life. They influence the success of the farmer in his work in the fields or the wife in her cooking or as she looks after the children. A tree or a hill is not merely an inanimate object but may possess unseen power. In order to cope with the everyday activities of life these powers must be recognized and patterns followed to avoid any harm from them.

In general, all people tend to use one of two basic analogies to describe nature and the world as a whole, and this applies to the concept of unseen powers. The first analogy is the impersonal, or mechanical, as would be applied to an inanimate force such as electricity. Considered in this way the power does not have a will of its own but operates in the same way as the law of gravity. Second, powers may be perceived in personal terms such as are used for living beings. When they are described in this way, such powers are regarded as having their own particular character, feelings, and ability to relate to other persons, as well as having a will of their own. Like people, they may be angered, placated, or turned to in time of need.

These two analogies provide a useful starting point in any attempt to understand the primal cosmology. In this chapter, the mechanical analogy will be considered together with the resulting repercussions in the everyday life of primal society. The next chapter will focus upon the personal analogy and so consider the common concepts of gods and spirits.

Mana

R. H. Codrington, a former missionary working in the Pacific Isles, wrote,

> The Melanesian mind is entirely possessed by the belief in a supernatural power or influence, called almost universally *mana*. This is what works to affect everything which is beyond the ordinary power of men, outside the common processes of nature; it is present in the atmosphere of life, attaches itself to persons and to things, and is manifested by results which can only be ascribed to its operation.[1]

The details of how this power is conceived and the name by which it is called differ from one language to another. The term *mana* is common in the Pacific, while the Iroquois of North America have the term *orenda*, which particularly refers to the mystic power derived from a chant. The Inuit (Eskimos) have a notion of *sila*, a force watching and controlling everything. The Chinese have the concept of *fung shui* (also commonly spelled *feng shui*), which particularly refers to the powers inherent within the contours of the earth and sea. Within folk Islam the term *baraka*, usually translated as "holiness" or "blessing," embraces many of these concepts.[2]

The word *mana* is one that has been most commonly used by anthropologists because it stresses the particular distinction of this form of power from what is more commonly understood by Western science. *Mana* is therefore the term that will be used in this text to describe this general concept of powers. To understand the concept of *mana* it is necessary to appreciate its particular characteristics.

First, *mana* is a power distinct from the ordinary powers of humankind. In Fiji, for example, there are two quite distinct words for power. *Calwa* refers to physical strength, while *mana* refers to supernatural power that may be possessed by an object or a person. If a person is conspicuous by his particular success in hunting, fighting, or powers of leadership, such would be considered to be proof that the person possessed *mana*. It is appreciated that the yams will grow naturally when planted in the earth, but they will not be very large unless *mana* comes into operation. Similarly a canoe will not be very swift unless it possesses *mana,* nor will a hunter be very successful unless he possesses *mana*. Codrington, writing about the Melanesian concept, sought to define *mana* in the following way:

> It is a power or influence, not physical, and in a way supernatural; but it shows itself in physical force, or in any kind of power or excellence which a man possesses. This *mana* is not fixed in anything, and can be conveyed in almost anything.[3]

The term *mana* acts as a verbal sign that, beyond a certain point, achievement is not because of human initiative but requires the assistance of the supernatural.

In case the reader is likely to distance himself from such notions, it is interesting to draw a comparison with the English meaning of the word *luck,* which derives from a Teutonic background. A businessman may consider his promotion to chairman as the result of his hard work and intellectual abilities, but he may also recognize that he was "lucky" to be at the right place at the right time. A person who has just won a lottery will reckon himself to be lucky. Similarly a person who is successful in growing plants may happily say that he has a green thumb.

Second, as has been stated earlier, *mana* may generally be understood as being an impersonal force very much like high-voltage electricity. Although this is a useful illustration, we must be careful not to take it too far. The way that the term is used implies that *mana* is descriptive of the possession of the power rather than the power itself, and so it is always connected to some person or spirit who may activate its effect. *Mana* may be transferred from a donor to a recipient by various forms and rituals, but these nearly always involve the act of touching. The Australian aborigine, for example, keeps hidden certain sacred stones called *churinga*, which in times of need he will handle to gain *mana*.[4] Similarly, a person may take hold of a charm to protect himself from impending danger.

The analogy with luck may be made yet again. Which English speaker has not heard of the story of the kissing of the Blarney stone? The tradition of touching wood for luck remains part of English folk magic. The sophisticated scorn of the "educated" for these practices may blind us, however. The Christian tradition of laying on of hands in order to confer a blessing has its origins from New Testament times. Acts 19 records the fascinating story concerning the apostle Paul. "God did extraordinary miracles through Paul, so that even handkerchiefs and aprons that had touched him were taken to the sick, and their illnesses were cured and the evil spirits left them" (Acts 19:11–12; see also Acts 5:15). These passages tend to be neglected by Western biblical scholars who often regard them as strange and primitive in the context of Christian revelation. However, this apparent anomaly may be the result of our own secularized worldview, with its particular assumptions, which hinders us from appreciating the implications of such passages.

A third characteristic of *mana* is that it may be conceived of as being intrinsically amoral. Whether it brings good or evil depends upon the possessor. A healer may use his *mana* to cure the sick, while a sorcerer may use his to cast a curse upon a person. It is the intentions of the person that give to the power its moral quality in much the same way as drugs may be used to heal or to kill. As Hiebert has commented,

> Many of the similarities between modern science, magic and astrology which have been pointed out by anthropologists are due to the fact that both use mechanistic analogies. Just as scientists know how to control empirical forces to achieve their goals, the magician and astrologer control supernatural forces of this world by means of chants, charms, and rituals to carry out their purposes.[5]

Fourth, *mana*, like any power, is valued by people. *Mana* can increase a person's prosperity, preserve a man from danger, and enable a barren woman to bear children. A charm has power to protect a person from danger because it bears the name of a powerful spirit or god upon it, or it has been made in a particular way such that the spirit has transferred *mana* to the article. *Mana* has something of a qualitative element about it. *Mana* can be built up within an object or a person by use of suitable rituals. In the pre-Christian Solomon Isles, the taking of heads was one way of building up *mana*. The heads of slain enemies were offered to the skull of the honored ancestor, and in so doing the latter's *mana* was increased, and so its effectiveness to protect the tribe increased. Tippett, writing of the Malaita bushmen, recounts the following scale in which the heads have an increasing *mana* value:[6]

pig → woman → man → warrior → chief → white man

An object or a person may either gain or lose *mana*. This observation brings an interesting reflection on the well-known story of Jesus and the woman with the issue of blood. There among the crowd of people Jesus was conscious of being touched in a particular way: "But Jesus said, 'Someone touched me; I know that power has gone out from me' " (Luke 8:46). It was only then that the woman came out of the crowd and confessed that she had touched him: "Then he said to her, 'Daughter, your faith has healed you. Go in peace' " (Luke 8:48).

Although the concept of *mana* is a useful introduction to the study of primal worldviews, it must not be regarded as a totally universal belief. It does, however, show that primal man sees his life in the context of a larger universe containing other forces and powers greater than his own. To cope with the issues of life, he must recognize these powers and come to terms with them.

Taboo

The major way of dealing with any power is to establish rules to protect the unwary from harm. With the concept of *mana* this is achieved by establishing a set of imposed restrictions relating to the object. If *mana* is likened to high-voltage electricity, taboos may be likened to electrical insulation. The oral knowledge of these taboos is as valuable as the sign warning of high-voltage electricity running through overhead power cables. Frazer, in his book *The Golden Bough*, joined the two terms of *mana* and *taboo* together into a common category of "contagious magic."[7] This has the advantage of identifying the association of the two, but it fails to explain the nature of their particular characteristics.

Every religion has some form of taboo, in the sense of supernaturally imposed sanctions to protect the devotee from harm. Some religions, such as those of the Polynesians, contained a multitude of such restrictions that applied to every area of life. These taboos identify the boundary between what is the sacred and the secular with regard to the religion of the people. Thus, through the awareness of such taboos, a society is made conscious of the presence of *mana* in a particular object or person.

Taboos may be of many forms.

Taboo People

Certain people are considered to be particularly powerful in *mana* and may be approached only with great care. In July 1874 the king of Cambodia was thrown from his carriage and lay insensible on the ground, but none of his courtiers dared to touch him because there was a strong taboo about touching the king without his express command. The king might well have died there on the ground if a passing European had not been willing to carry the injured monarch to his palace and care for him until he regained consciousness and gave permission for the local doctors to treat him.

It is not only a person that may be taboo, but also the things that he owns or uses may become deposits of *mana*. The cape of a Maori chief, for example, was regarded as being particularly strong in *mana* and could kill an unsuspecting person who accidentally touched the cape. Frazer tells the story of how a Maori chief's tinderbox became the means of killing several people.[8] The chief lost the tinderbox, which was found by a group of men who used it to light their pipes. On hearing that this was the chief's lost property the men quickly became ill and died. It would be easy to seek to explain such cases in terms of Western categories of thought and dismiss the cause of death as shock. However, this fails to recognize the inadequacies of our medical science to fully explain such phenomena. For the primal religionist living in a world of powers, the explanation of the broken taboo would appear far more convincing.

Priests, as people who handle supernatural powers, are expected to observe particular taboos. For example, among the Ga of Ghana the priest must not eat salt except in the form of seawater. No one must speak to him while he is eating, and neither must he eat on any day until the sun has shone. He must also refrain from sexual intercourse on certain days of the week as well as before performing certain rites.[9]

Not only are chiefs and religious leaders considered to be taboo, but so are ordinary persons at particular points in their lives. The avoidance of menstruating women is a common practice in many parts of the world. Among the Ga, a menstruating woman is considered to be particularly polluting so that even a river (or spirit of the river) may object to such a woman being ferried across and upset the boat.[10] In other parts of Africa, the pots that a woman touches while she is menstruating must be destroyed.

Taboo Foods

The soldiers of Madagascar were once forbidden to eat hedgehog because it was a timid animal that rolled up in a ball when alarmed. This is the very opposite of those qualities that should characterize a soldier. Jews and Muslims refuse to eat pork because it is regarded as unclean by their respective religions. Hindus similarly will not eat beef because to them the cow is a sacred animal. At this point the concept of taboo overlaps with that of sin and pollution, which will be discussed in chapter 7.

Some of the most elaborate food taboos are those recorded in the Pentateuch. To understand the importance of these it is necessary to see that holiness has been given a physical expression in its encounter with the animal kingdom: "Every creature that moves about on the ground is detestable; it is not to be eaten.... Do not make yourselves unclean by means of them . . . consecrate yourselves and be holy, because I am holy" (Lev. 11:41–44). The distinction between the sacred and the secular is being clearly established through the whole of life, and the Israelites are directed to associate themselves with the holiness of God by following these taboos.

Taboo Objects

Taboo objects are mostly images of deities or ritual objects associated with the spirits. A grove of trees, for example, may be considered as being particularly significant to a deity and therefore taboo to all but the priests. A person cutting down such a tree would be likely to die in a short period of time unless protected by a greater *mana*. The Holy of Holies in the tabernacle of ancient Israel was an area of taboo to all but the high priest who was allowed beyond the inner veil only on the sacred Day of Atonement.

Don Richardson, writing of the Yali people of Irian Jaya, tells of the special walled gardens that only the men were allowed to enter: "Any female who trespasses that stone wall, or even touches it, must be cast into the rapids of the Heluk river! Even males not yet consecrated to the *kembu* spirits must die if they set foot upon the sacred ground!"[11]

Taboo Names

Many societies see a name as not merely being a form of label to identify an individual but a distinct part of that individual's personality, just as much as an eye or an ear. Injury may be caused by maliciously handling a person's name with results similar to those of a physical attack. For this reason a person's name may be kept secret because knowledge of it can give another the potential for harm. Among the tribes of central Australia every person has a secret name bestowed at birth by the old men in addition to the personal name that is in common use. This secret name is never used except at sacred rites.

Countless illustrations of strange and exotic or ordinary and mundane taboos could be given. These merely stress the importance of the concept of powers to those who adhere to a primal worldview. These powers are regarded as penetrating what the Western man would call the empirical reality and so may affect an individual's life for good or for ill.

Christianity and Powers

The strength of belief in *mana* held by many peoples of the Third World leaves the Western Christian in something of a dilemma. Can one accept the reality of such powers, or must they be rejected as the views of primitive, uneducated people? Once again, two main options present themselves. Either one holds to a materialistic view of the world and so one must reject all notions of unseen powers, or one can seek to adopt a worldview that recognizes the reality of such powers.

The first position leads of necessity to a total rejection of the primal viewpoint. Primal societies, in this case, need to be educated toward a more scientific and mechanistic view of the world. Only when this view is adopted can the person then begin to appreciate what the advocate would regard as a correct understanding of the gospel message. However, as history has shown, for most societies such a process will not be achieved in a single generation, and an awareness of unearthly powers will remain for centuries. Rigidly held taboos may in time become superstitions and in later generations merely quaint customs.

If this approach of rejecting the primal worldview is followed, Christianity will appear to the primal religionist as being irrelevant to him because it does not seek to relate to his needs. It fails to answer the problems he has with spirits, ghosts, and witchcraft. Further, it needs to be recognized that such an approach will result in the "demystification" (to use Max Weber's expression) of their worldview as it has done to the Western worldview. A rejection of spiritual powers can often lead ultimately to the rejection of a spiritual God and therefore to an entirely secular perspective.

The second option is to accept the reality of such powers and be willing to examine critically our own Western world-view. This will require the Western Christian to recognize the pervasiveness of materialistic thinking even in his own worldview and to listen more humbly to the growing churches of the Third World who are affirming the reality of such powers. The Lausanne Continuation Committee convened a consultation in 1978 and produced a paper known as *The Willowbank*

Report. In that report they made the following statement:

> We wish to affirm, therefore, against the mechanistic myth on which the typical Western worldview rests, the reality of demonic intelligences which are concerned by all means, overt and covert, to discredit Jesus Christ and keep people from coming to him.[12]

This option requires that the primal societies must see the gospel not merely as a set of intellectual truths but as Jesus Christ, the Lord of *power*. People will respond to the claims of Christ when they see that His power is superior to the magic of the sorcerer or that of the ancestors. The missionary needs to stand with the convert, and together they need to appreciate what Jesus meant when He said that "all authority in heaven and on earth has been given to me" (Matt. 28:18). This authority He delegated to His disciples so that they could minister in His name: "When Jesus had called the Twelve together, he gave them power [Greek *dunamis*] and authority [Greek *exousia*] to drive out all demons and to cure diseases, and he sent them out to preach the kingdom of God, and to heal the sick" (Luke 9:1–2).

Throughout the Old and New Testaments, the reality of unseen powers is accepted. During the last three centuries some Western Christians have sought to explain such events in terms of the closed universe until they have come to a point of denying the miraculous altogether. In seeking to understand the thinking of the animist, it is therefore necessary to interact afresh with the Scriptures in order to determine how to make Christ relevant within his experience. As we do so, the Scriptures will take on a new meaning and significance often previously unrecognized by Western Christians. This may well challenge us to formulate a more meaningful worldview than one that is merely an adaptation of the secular worldview.

While traveling through northern Nigeria I was approached by a bright, well-educated young man. We had met in a church one Sunday morning. He came up and challenged me. "You have a different Bible from us!" he exclaimed. I was puzzled over what he meant. Did he mean I had a different translation? But before I could reply, he continued by saying, "My Bible mentions evil spirits on many occasions, but you missionaries never speak about them." Here was a cry for the gospel message to be presented with a relevance to the local situation, which had previously been ignored.

Notes

1. R. H. Codrington, *The Melanesians: Studies in Their Anthropology and Folk-lore* (Clarendon Press: Oxford, 1891), pp. 118–20.
2. Mary Douglas, *Purity and Danger* (Routledge & Kegan Paul: London, 1966), p. 109.
3. Codrington, op. cit., pp. 118–20.
4. Anthony F. C. Wallace, *Religion: An Anthropological View* (Random House: New York, 1966), pp. 60–61.
5. Paul G. Hiebert, "Folk Religion in Andhra Pradesh," in Vinay Samuel and Chris Sugden, *Evangelism and the Poor* (Partnership in Mission—Asia: Bangalore, 1983), p. 88.
6. Alan R. Tippett, *Solomon Islands Christianity* (William Carey Library: Pasadena, 1967), p. 9.
7. Sir James G. Frazer, *The Golden Bough* (Macmillan: London, 1978).
8. Ibid., p. 270.
9. M. J. Field, *Religion and Medicine of the Ga People* (Oxford University Press: London, 1961), p. 8.
10. Ibid., p. 112.
11. Don Richardson, *Lords of the Earth* (Regal Books: Glendale, 1977), p. 22.
12. *The Willowbank Report* (Lausanne Committee for World Evangelisation: Wheaton, 1978), p. 21.

3

Gods and Demons

In primal religions, unseen powers are perceived not only in mechanistic terms but also as personalities. The universe is seen as being alive with many and varied spiritual beings. These may be classified by the use of Western terms such as *gods*, *spirits*, *demons*, or *angels*, but these terms can lead to confusion. Ideally these beings must be classified according to the actual words that the people employ. Some primal societies have a complex and distinctive cosmology in which the seen and unseen world is ordered, while others have only hazy ideas that often may appear contradictory. Frequently the ordinary people are not aware of the complexity of the spiritual world and prefer to leave the matter to religious specialists upon whom they can call in times of difficulty.

The Central Luo of Uganda call their particular supernatural power *Jok*. Yet it cannot be simply equated with the impersonal *mana;* neither may it be regarded as purely a god.[1] *Jok* is what is present in and explains extraordinary natural phenomena, such as a great waterfall or a fertile valley. It is the power that an important shrine may possess. However, it may also be considered as a kind of great spirit.

Although one must appreciate the wide variety in humankind's conception of spiritual beings, it is possible to identify certain common features among most societies: the supreme creator-being, and the deities.

The Supreme Being

Every African people has a belief in the existence of a supreme

35

being who is the creator of all. He is known by many names. The Nuer call him Kwoth; the Ibo, Chukwu; the Krobo, Mau; and the Karimojong, Akuj. The Akan use the name Onyame, meaning "a shining being living beyond the ordinary reach of man, but revealed through his own light."

Among the Akan people of Ghana, God is supposed to have made the universe in an orderly fashion. First he made the sky, then the earth, rivers, waters, plants, and trees:

> Then he made man, and for man's use he made animals. In order to keep the animals alive, he ordered them to eat plants, which men were also to eat in addition to eating the animals. Then God made spirits of the waters, forests, and rocks, in order to protect man.[2]

The myths of creation have been passed on through oral tradition from one generation to another. These myths are not merely the equivalent of Western fairy stories but provide explanations of how the world came to be as it now is and also reveal the creator as the one who also created the established social order:

> The Luyia of Kenya say that when God had created the sun he wondered for whom it would shine. So he made the first man, called Mwambu. Since the man could talk and see he needed a companion, and God made the first woman, whose name was Sela. They wanted something to drink, so God made water fall from heaven which filled up the holes and valleys to make lakes and rivers. God instructed Mwambu and Sela in the flesh they could eat, some animals were allowed for food but others were taboo. They were forbidden to eat crawling beasts like snails and lizards, or birds that feed on carrion like hawks and vultures. One day God surprised a buffalo cow with its young, and it ran away leaving the young ones, which were male and female. God took them and gave them to the man and woman. They fed them on an ant-hill, and some people say that originally cattle came from an ant-hill. Mwambu and Sela lived in a house supported by posts, because they were afraid of earthly monsters. Their children came down and lived on the ground, but tree-houses are still used sometimes in forests, and houses on piles stand in the waters at the edge of lakes.[3]

One may expect such a god to be at the very center of such primal religions, but this is rarely the case. The supreme being usually has neither temples nor priests. He is regarded as a transcendent being too exalted to be concerned with the affairs of men. There are often myths to explain this strange aloofness. One story tells of a woman who was pounding her fufu (a staple West African food) with a pestle and mortar. Heaven used to be much closer in those days. This woman had a particularly long wooden pestle so that whenever she pounded her fufu her pestle reached so high in the sky that she struck God. When the woman refused to stop, God became angry and moved away from the world. Another common story is of a people who did not like to have God living so close by, so they migrated to another land.

For these reasons it is frequently the gods and spirits that are of greater concern for the majority of the people. However, it is not correct, as some writers have said, that the supreme being is totally transcendent over the world. As with the case of the Karimojong and their rainmaking ceremony, it is to Akuj they call. Among the Bantu, the people usually turn to the supreme being only as a last resort when the other spiritual beings have failed. John V. Taylor tells the story of a hunting expedition in Malawi that had no success for two weeks. In desperation the leader of the hunt exclaimed, "I am tired of asking the shades [ancestors], let us pray to God."[4]

It is worth noting that the peoples of Africa believed in a supreme creator god long before the arrival of Christian missionaries. Writers such as John Mbiti have shown that such gods were understood as having characteristics very similar to those of the Christian God.[5] Almost by definition the creator god is seen as being inherently good. While there are many similarities, there are also differences, the major one being that he is considered to be distant from humanity and indifferent to their needs. A second difference is that the creator god is often considered as manifesting himself through intermediaries that we will call divinities. The word for god is often used in the plural as well as the singular. The Turkana will speak of Akuj, but they will also use the word in the plural for many gods.

Divinities

A belief in a pantheon of divinities is common among many

peoples throughout the world, and as we have seen they are often more important than the supreme being. These deities are frequently believed to form a hierarchical order depending upon their local importance and power. The divinities are perceived to be related to some particular aspect of nature or some area of life over which they rule. The pantheons of Greece and Rome are examples of these patterns of belief. Neptune was the god of the sea; Apollo, the god of medicine and the fine arts: Venus, the goddess of beauty, love, and marriage; and Pluto, the god of death and the underworld.[6] For this reason these beings have often been called "nature spirits."

The supreme being of the Yoruba of Nigeria is called Olodumare, and his position is like that of a traditional king who works through his ministers. The general name for the subordinate gods is *orisha,* which means "head-source." Orisha-nla or Obatala is the chief *orisha* and executes the creative functions of Olodumare. He is the one who gives a man riches or poverty, strength or deformity. Ogun is the god both of war and of iron, and so he is worshiped particularly by warriors and blacksmiths. Shango is the god of storms and is often regarded as the anger of Olodumare. Shopona is the power of smallpox and most fevers including boils and other skin eruptions. There is a parallel here with the way that the Romans worshiped Febris, the power of malaria. Eshu is considered as the power of mischief, and so is regarded with dread by most of the people. The Yoruba have often represented these gods by wooden or bronze images.

On the other side of the world from the Yoruba, the Chinese have beliefs in a wide range of gods.[7] Often Western visitors do not consider the Chinese to be very religious, but in fact they have a very pragmatic view of the deities and prefer to leave them alone if at all possible. As one may expect in such a numerous people, there is a complex belief system. However, one thing that is found in nearly every Chinese household is the family altar. This is a small shrine, often in the shape of a tiny house hung on the wall in a position of honor in the main room. A variety of deities will be placed on the altar according to the traditions of the family. A mixture of religious influences may be observed with the Taoist Commanders of the Heavenly Army, the Buddhist Kwan Yin, and various household gods.

The altars of today are illuminated by little red electric light bulbs, and offerings of rice and burning incense are still regularly made to the deities. Nearly all Chinese shops in Hong Kong and Taiwan have such small altars on display. Every police station in Hong Kong has within it a small shrine to the deity Kwan Tai. Even in Europe and North America the practice continues, and the deity of the business smiles down on the sales of chop suey.

Where the people believe in the existence of a supreme benevolent creator, they are immediately faced with the problem of the presence of evil and suffering in the world. How can a god who is ultimate goodness create evil? In the major monotheistic religions the problem is answered by the concept of an adversary to the creator god. In the Judeo-Christian tradition this anti-God is called Satan, which means "adversary." In the Hindu pantheon Vishnu is associated with light and the heavens, while Kali, "The Black One," lurks in darkness and the battlefield. In Babylonian tradition, at Akitu, the New Year festival, the great epic of creation was recited, celebrating the victory of the god Marduk over the dragon of chaos. These antigods are created beings who are in rebellion against their creator and therefore by definition are evil. There is a strange attractiveness about such an antigod that draws some people in every society to worship this spirit. The devotees of Kali have been known to practice human sacrifice, and among Europeans there has been a growing interest in satanism.

An alternative explanation of the presence of good and evil in the world is provided in many societies by regarding the gods as having an ambivalence that makes them very like human beings, able to do good or evil. Some are more evil by nature, such as the god Eshu of the Yoruba or the spider Anansi of the Ashanti. These are perceived as having little power in themselves and so employ cunning to achieve their ends, very much like the Teutonic Loki who relies upon his handsomeness and charm to bring about the pain and suffering he longs to create.

Some of the spirits are regarded as of greater importance than others. These may range from powerful spirits that must be treated with respect to relatively insignificant spirits of the forest, field, or water who may merely cause a nuisance to humans. The water nymphs of Roman mythology would be an example of this, as would fairies, goblins, and elves in traditional English beliefs.

The Chinese tend to regard these spirits as powerful but easily fooled, and as such, though they receive attention, they do not receive the respect of the people. One may identify three sets of such gods: the kitchen gods, the door gods, and the earth gods of an individual household. The kitchen god is located in the kitchen and resides in his own red illuminated temple. The door gods are supposed to protect the house from evil, while the earth gods (Tu Di) are more akin to the traditional nature spirits. All these gods are known as *shen,* but care must be exercised in the use of this term because it has a wide and complex meaning in Chinese thought. Whether many Chinese today actively believe in the benefits of these divinities is debatable, but they are certainly regarded as a form of supernatural insurance.

Folk Islam has much to say about the *jinn,* and it is still an important aspect of the beliefs of many Muslims in the world today. The respected business magazine *Middle East* reported a few years ago,

> In Morocco, as in other countries of the Muslim world, not all demons, or *jinn,* were sealed in bottles by magicians. Here, at least, the *jinn* are alive and well, living in caves, running water, streams, rivers and in dank drainpipes. Their presence is woven into the fabric of everyday life. No one pours hot water down a sink, for the wrath of a scalded *jinni* is fierce indeed. Nor should anyone cross a stream without first saying a cautious, "Bis Mi'illah" (in the name of God).[8]

The Ga of southern Ghana believe in dozens of gods, called *kple.* These include some of the traditional deities of the area worshiped before the coming of the Ga tribes. Chief of these are the gods of the lagoons, which are found along the coast. In addition there are nature gods and war gods who are worshiped with singing and dancing and the offering of food at feasts. The worship of the *kple* has traditionally been focused upon Labadi, which is now a suburb of modern Accra.

Whereas nature spirits have no direct kinship with people, there is a strong belief in many primal societies concerning humans who for various reasons have taken their place among the gods and permanent spirits in the world. The subject of ghosts and ancestors will be dealt with in chapter 5, and there a distinction will be made between ghosts and spirits. Spirits are those supernatural beings who have always existed in that form, while ghosts were formerly human beings but after death have taken on a different form of existence. Together with the class of deified ancestors, there is that class of humans whose lives have been so meritorious that they did not become mere ghosts but have taken their place among the permanent spirits in charge of the world. Often the nature spirit has become merged with the human aspect.

The belief in deified humans is common among the peoples of the Pacific area. Hong Kong has always been a place dependent upon the sea. Even today there are an estimated 60,000 fishermen and boat people who live on junks and depend on the sea for their livelihood. One of their most important deities is Tin Hau, or Queen of Heaven, who is still worshiped by an estimated quarter of a million people. Like many of the Taoist deities, she began life as a mortal, living in Fukien Province at the end of the tenth century. She was said to perform miracles, and one in particular was to save her family's junk from a storm. She is said to have died young while she was still a virgin and was canonized by imperial edict.

Although Tin Hau is the goddess of seafarers, she is worshiped by many different peoples. Among the modern skyscrapers of Hong Kong her birthday is still celebrated at the beginning of May. People throng to her temples and light incense sticks and hold feasts.[9] The contrast between the Western appearance of Hong Kong and these traditional beliefs is striking. This observation only goes to stress the fact that the primal worldview is not restricted to isolated tribal societies— nor is it merely the result of a lack of Western learning.

This kind of belief is also found within some forms of Christianity. In Roman Catholicism, a few people who have lived exemplary lives are recognized by the church as saints. An appeal may be made to these saints to intercede on behalf of the living before the throne of God. In folk Catholicism the saints, together with Mary, may take a more prominent place in the lives of the people than Jesus Christ Himself.

The honor of being ascribed deity has not been limited to the dead. Many societies have deified humans while they are still living. Usually these have been kings and political rulers. The Pharaohs of Egypt were regarded as divine. The emperor of Japan renounced his divinity only in 1945. The early church had one of its greatest conflicts with the Roman Empire because the members refused to offer sacrifices to the emperor. The Kumari, the virgin goddess of Katmandu, gained international publicity with the visit of Queen Elizabeth to Nepal in 1986. The Kumari is chosen for goddesshood when she is five years of age on the basis of thirty-two physical characteristics. These include well-proportioned nails, long toes, the eyelashes of a cow, and a good complexion. She remains in isolation in the temple until she reaches the age of puberty.[10]

The Transformation of the Concept of God

The major obstacle confronting a missionary when communicating the Christian message is that the people already have their own cosmology with its view of gods and spirits. It is not as though the missionary is coming to a blank sheet of paper onto which he has to pen his message, since he finds a complex script already present. He may either seek to discard the original piece of paper and replace it with new or seek to modify the existing writing to make it more akin to that of the biblical revelation.

The question of these options is one that will be met continually in this study, and it needs to be considered carefully. If the missionary resorts to the first option of rejecting their traditional cosmology, he may seem to achieve a start for his communication that is free from compromise. However, it does raise several problems.

First, the notions of God held by a society provide a most vital key to an understanding of the deepest of human feelings. As William Reyburn has written,

> In fact, the missionary who will know his people will have to first know their God. How a people symbolise the supernatural, and the way they think and feel toward their God or gods is not only a clue to the stuff of which the society is made, but also an indication of what in Christianity will be immediately relevant.[11]

Second, to reject the religious system of a people is to reject the heart of their culture. This results in a break with their traditional culture and a total adoption of another, which is usually that of the missionary. The process of becoming a Christian is therefore one of cultural conversion as well as Christian conversion. This was the central theme within Paul's letter to the Galatians, where Paul objected to the practices of the Judaizers who wanted gentile converts to take on Jewish culture.

Third, the majority of people do not want to leave their traditional culture, and so they seek some way of reconciling the many views that are open to them. Outwardly they may practice Christianity, but inwardly the traditional beliefs play a far more significant role in everyday life.

For these reasons missionaries have often preferred the second option and have commenced with the ideas that people already have of a creator god and try to transform these concepts into those revealed in the Bible. For example, in Bible translation, the local name for the supreme being is often taken and used for the word *God* in our English translations. Among the Karimojong the word that is used is *Akuj,* which the people understand as meaning the supreme creator. Within the context of the Scriptures the Karimojong will have their original ideas of Akuj modified to one that is more biblical. In case the reader is surprised at this process, it is necessary to state the Paul was willing to use the Greek word *theos* as a translation for the Hebrew name of God. Through teaching, the Greeks, who mostly practiced primal religions, came to appreciate the character of God as revealed in the Old Testament. A similar process occurred with the English word *God,* which originated from a name of one of the Teutonic hierarchy of gods. A biblical content was given to each of these names, which mixed a familiarity of the term with a new interpretation. Communication commenced where the people were, and not with a negation of their beliefs.

Although it is an obvious and easy road from the traditional concept of a creator god to that of the God of the Bible, it is not without its dangers. A clear distinction must be made between any association of the Christian revelation of the supreme being with that of any of the lesser created deities. The Bible teaches a dichotomy between the Creator and the creation (see Figure

3.1). Paul refers to the altar "to an unknown god," a concept that is common among many polytheistic peoples, but goes on to proclaim "the God who made the world and everything in it is the Lord of heaven and earth and does not live in temples built by hands" (Acts 17:24).

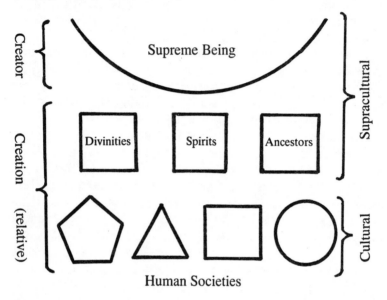

Figure 3.1. The main features of a biblical cosmology

Further, in tribal mythology the creator god is remembered as one who created and has moved away. He is considered as being remote from the daily lives of ordinary people, in a way similar to the philosophy of Deism in the West. As Alan Tippett has stressed, "The only way of distinguishing this retired creator from the God of the Bible is to insist that our Creator God is alive, still creating and providing, and indeed is the same One as our Heavenly Father."[12] People therefore need to see that God is active in the world today, and He is concerned about their felt-needs.

Another difficulty concerning the nature of deity is illustrated by the Navaho, the largest tribe in the U.S., numbering over 90,000 people. Their traditional mythology gave great importance to a female deity called "Changing Woman" who transformed the world to make it as it is today. The Navaho have found it difficult to accept the Bible, which speaks of God only in masculine terms. In addition, the concept of a God who is entirely good is also hard for the Navaho to understand, for their worldview insists that all beings have an evil as well as a good side.[13]

Care must also be taken when missionaries use the many names of the creator god found in the different languages of the world. The impression can be given to converts from a polytheistic society of a system of tribal gods. It is important to stress that there is but one God traditionally known to people by different names but now revealed fully in the Scriptures through the life of Christ. For primal societies it is essential that Christian doctrine is examined as it would be seen through their eyes and instruction given in the whole teaching of the Scriptures.

Notes

1. Okot P'Bitek, *Religion of the Central Luo* (Kenya Literature Bureau: Nairobi, 1978), pp. 41–58.
2. John S. Mbiti, *Concepts of God in Africa* (SPCK: London, 1971), p. 49.
3. Geoffrey Parrinder, *African Mythology* (Paul Hamlyn: London, 1967), p. 44.
4. John V. Taylor, *The Primal Vision* (SCM Press: London, 1977), p. 80.
5. Mbiti, op. cit.
6. H. A. Guerber, *The Myths of Greece and Rome* (George G. Harrap: London, 1925).
7. Frena Bloomfield, *The Book of Chinese Beliefs* (Arrow Books: London, 1983).
8. *Middle East*, February 1979, p. 59.
9. Joyce Savidge, *This Is Hong Kong: Temples* (Hong Kong Government Publications: Hong Kong, 1977), pp. 34–57.
10. *The Daily Telegraph*, February 20, 1986, p. 19.
11. William D. Reyburn, "The Transformation of God and the Conversion of Man," in W. A. Smalley, ed., *Readings in Missionary Anthropology* (William Carey Library: Pasa-

dena, 1974), p. 26.
12. Alan Tippett, *Introduction to Missiology* (William Carey Library: Pasadena, 1987), p. 81.
13. Clyde Kluckhohn and Dorothea Leighton, *The Navaho* (Doubleday: New York, 1962), p. 133.

4

The Human Soul

What is man? This is a question not limited to the Western peoples but asked and answered by all. The answers given can vary greatly from those commonly understood in the West, and yet it is essential to appreciate the different conceptions of human personality if one is to understand many of the practical aspects of primal worldviews. Before one studies these various concepts, it is essential to appreciate the lack of any clear philosophy existing within Western understanding of this subject. For example, how do personality, spirit, mind, will, soul, and emotions all relate? What is lost when a person dies? Other societies seek to grapple with these questions and formulate distinctly varied answers.

The Multiple Self

Central to the view of personality in many societies is the concept of the "multiple self." Unlike the Western notion where personality is assumed to be an integrated whole, many societies picture the human self as consisting of separate entities rather loosely held together, each with its separate source and function. This is especially significant in Africa.

According to the Ga of Ghana, a human being consists of three distinct entities: the *sumsuma,* the *kla,* and the *ghomotfo* or body.[1] The *sumsuma* (see Figure 4.1) is able to leave the body in dreams and mind wandering. The *sumsuma* is not only conscious but may be wiser than the man himself. When an orator speaks with such eloquence that the attention of his audience is held, then the *sumsuma* of the one is said to have

Figure 4.1. The Akan symbol for the sumsuma *or* sumsum, *which is often used as a design in cloth*

grasped the *sumsuma* of the listeners. Here is a phenomenon that all have known at one time or another. In English, we say that a theatrical performance was gripping, or that the time seemed to pass so quickly it was like being under a spell.

The Ga believe that not only do people have a *kla*, but so do all living objects. If the *kla* leaves the body, then life also departs. An individual of powerful personality but frail physique is said to have a strong *sumsuma* but a weak *kla*. When a person dies, both the *sumsuma* and the *kla* leave the body. Although the *kla* is believed to be invisible, it is regarded as having arms and legs corresponding to a visible body.

The *kla* is the part of the individual that is passed on in reincarnation. When a man dies, he gives up his *kla* and becomes a ghost (*sisa*). When the *kla* is reborn, this does not affect the *sisa*. Thus it can be seen that over a period of time the number of *kla* will remain the same although the number of *sisa* increases. The fact of the reincarnation of the *kla* shows the importance of the unity of the individual with that of the tribe as a whole. This is an important aspect of the belief systems of all primal societies.

Every family gives to each of its children what is called *gbefi*, which may most simply be translated in English as "luck" or "fate." Even so, the notion is personified as something external to the owner and not an integrated part of the man's personality. The *gbefi* usually walks behind the man, but if the *gbefi* starts to walk in front of him, it could get out of hand and lead him into trouble. The *gbefi* may become so evil that it must be driven away.

The complexity of the Ga view of personality is not unusual, especially among African peoples. Among the Dahomeans of Benin a man is supposed to have four souls, while a woman has only three. The first soul is inherited from an ancestor and accounts for the physical resemblance that a child may have to an elder. The second soul is what characterizes the person as a particular individual. This is often associated with the voice, and when it leaves the body, the person dies. The third soul is a small piece of the supreme being, which allows some control over human beings. When the person dies, this soul is taken back by the god. The fourth soul, which is one's fate, is acquired by a man at his initiation to adulthood. This soul is concerned not only with the welfare of the individual but with all the other members of a man's household.[2]

It is essential that in any attempt to understand such concepts, one uses the terms used in the people's own language. Trying to fit Ga concepts into English terms is liable to result in confusion. However, when it comes to translation, one has to find an equivalent term, and in the Ga Bible the term *sumsuma* has been used to translate the word *soul* as in "Bless the Lord, O my soul."

The External Soul

The repercussion from the Ga example quoted above is that the concept of the multiple self leads to an external dimension to the self. This is generally an alien concept to the Western worldview, and for this reason the Westerner often fails to appreciate the consequences of the external character of the soul as found in many societies.

In many areas of the world, the soul, or one component of the soul, may be likened to a little man within the person's body. This soul may be located behind the eyes or in the heart or liver. It is able to leave the body, as may the *sumsuma* in Ga thinking. This has a number of important effects.

First, dreams are considered to result from the soul's leaving the body while the person is asleep. With the Ga it is the *sumsuma* that leaves the body. Sometimes it is said that when a child struggles in its sleep, its *kla* and *sumsuma* are fighting together. When the *sumsuma* does leave the body, it is supposed to travel along an invisible cobweb. If a person is awakened suddenly, his *sumsuma* may not be able to find its way back, and the person may become ill.

The primal understanding of dreams is therefore very different from that of the Westerner. The latter may regard dreams as the result of eating cheese late at night and having no reality in themselves. The Ga, on the other hand, understand dreams as real experiences encountered by the *sumsuma* while other elements of the self sleep. Dreams therefore are taken far more seriously than by Westerners, and one may often hear people talking over what could be the meaning of a particular dream.

Among the Iban of Sarawak a distinction is made between good dreams and bad. A bad dream is regarded as a warning, and after one, the dreamer would not leave his long house in the morning, otherwise something bad might happen to him such as being bitten by a snake or attacked by a crocodile while he bathed in the river. Alternatively, some dreams are regarded as being signs of good fortune. One Iban evangelist told me the following story: "I know one Iban man who hated the Christians, but one night he had a dream. In the dream he met a white man who showed him the life of a Christian and a non-Christian. When he awoke he burned his fetishes and accepted the Lord Jesus as his saviour."[3]

The second repercussion of the external concept of the soul is that the failure of the soul to return to the body can cause sickness. This is why in many Muslim countries a person is not awakened suddenly, but the little finger is touched and a prayer recited, *"Bismillah"* (in the name of God). The soul may also be alarmed while the person is awake and in fright may leave the body. The person will be left in a state in which he is withdrawn from the world and even unable to communicate to others. Among the Batak of Sumatra, parents are cautious in chastising their children lest their sensitive souls leave them and they die.[4] These are symptoms that a Western doctor would diagnose as shock.

The Buryat are a people living in the USSR near the border with China.[5] They consider that humans each have three components to the personality. The first is housed within the skeleton of the person. It is an invisible copy of the skeleton and may be broken if the bone is broken, and it disintegrates after death, as does the skeleton. The second has the form of a little person resident in the trunk of the body. It may take a form that can fly like a wasp or a bee. It is the loss of this aspect that results in sickness, and the healer, called "*shaman*," needs to retrieve this lost soul if the person is to be healed. A fuller description of the work of the *shaman* will be given in chapter 14. The third and highest soul is similar to the second, except at death it is called by the chief god to the afterworld. There it lives for a term as it had on earth and then is born again.

A third aspect of the externalizing nature of the self is that of anger. In Africa there is a common belief that anger can take on a life of its own. It continues to be part of the self, but it also moves out beyond the person and can become an independent agent. As such it can act upon the person or object that has caused the anger. An Akan proverb says, "Anger is like a stranger; it does not stay in one house." A man may cause another to become sick simply by brooding in anger at the other's insults. At times of severe offense to his father the anger so generated can cause the death of the child. Supreme respect for one's father and paternal kin is therefore expected of every individual if health, peace, and tranquillity are to continue.[6]

Continuity of the Soul

In order to understand the complexity of how a people perceive the human personality it is necessary not only to know the nature of the soul in life but also to know where the soul originated and to where it goes. The problems with this can be seen in the difficulties faced by Christians in answering the question of the origin of the soul. During the history of Christian theology, three main views have been proposed.

1. *Creationist.* God creates a new soul at the birth of every individual. This is a view that has often been held by the Eastern church.

2. *Preexistent.* Human souls were created by God at an earlier time and are joined to the particular body at its biological birth. Origen was a major exponent of this view.

3. *Traducian.* The souls of men are propagated along with their bodies by the natural process of procreation.

It is interesting that Augustine could not choose between creationism and Traducianism. Strong tends to prefer the Traducian view, while Berkhof shows a preference for the creationist view.[7] Not only does this confusion show the lack of precision within Christian theology, but it warns us about criticizing a similar lack of precision within the primal worldviews.

Most primal worldviews hold to some form of preexistence of the soul, and this requires the assumption of some mysterious spiritual world. Among the Baoule of the Ivory Coast this spiritual world is called *blolo,* about which little is known. All life comes from *blolo,* and after a short or long stay it returns there. It is a world that transcends the biological world but in some way duplicates this world, apart from being impervious to death.

Father Vincent Guerry tries to describe the Baoule view of life in these words:

> When the boy—whom we shall call Yao—was born, he came straight from the *blolo* and was given a body and a "double"; but until he gets to the age of reason, Yao remains what he had been there, a little ancestor. During this whole period, he remains in contact with the other ancestors and talks to them. And when he dies he will become an ancestor again. But when I ask just who it is who goes to the *blolo,* the answer is: not the body, not the double, but Yao himself, the Yao who existed before he had either a body or

a double. . . . The double is but a shadow.[8]

The concept of a spiritual double is one spread throughout much of West Africa. Among the Yoruba it is called *ikeji;* among the Igbo, *chi;* and *ehi* among the Bini people. The concept does not allow precise translation into English and has been described in anthropological literature as "guardian angel," "transcendental self," or "invisible half." A man's double is associated with him as soon as he is born, and from then on the person's abilities and faults, and his good and bad fortunes, are ascribed to his double. Among the Bini, the double is regarded as being in constant spiritual communication with the man. The double may be seen in dreams, or a diviner may reveal the *ehi*'s wishes.[9]

From the Baoule description, one can see that in this way that part of the ancestor's self (the transcendent soul) reappears in the transcendent soul of the child. The external characteristic of the multiple self allows a continuity of the soul while also recognizing a decay of the worldly existence.

The African concept of "partial" reincarnation must be distinguished from the "total" reincarnation in Buddhist and Hindu thought. An inherent element of Hindu thought is the doctrine of *samsara* with the allied concept of *karma*. *Samsara* is the cycle of birth and rebirth to which all souls are subject. What determines the body or form into which the soul is born is the cosmic law of *karma*. It is through the law of *karma* that one can understand why different souls are born to different levels of status and fortune. Although the beliefs of the village Hindu are vague as to what happens to the soul after death, there is a commonly held view about numerous heavens and hells. The description of the heavens and hells, however, varies almost from individual to individual.

The tortures of hell are pictured on sheets sold in many Indian bazaars. Bodies are pictured as being eaten by dogs or transfixed by spears or even plunged head downward into a sea of mud. In contrast, the heavens are depicted equally vividly, as individuals are dragged safely across the monster-ridden plains of existence. The soul is considered as going to heaven or hell until its merit or sin runs out, after which it is reborn into an appropriate form.

This reveals one of the major differences between the African and Indian view of the afterlife. In the Indian concept the afterlife is seen as being divided into two possible domains: heavens and hells. In the African worldview there is only one domain, that of the ancestors. There is therefore no notion of judgment or punishment. African primal religions are very pragmatic, being concerned with survival and betterment in this life. This includes attaining a respected position in the community, having children, living to an old age, and not dying a bad death resulting from witchcraft. The Hindu worldview recognizes the importance of this pragmatic aspect, but it also recognizes the need to acquire merit so that one may achieve a good rebirth and, if possible, the eventual liberation from the law of *karma*.

"Soul-Stuff"

Many societies hold the belief that in some way the very personality of the individual is contained in elements of the body such as the hair, fingernails, or spittle. It is as if these elements contain the *mana* of the person and, if lost, will be to the detriment of the individual. Care is therefore taken with the disposal of such items, lest an enemy get hold of them and use them for harm. The concept has often been given the rather colloquial expression "soul-stuff." It does, however, provide a way of appreciating a whole range of ideas and practices that are common in primal societies.

The following extract illustrates the typical practice of a Yoruba sorcerer:

> You take the hair of a man's head. You prepare medicine and put it with the hair and put them both in an ant hill. As the ants are circulating about the medicine, so the victim will feel it inside his head, or you may put the medicine and the man's hair under an anvil, and every time the blacksmith strikes the anvil so he will feel it inside his head.[10]

Hair and nails are looked on as containing soul stuff in surpassing measure because they are constantly growing, a proof of their indestructible power. Blood and the sex organs are frequently regarded as being rich in soul-stuff. When the government of Papua New Guinea was planning to establish a blood bank, it found a great hesitancy among the people. The rumor was that when you gave blood, the government would have power over you. Only after an extensive education program were some people willing to give blood.

Many people have a fear of the camera because they believe that something of the soul may be caught by the camera. This can then be used as power over that person. There is a concern among some in the Ivory Coast that the spittle used to seal envelopes can be used for sorcery. Some primal societies even regard the perspiration of an individual as containing soul-stuff, and so clothes that have become saturated with it have gained soul stuff. Footprints can even be used as a source of sorcery by means of the sweat that adheres to them.

Likewise, personal names are often regarded as being far more than a label but a part of the individual's personality. The shadow may be considered in a similar way. It is regarded as a projection of the living soul, and for this reason many societies believe that ghosts cast no shadow. Among the Batak, it is forbidden to walk on anyone's shadow or to beat it:

> The shadow of man must not fall on a grave or a place where evil spirits dwell, otherwise the spirits will get the owner into their power. A man must not let his shadow fall on other people's food, else the eater will appropriate with the food the man's soul power, and he will pine away.[11]

In order to comprehend the primal concept of personality, one must enter into a world that appears very strange to the Westerner. Gone is the apparent impervious wall that protects the individual from the outside world. Gone is the integrated view of self that makes the Westerner feel as though he is a distinct isolated being. Instead one finds an interrelatedness of people in an integrated community. The strong sense of individualism that is so common in Western societies is not known in primal societies. The individual is part of nature and part of the tribe as a whole. As John Taylor has said, "In Africa 'I think, therefore I am' is replaced by 'I participate, therefore I am.'"[12]

Notes

1. M. J. Field, *Religion and Medicine of the Ga People* (Oxford University Press: London, 1961), pp. 92–99.
2. William J. Goode, *Religion Among the Primitives* (Free Press: Illinois, 1951), pp. 191–94.
3. Personal comments from an Iban evangelist, 1987.
4. Johannes Warneck, *The Living Christ and Dying Heathenism* (Baker: Grand Rapids, 1954), p. 47.
5. Lawrence Krader, "Buryat Religion and Society," in John Middleton, *Gods and Ritual* (University of Texas Press: Austin, 1967), pp. 103–32.
6. Kofi Appiah-Kubi, "The Akan Concept of Human Personality," in E. Ade Adegbola, *Traditional Religion in West Africa* (Asempa Publishers: Accra, 1983), p. 259.
7. Louis Berkhof, *Systematic Theology* (Banner of Truth Trust: London, 1969), p. 201.
8. Fr. Vincent Guerry, *Life with the Baoule* (Three Continents Press: Washington, 1975), pp. 137–44.
9. Matthew Omijeh, "Ehi—The Concept of the Guardian Angel in Bini Religion," in Ade Adegbola, op. cit., pp. 265–69.
10. Raymond Price, "Indigenous Yoruba Psychiatry," in Ari Kiev, *Magic, Faith and Healing* (Free Press: New York, 1964), p. 90.
11. Warneck, op. cit., p. 45.
12. John V. Taylor, *The Primal Vision* (SCM Press: London, 1977), p. 85.

5

Ghosts and Ancestors

Ghosts—the very word brings to mind a whole host of ideas and feelings. It is a striking fact that a belief in what may loosely be called ghosts is found in every culture. The notion of the character and formation of such supernatural beings may vary, but the idea of some ongoing existence of the dead that has an influence upon this world is one that is common to all. This was the very point that led Sir Herbert Spencer to argue for an evolutionary development in religious thought, originating with a belief in ghosts, moving to belief in ancestors and finally to religion.[1]

The tenacity of the belief in ghosts can even be seen within Western society where it is retained, despite a strong adherence to the philosophy of materialism. As the African writer Idowu concluded about Western society,

> Modern sophisticated man may wish...to dismiss as puerile stories of experiences of ghosts and of haunted places; but deep down in the minds of thousands of men and women of every level of spiritual or intellectual attainment is the... persistent notion, that the deceased still have a part to play, for better or for worse, in the lives of the living.[2]

In 1882, the Society for Psychical Research was founded in Britain by some eminent scholars. Its aim was to investigate in a scientific manner apparently inexplicable phenomena, such as ghosts. Throughout the past hundred years this society and other similar organizations have documented numerous cases. Much trickery and illusion have been revealed, but there have always been a few stubborn remaining cases that have baffled the natural mind.

Although the concept of ghosts is one that is surprisingly

common, the ways in which it is understood by people vary greatly. It is rarely regarded as part of the main religion of a people, but it is part of the oral traditions that run parallel to recognized religious belief and practice. Because of the wide variety of ideas among peoples, it is necessary to be careful to define what one means by the term *ghost*. First, we will make a distinction between ghost and spirit (or god). A spirit may be regarded as having always existed in the one form, which is that of a "supernatural" being, while a ghost has, at one time, been a natural living being. Second, the notion of a ghost relates to the concept of the nature of the soul and to the element that continues to exist beyond biological death. Third, the possibility of a kinship link with the deceased person can lead to a special relationship with the ghost, which we will therefore specify by using the term *ancestor*. It is important to retain a distinction between ghost and ancestor because the concept of a kinship link implies the continued interest of the ancestor in the well-being of the family, while if a ghost is unrelated to a particular person, it may seek to cause mischief and harm.

Ghosts

Among Hindus there is a common and strong belief in ghosts, or *bhootha*. These may be either male or female, called *bhooth* or *churail,* respectively.[3] Anyone who dies in irregular circumstances may become a *bhootha,* but especially those who die by drowning, fire, murder, violence, or suicide. They haunt the places where they met their deaths, cremation grounds, isolated fields, dark clusters of trees, deserted houses, and similar places. Because of their envy of the living, such ghosts can cause harm in many ways. This idea of a ghost resulting from a "bad death" is common among many societies, and especially so among the peoples of Africa. This is similar to the Western notion of ghosts as being those who have died as a result of murder or execution.

In Africa today, there is still great concern at a bad death. This may lead to considerable fear in which a man's house may be abandoned in case the ghost will return and cause harm. It could be that a whole village will move to another locality.

However, more usually a diviner would be called in to identify the cause of death, especially if it is feared that it could be as a result of witchcraft. Once the cause has been identified, some offering may be necessary to pacify the ghost and encourage it to leave and cause no more harm to the people. Among the Bimoba of Ghana one of the worst forms of bad death is that of a woman dying during childbirth with the baby undelivered. In this case

> the woman's room is broken down, every trace of it is cleared, and all her belongings are thrown away. No funeral ceremony can be performed in such cases, for the spirit (ghost) refuses to go to God; it just wanders about, and is called *kpeeyiok*, (literally meaning "dead person without an owner").[4]

John Beattie recounts the story from an elderly man of the Banyoro of Uganda:

> Nameless ghosts generally come from outside the household, perhaps from very far away. They come especially from men who were killed with women (i.e. in war); perhaps speared and thrown into pits. . . . These nameless ghosts may make impossible demands. I once heard of one which asked for buffalo milk, a dog's horn, and the tendon of a *nkuba* (a fabulous fowl associated with thunder and lightning). It said that it wanted to drink buffalo milk in the dog's horn. If it doesn't get what it wants, it may kill off a whole settlement. One such group of [ghosts] lived in Kiswaza, and now not a single person of that group remains.[5]

The Banyoro do not believe that ghosts can be seen, but that they appear only in dreams in the image of the dead person. However, most societies tend to believe that ghosts may materialize in some form that can be seen by the living. In northern India, the *bhootha* are believed to be able to appear at night in the form of human beings. There are two notable differences: first, they do not cast a shadow, and second, their feet point backward. In the villages of India the fear of such ghosts is strong, and a person would avoid being in isolated fields when night has come. In case the Western reader is tempted to laugh at such fears, who has never felt a sense of fear of the unknown when walking in a dark, lonely area?

Another common characteristic of the belief in such wandering ghosts is the possibility of a person becoming possessed by them. A *bhootha* may lay hold of any passerby who may have unwittingly trespassed within its domain or may have roused its interest. The ghost is said to "lay hold of" the person, and the victim has to resort to exorcism for deliverance. This can take various forms, but a discussion of this topic will be left until chapter 13 in which the whole subject of possession will be considered.

Ghosts may be considered to have varying degrees of human characteristics. Not all are considered to be harmful and wanting revenge. Some, such as those of traditional Chinese mythology, are delightfully human. The Chinese have stories about female ghosts who come to a poor scholar in his mountain retreat to live with him and minister to him in his sickness. Other stories tell about a female ghost who returns to her lover and bears him children. The period of cohabitation may last from a few weeks or for a generation until she has borne him children and they have reached adulthood. These children, after they have succeeded in their examinations, come back for their mother only to find that the gorgeous mansion of their youth has disappeared and in its place is an old grave, with a hole underground, where lies a dead old mother fox. Sometimes she leaves behind a note saying that she was sorry to leave them, but that she was a fox and only wanted to enjoy human life, and now since she has seen them prosper, she is grateful and hopes they will forgive her.[6]

Ancestors: African Concepts

Among many societies a belief in the immanence and concern of ancestral ghosts is a common, although varied, notion. To illustrate the variation and importance of such beliefs we will consider the general ancestral cults found in Africa and in the Orient.

The Westerner frequently fails to appreciate the priority of ancestors within African beliefs. This is due to the individualistic view he has of life, unlike the African for whom the family and tribe are more significant. The family includes both the living and the ghosts of the dead. Just because persons have moved from the world of fleshly order and existence, this does not mean that they have ceased to exist as part of the tribe. The nearest Western equivalent that one can see is that of the church visible and invisible. The church visible consists of those members of the church who are alive at this moment, while the church invisible consists of those members who have died and are "with Christ." To stress this relationship between the ancestor and the living, John Mbiti has used the term *the living dead* for the ancestors.[7]

The fact that the ancestors have left this world means that they have become freed from the restrictions imposed by the physical world. Therefore, they have greater power and can influence the lives of their earthly descendants. Just as a living father or mother has the power to bless or curse the undertakings of the children, so an ancestor has a similar and possibly much greater power. An ancestor may come near to a person when he sleeps and by dreams warn him of impending danger. John Beattie tells the story of a Banyoro man who was warned in a dream by his deceased father that sorcery was being worked on him by a neighbor. However, the father protected his son, and in the morning the man found the horn that had been used in the sorcery and destroyed it by burning. Two days later the neighbor died.[8]

Not only may the ancestor bring blessing, but it may also cause harm to those who displease it. This may be in the form of sickness, barrenness of women, or crop failure. For this reason care must be taken to respect ancestors and even offer them sacrifices. Many African peoples, like the Ga, never eat or drink without tipping a small portion on the ground for the ancestors.[9] In many parts of Africa, the head of the family pours out beer, water, or milk as a libation to the ancestors. The Ga hold special celebrations once or twice a year where libations are poured out for the ancestors at specific spots in the homes. The stools of the family heads are purified with the sacrifice of fowls and the ancestors invoked to partake in special ritual meals.[10]

The anthropologist M. J. Field gives an account of the Ga that illustrates many of these points:

An old man of Labadi abruptly refused to tell me any more of his family affairs. He said that since he last saw me he had been very sick. His gums, mouth, and lips had swollen and become very sore and painful, and all at once it came to him that his forefathers were angry with him for chattering about their affairs and had smitten his mouth in warning. He rose immediately and poured out rum and apologies and promised not to offend again. His mouth then quickly healed, leaving him convinced that any further transgression would cause his speedy death.[11]

The period of ancestorhood tends to be conceived of in one of two ways: linear or cyclic. In the linear model the ancestor is supposed to have an existence for a period, but it does not return to have further human existence. The cyclic model assumes the possibility of a reincarnation of the ancestor in the form of a newborn child (see Figure 5.1).

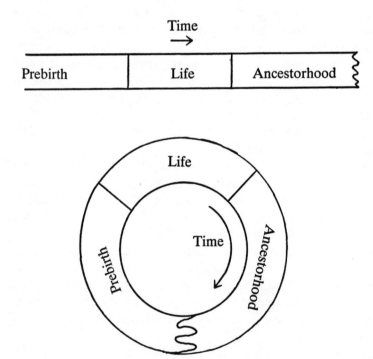

Figure 5.1. Cyclic and linear concepts of existence

For those societies believing in a linear view of ancestorhood one could see that with time the number of ancestors would become multitudinous. For this reason there is some form of limit on the number of ancestors with which one must reckon, and the most common is the limit resulting from the loss in remembrance. So long as the ancestor is remembered by some living person, the ancestor has some existence, but with the death of the last person to remember the ancestor, the ghost ceases to have the same existence. The ghost may wander lost or congregate with other ghosts in the world of the ghosts. Exactly what is the final state of the ghost is often unclear.

Many African peoples do in fact believe in the reincarnation of the ancestor. This is an important belief among the Ga, who consider that the dead will be reborn only in their own families, a grandfather as a grandson or a dead first child as a second child. One can therefore see the great curse that childlessness is to an African family and even how this reflects on the whole concept of contraception. The Ga word for this reincarnation is the same as that used for a vine twining around a post so that it reappears again and again all the way up the post. This is an important aspect in the ancestral beliefs of the Nilotic peoples of eastern African such as the Masai or Karimojong. The whole of the Karimojong view of adult life is a cycle made up of various age sets, which make up four generations, of which about half the members are ancestors (defunct age sets) at any particular time.[12]

Frequently when a child is born, people will study the child to see which of the ancestors he or she resembles. When a child dies at birth, it may be persuaded to be born again, and this time to stay with the living. The Ga provide us yet again with an example of this. When a couple lost a child, both father and mother were traditionally shut up together for seven days fasting and mourning. During these days they were supposed to focus their thoughts on the child and tell him aloud that they wish for his return. On the eighth day they were taken to the beach and purified. The woman was thereafter assumed to become pregnant and the child born again.[13]

Thus, in African society the dead are not really forgotten but are considered to be sociologically alive, at least for a period of time. They are remembered by offerings and respect, and the ancestors in turn are considered as helping the living.

Ancestors: Oriental Patterns

Ancestorhood is a notion not limited to Africa; it is found in many parts of the world, and nowhere more so than in the Orient. In China, Japan, and Korea the ancestor cult has remained strong even in sophisticated societies, mainly through the rationale given to it by Confucianism. As the Confucianist classic states: "When one lives one should think of his ancestors, and when one drinks one should think of the spring from which the water comes." Or, in a more direct translation, "To live, one should not forget one's origin; to drink, one should remember its source."

The Chinese believes that the ancestors fly around the houses of his family, and as with the African pattern, they can bring fortune or misfortune to the living. To show their respect for the departed the Chinese take meticulous care of the graves of their ancestors. Especially at the Ching Ming festival (April 5) one will see thousands of people in Hong Kong visiting the graves of their families to clean them and present them with food offerings and yellow paper money. The vast majority of Chinese have a great concern for or even a fear of the ancestors. A family will spend much money to obtain an auspicious grave site and then make many offerings to appease the ancestor. If anything goes wrong in the family soon after the death of the person, they will assume that the ancestor is unhappy and will call in a medium to investigate. The role of the medium will be considered in chapter 15.

Most Oriental homes have an ancestral shrine that is the center of the family veneration. The focus of the shrine is an ancestral tablet, which lists the names of the ancestors of the particular family. The rituals involved were once very complex, but in recent years these have been greatly simplified. Worship is usually led by the eldest son, who offers prayers, burning incense, and food and drink offerings. It is usually believed that the ancestor comes to the tablet to receive the offerings. Special considerations are given to the ancestor at the New Year and the anniversary of the death of the person.

To the Chinese it is an unforgivable breach of filial piety to fail to make offerings to one's ancestors, and it is a great tragedy for a couple not to have a son to do this for them. Daughters marry out of the family, and if there is no son to make them offerings, they may become "hungry ghosts," lost and homeless. For this reason many Chinese parents have objected strongly to their children becoming Christians.

The importance of ancestor veneration within Oriental society means that for many first-generation Christians a major question they must face is how they participate in their family ancestral rituals. Many young Christians have faced great social pressure or even violence because they have refused to participate in the family rituals.[14]

Ghosts and the Bible

There are two common assumptions about ghosts made by Christians, namely, that the dead are unable to contact the living, and that the materializations are evil spirits in disguise. The first assumption is based on verses such as Job 7:9: "So he who goes down to the grave does not return." However, it must be realized that some of Job's statements question the traditional Hebrew religious views, and some would say border on blasphemy (e.g. Job 9:14–35). It would therefore be unwise to base any doctrine totally on his statements. A more reliable basis is the parable of the rich man and Lazarus in Luke 16:19–31. Even so, we cannot conclude that ghosts are unable to communicate with the living. A careful reading shows that Abraham does not tell the rich man that it is impossible for the dead to return, but that it is spiritually useless: "He [Abraham] said to him, 'If they do not listen to Moses and the Prophets, they will not be convinced even if someone rises from the dead'" (Luke 16:31).

One may in fact make a case for the reality of ghosts from the Bible. In the well-known story of the so-called witch of Endor (1 Sam. 28), the medium was surprised that Samuel actually rose from the dead. This did not seem to be what she expected. Also in the New Testament one finds Moses and Elijah conversing with Jesus on the Mount of Transfiguration. Although these are unique cases, they do not discount the possibility of ghosts.[15]

One must therefore conclude that the Bible does leave open the possibility that the dead may communicate with the living. Scripture, however, is emphatic that any attempt to communicate with the departed is sin. In Israel there was to be a total ban on anyone who "consults the dead" (Deut. 18:11). One of the sins of Israel condemned by Isaiah is that the people tried to consult the dead: "When men tell you to consult mediums and spiritists, who whisper and mutter, should not a people inquire of their God? Why consult the dead on behalf of the living?" (Isa. 8:19). One must conclude that the Bible absolutely forbids Christians to communicate with ghosts even if they are ancestral ghosts.

The Bible exposes death as being a radical break with life. If this is true, then one may also agree with the statement of the Asian Consultation on Ancestor Practices:

> "Ancestors' spirits" have no supernatural power either to bestow blessings or to inflict curses upon the descendants. We, therefore, encourage Christians confronted with the problems of ancestor practices not to be controlled by a sense of fear, trust, or adoration of the ancestors nor create an impression of such to the surrounding society and to fellow Christians.[16]

On the other hand, the Asian Consultation recognized the need to stress the obligation of children to "honor your father and your mother" (Exod. 20:12).

This consultation has shown the necessity for Third World Christians to reassess the Scriptures in the light of their own cultural heritage. This is a complex subject, and the Westerner must approach it with humility. It may be easy for him to condemn the ancestral shrines of the peoples of the Orient, but where does the line fall between that and his own act of placing flowers on the grave of a departed loved one or even a Christian memorial service?

How may one answer the African Christian who affirms that it was his deceased father who spoke to him in a dream and so saved him from harm? These may easily be considered as hallucinations due to emotional stress, but could they just as well be warnings from God in the same way as they are found in the Bible? As Robert Cook has written when he paraphrased the seventeenth-century philosopher, Thomas Hobbes, "When a man claims that an ancestor spoke to him in a dream, this is no more than to say that he dreamed that an ancestor spoke to him."[17]

Notes

1. Herbert Spencer, *The Principles of Sociology* (Appleton: New York, 1880–96), vols. 2 and 3.
2. E. Bolaji Idowu, *African Traditional Religion* (SCM Press: London, 1974), p. 178.
3. Uma Anand, "Ritual Arts at Wayside Shrines," in *Gods of the Byways* (Museum of Modern Art: Oxford, 1982), p. 11.
4. Peter Barker, *Peoples, Languages, and Religion in Northern Ghana* (GEC: Accra, 1986), p. 164.
5. John H. M. Beattie, "The Ghost Cult in Bunyoro," in John Middleton, *Gods and Rituals* (University of Texas: Austin, 1967), p. 262.
6. Lin Yutang, *My Country and My People* (Heinemann: London, 1962), pp. 90–91.
7. John S. Mbiti, *An Introduction to African Religion* (Heinemann: London, 1975), p. 119.
8. Beattie, op. cit., p. 257.
9. M. J. Field, *Religion and Medicine of the Ga People* (Oxford University Press: London, 1961), p. 196.
10. Personal comments of Richard Foli, himself a member of the Ga-Adangme tribe (1985).
11. Field, op. cit., p. 196.
12. John Lamphear, *The Traditional History of the Jie of Uganda* (Clarendon Press: Oxford, 1976), p. 41.
13. Field, op. cit., p. 202.
14. Bong Rin Ro, *Christian Alternatives to Ancestor Practices* (ATA: Taichung, Taiwan, 1985), p. 4.
15. Paul Bauer, *Christianity or Superstition* (Marshall, Morgan & Scott: Edinburgh, 1966), pp. 69–76.
16. Bong Rin Ro, op. cit., p. 9.

17. Robert R. Cook, "Ghosts," *East Africa Journal of Evangelical Theology* 4, no. 1 (1985): 45–46.

6

Totem

For most Westerners the word *totem* is immediately linked with the totem pole, which is part of our popular image of the North American Indians. However, this association is misleading because for the few American tribes who did actually make totem poles, these were symbolic representations of their history rather than what the term *totem* has come to mean.[1]

The word *totem* was introduced into the English language at the end of the eighteenth century from an Ojibwa word. The Ojibwa people, who live in the region north of the Great Lakes of North America, have an expression, *ototeman*, which means "he is a relative of mine." The first accurate report about totemism was written by a Methodist missionary, Peter Jones, himself an Ojibwa chief who died in 1856.[2] He explained that the Great Spirit had given five totems to the Ojibwa and each of these have animal names. Members of a particular clan feel a special relationship not only with the other members of the clan but with the totem animal of their clan.

The term *totem* has come to cover a wide range of magico-religious phenomena that are found among many peoples of the world. The definition by Rivers provides a useful starting point in the understanding of totem:

> The term totemism is used for a form of social organisation and magico-religious practice, of which the central feature is the association of certain groups (usually clans or lineages) within a tribe with certain classes of animate or inanimate things, the several groups being associated with distinct classes.[3]

One can see from this definition that totemism is a way of classifying the various clans of a tribe according to animal and

69

plant species. However, in all cases, the association goes much further than just being a useful nomenclature for denoting a social system to become one that has important magical and religious meanings. The human world and the natural world are somehow related to provide a comprehensive view of life. The human, natural, and supernatural are seen as being linked in some particular way and able to influence one another. Nevertheless, the boundary between the human social world and the nonhuman natural world is still regarded as an area of ambiguity and danger.

Tribal Totemism

Totemism is essentially a way of classifying a people group, and as such it affects the way in which the tribe exists and how it sees itself in relation to the world. Totemism may, however, have an individual dimension in which it is related to a particular person. In order to consider the basic characteristics of totemism we will first consider the tribal aspect before looking at the individual manifestation.

First, totemism assumes a mystical association of the tribe with animal, plant, and even inanimate objects. The totem may be supposed to represent or even actually be the ancestor of the tribe or clan. Thus the clan in relation to the totem find a mutual identity with each other. The nature and origin of this relationship are usually expressed by the people in terms of a myth. The Ojibwa, for example, have a myth that explains the origin of their five clans and their totems. Six supernatural beings, they say, emerged from the ocean to mingle with human beings. One of them had his eyes covered and dared not look at the people although he had a great desire to do so. Finally curiosity overcame him, and he partially lifted his veil. As soon as his eyes fell on the form of a human being, that person fell dead as if struck by lightning. Although the intentions of this great creature were friendly to men, his glance was too powerful, and so the other supernatural beings caused him to return to the ocean. The five others remained among the Indians to help them, and it was from them that the five great clans or totems arose: catfish, crane, loon, bear, and marten.[4]

The actual nature of the relationship of the clan with the totem may be expressed in various ways. For example, one people may regard itself to be directly derived from a particular totem. A story may be told of an animal progenitor who was turned into a human being and from whom descended both a human clan and an animal species. These two groups therefore have an intrinsic union and mutual relationship.

In other cases, the founder of the tribe may have had some favorable or unfavorable experiences with an animal or a plant and so ordered that his descendants had to respect the whole species of that animal or plant. Evans-Pritchard recounts the Nuer story (from southern Sudan) of how one clan gained its totem:

> The story is told that long ago some people of Gangni were dying of thirst on a journey. They were wandering, light-headed with thirst and the heat of the sun, when they saw a monitor lizard in a thep-tree. They intended to kill it but it escaped them and following it brought them to water, to which, being a water creature, it naturally made. Ever since, their descendants have respected the lizard and dedicated cows of their herds to the lizard-spirit.[5]

Second, totemism provides a pattern of social organization that gives a sense of social identity and system of marriage between clans. For example, let us imagine two groups living in separate territories but being bound by rules of exogamy (i.e., marrying out of their own clan). A man of one clan must marry a woman of the other clan, and the wife and her children shall reside with the man. Levi-Strauss has presented the following helpful analogy:

> Let us call the two matrilineal moieties Jones and Smith, and the two local groups Oxford and Cambridge. The rule of marriage will then be: If a Jones man of Oxford marries a Smith woman of Cambridge, the children will be Smith (after their mother) of Oxford (after their father).[6]

The son, who would be a Smith of Oxford, would then be required to marry a Jones of Cambridge, and their son would be a Smith of Cambridge, and so the cycle rotates (see Figure 6.1). This is usually called a four-sectional system, but the important point is that these four sections are often named after particular totems, as they are among the Kariera of Western Australia. It is

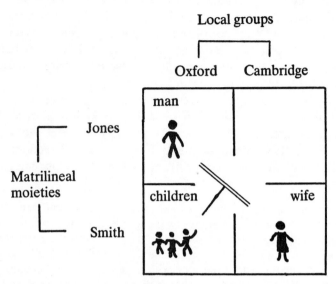

Figure 6.1. Four-sectional system of marriage arrangement

in fact a way of dividing the tribe up into ceremonial groups by means of the method of marriage arrangement.

A third aspect of clan totemism is that of taboo. There is usually some restriction on the eating or even touching of the particular totem. Among the Nuer, for example, the clan that has the monitor lizard as its totem, it is taboo for a man to kill a lizard. If a man knowingly eats the flesh of a lizard, he will die, and even if he should eat it unknowingly, he might fall sick or become crazy. If a man of the clan harms a lizard, his next child may be born with deformed legs resembling those of the lizard.

The Birhor of India have at least thirty-seven clans, twelve being based on animal totems, ten on plants, eight on Hindu castes, and others on inanimate objects. The Birhor think that there is an organic union between the clan and the totem such that any harm done to the totem will result in a corresponding harm to the clan. If a person comes upon a dead totem animal, he must smear his forehead with oil or red dye, but he is not to mourn over it or bury it.

This taboo on the causing of any harm to a totem is almost

universal in totemic societies. The Norwegian missionary Johannes Gausdal, working among the Santals of India who have a system of clan totemism, drew a parallel with the restriction of Genesis 32:32. The text refers to Jacob's wrestling with an unknown man (God) at Peniel where he was touched in the socket of his hip: "Therefore to this day the Israelites do not eat the tendon attached to the socket of the hip, because the socket of Jacob's hip was touched near the tendon." Gausdal points out the similarity in attitude to the way in which a Santal of today regards his *khut* (totem).[7]

Fourth, a common feature of clan totemism is that of totemic rituals. These take many forms, but there are two common classes: commemoration rites and increase rites. Among the Australian aborigines a knowledge of totemism is extremely important in understanding their whole culture.[8] The clan frequently comes together at ceremonies known as "corroborees" to perform rites at certain sacred sites at prescribed times of the year. The rites are usually kept secret and are sanctified in the minds of the people by an ancient mythology. The purpose of these rites is to cooperate with nature so that a particular species should increase. These rites are not an attempt to bring about some extraordinary changes in nature`but a desire to maintain the basic cycle of nature that already exists.

These increase rites may also involve a commemoration of the foundation of the clan and the totem. It may be that it is only at this time that the clan is able to eat the totem, and it does so as a sacred feast. The Holy Communion of the Christian church is an obvious parallel to this rite, which is symbolic of eating the body and drinking the blood of Christ. Such concepts of a sacred feast may provide an important bridge in communicating Christian truth to a primal society.

Group totemism is found in many parts of Africa, India, Oceania, and North and South America. In West Africa, most tribes have some particular totem. For the Ga, it is the duiker (a small antelope); for the Akwamu, the buffalo; for the Fon of Benin, the leopard; and for the Anona clan of Winneba, the parrot. Totemism reveals a close relationship with nature and the dependence that the people have upon nature for their very survival.

Individual Totemism

Not only is totemism a concept that is applied to a particular group, but it can also relate to an individual inasmuch as the person has an intimate relationship with a totem. Here the concept is connected to definite ideas of the nature of the human soul, or souls. A kind of simultaneous existence is assumed between the totem and the person so that the fate of the one affects the fate of the other. If the totem is hurt or killed, then the person will be likewise affected.

Among the Loma of Liberia many items are regarded as possible totems of an individual. These consist of animals such as the leopard, snake, or elephant, or plants such as plantain, cola tree, cassava bush, yam, or pepper plants. The term used by the Loma comes from the root word "thing at the back of a man." This reveals something of the concept of the totem as what accompanies a person to guide and help. An individual's totem may be known by the qualities it imparts to the individual.

For example, George Schwab records some of the comments concerning totems by various Loma informants: "If you see a person who is a very swift runner, that person is sure to have a leopard behind him." "When you see a woman who has a fair number of children, you may feel reasonably certain that she has the banana or plantain tree for her totem. These help women to get plenty children." "Those who have pepper (capsicum) for their totem will often be found growing wealthy."[9]

A man may receive his totem from his father or a daughter from her mother. It is, however, taboo to tell anyone your totem because it will mean that the power of the totem is lost, and so the identity of the totem is made by suggestion to the child. Alternatively, a person may come to an agreement to accept a particular totem as his special helper. One of the most common and feared totems among many peoples of western Africa, including the Loma, is that of the snake.

"If a snake wants to be your totem, it may meet you on the path as you are going somewhere and tell you so. If you accept, you make an agreement with it. If not, it may keep on following you until you agree."[10] With the help of a snake totem, a person is believed to be able to kill anyone he chooses and to accumulate wealth and so become a powerful man in the community.

Among the Iban of Sarawak, it is believed that a man may dream of an ancestor who comes to help him and names an animal in which he is manifested. The Iban observe the mannerisms of a person and so recognize the protector spirit that is embodied within him. Sometimes, the person may even carry with him a part of the animal. Young men eager to receive a powerful spirit may even sleep on the grave of a prominent person and fast to receive a dream in which they are granted the totem of the dead person.

As with group totems, there are often strong taboos concerning individual totems. As the Loma say, "Your totem is yourself. If you eat it, you eat yourself." The offense is all the greater if you actually know that you are committing the act. For this reason the Gagua of the Ivory Coast have the proverb, "Don't ask what meat was in the sauce, you might have eaten your totem."

If a person breaks a taboo related to his totem, he will be punished by the totem. For example, the Loma say, "If you do something to offend it, your *plege pulu* [totem spirit] can come at night and beat you so that you fall down senseless." To appease the totem it is therefore necessary to make an offering of a fowl. The snake totem is considered the most difficult totem to please. It begins to demand greater and greater sacrifices. It may start with wanting a fowl, then a goat, then even a child. It may even later require a human adult as a sacrifice and even a close relative of the person. Ultimately, it will require the person himself!

The totem is believed not only to communicate power to an individual, but it may well draw the people with the same totem together into some form of association. Among the Kpelle of Liberia, there is much talk about the leopard society, which is a secret society seemingly emerged from such a relationship.

Healers, sorcerers, or medicine men of various kinds are generally regarded to have a powerful totem. In several areas of Australia, the totem, called *bala*, is considered to act as the medicine man's assistant going forth to do his work. This is conceived as being a spirit, or second self, and also externalized in the particular animal or plant species. The totem is believed to have been tamed by the medicine man to do his will.[11] The totem guards the man while he is asleep, but normally it resides in the body of the man. When the medicine man goes into a trance, he can send out his totem to gather information or in some cases to kill a person. This notion merges with that of the "familiar spirit" of the *shaman*, which will be discussed in chapter 14.

In southeast Australia, the aborigines believe that a dying medicine man may leave his totem to someone else.[12] The totem may be transmitted to the initiate who will have the totem placed on his chest as he lies on the ground. As the other medicine man chants, the totem is said to sink into the body of the initiate, and it finally disappears. The candidate is then instructed in the taboos of the totem. These rituals are usually surrounded in secrecy, and so little has been documented.

Pseudototemism

Totemism is found among many different peoples and in different forms. The significance of the concept within the life of a people can often go unnoticed by an outsider. However, it can play a most important role as it gives a cohesion within the society. For a person to be cut off from the totem means that he will automatically be cut off from his own people.[13] This, obviously, makes many unwilling to change their religious beliefs.

So as not to lose the immediate significance of the ideas of totemism to Western society, Ralph Linton described the strong sense of group solidarity that formed about a U.S. military unit in the First World War. Similar principles have been identified more recently with soccer crowds. Desmond Morris, with his own unique style, sought to consider some of these aspects in the book *The Soccer Tribe*. He writes,

> Like native tribes, each soccer club has its own sacred sign. Known as the "official club emblem", the design is usually protected by copyright, so that nobody may copy it or use it without permission of the Tribal Elders. In this way, it becomes uniquely associated with the club and takes on the role of a Totemic Device, to be respected, protected and rallied around, like a regimental flag or a royal standard.[14]

Allied to the "official club emblem" are the club colors worn boldly by all followers of the team, often in the form of a scarf. Some may make a special dress in the team colors or a flag or even paint themselves. This all gives a strong sense of group identity and distinguishes them from "the others." People who have never met before quickly establish a common identity and a common dislike of the supporters of the other team.

There is often a strong taboo against others making use of the team colors or emblem. It distinguishes the team property and is treated by the supporters with reverence. Abuse by others calls for often violent retaliation. The emblems adopted are often powerful animals, such as lions, tigers, and wolves. Birds of prey, such as eagles and hawks, are also used. These are symbols of force and aggression, which the team is regarded to manifest. Many clubs have chosen what at first sight may seem rather inoffensive emblems, such as canaries, robins, and blackbirds. However, these birds possess qualities other than strength: they are swift and able to dart around obstacles. The qualities of these pseudototems are seen as being manifest within the team itself.

Sometimes the emblem may be taken up as an unofficial mascot whose presence at the game is essential if the team is to succeed. In the case of Carlisle Football Club, the emblem is the face of a fox, and one ardent supporter regularly carries a stuffed fox with him to matches to ensure good luck for the team. Some supporters even dress themselves up in animal costumes or wear "lucky" coats or perform "lucky" rituals before going to the match. Superstitions and lucky charms of various sorts are not only common to supporters but also to the players themselves. Some players wear a "lucky" medallion, others carry a rabbit's foot, while others must be the last to get dressed or put their clothes on in some particular order. Failure to do any of these rituals would bring bad luck.

We have called this pseudototemism, but it is surprising how many parallels one finds with tribal totemism in many parts of the world. An appreciation of the behavior of the soccer tribe can give some additional insights in the beliefs and practices of totemic communities. Perhaps it also shows that within the

Western worldview there is an underlying superstitious belief that is more important than one would first assume.

Notes

1. Claude Levi-Strauss, *Totemism* (Beacon Press: Boston, 1963).
2. *Encyclopaedia Britannica* III, 18:529.
3. Royal Anthropological Institute, *Notes and Queries on Anthropology* (Routledge & Kegan Paul: London, 1951), p. 192.
4. Levi-Strauss, op. cit., p. 19.
5. E. E. Evans-Pritchard, *Nuer Religion* (Oxford University Press: New York, 1977), p. 66.
6. Levi-Strauss, op. cit., pp. 34–35.
7. Per Juliusson, *The Gonds and Their Religion* (University of Stockholm: Stockholm, 1974), p. 131.
8. A. P. Elkin, "The Nature of Australian Totemism," in John Middleton, *Gods and Rituals* (University of Texas Press: Austin, 1967), pp. 159–76.
9. George Schwab, *Tribes of the Liberian Hinterland* (Peabody Museum: Cambridge, Mass., 1947), pp. 351–52.
10. Ibid., p. 353.
11. Elkin, op. cit., p. 160.
12. Ibid.
13. Juliusson, op. cit., p. 130.
14. Desmond Morris, *The Soccer Tribe* (Jonathan Cape: London, 1981), p. 207.

7

The Pollution of Man

The cycle rickshaw bumped me along the crowded streets of Madras. Cars, cycles, people, and cows all milled together for space on the busy street. The cow in front of us casually lifted its tail and began to do what comes naturally. Immediately the cyclist next to us jumped off his bike and rushed for the falling offerings, caught some in his hands, and pressed the warm dung to his forehead. The rickshaw trundled on with its thoughtful English passenger.

Why is cow dung, which is seen as dirty and polluting to an Englishman, a valuable cleansing product to an Indian? European notions of dirt are bound up with concepts of bacteria and hygiene, but these ideas entered the secular worldview only in the last century. Even before that time cleanliness and holiness were part of the European life. In primal societies, the notion of pollution can be far ranging and is seen primarily as a religious offense. This concept is interwoven with the concept of sin, and yet it retains its own character in the practical living of many peoples. Nowhere is the concept of pollution more clearly seen than among the Hindu peoples of India.

Most Europeans tend to think of Hinduism as being one religious system with an orthodox body of doctrine. In practice, the term *Hinduism* embraces a heterogeneous mass of beliefs and practices of Indian people. At one end of the scale are primal beliefs concerned with magic and malignant powers. At the other end is the pantheistic belief that all personal gods and goddesses are merely aspects of the one nameless, indescribable reality that underlies everything. Between these two extremes, one can find a wide variety of religious belief and practice. Although Hinduism is not normally classed as a primal religion,

in many of its manifestations it does contain such features.
These especially reveal themselves within the "folk" aspect of
Hinduism as practiced by the vast majority of the people in the
villages of India.

Pollution and Purification

Within the worldviews of Hindu people, a person is regarded as
being in one of two possible states: purity or impurity. A person
in a pure state is always in danger of being polluted and
becoming impure. The sources of pollution are manifold. They
may be natural human emissions such as saliva, urine, feces,
semen, or menstrual blood. The most potent source of pollution
is death and decay. Not only are those who handle a corpse
deeply polluted, but the whole household and other members of
the lineage of the dead person become impure. This is a state
that may last for days until all the funeral rites have been
completed, and during this time the people are subject to
various kinds of prohibitions.

The hierarchy of the caste system of India comes about
because each caste regards various other castes as a potential
source of pollution. Pollution may occur through contact with
someone of a lower caste, by touching, by taking food from or
eating with an impure person, through sexual intercourse, or
even marriage, which is regarded as a source of great pollution.
For this reason the various castes keep themselves separate and
tend to be endogamous in their marriage practices.

There is no way for any individual to escape from being
polluted, to some degree, in the course of everyday life. The
necessary task of the daily toilet or washing causes pollution,
which must be removed. The purification may be achieved in
many ways depending upon the caste and the nature of the
pollution. Perhaps the most universal method is the Indian-style
bath, where one pours water over oneself because running water
is regarded as a particularly effective purifying agent. Sometimes purification may require the payment of a sum of money
to the caste or even a sacrifice.

The purificatory measure depends upon the nature of the
pollution and the scale by which it is measured. It also depends

upon whether the pollution occurred voluntarily or involuntarily. Involuntary pollution occurs as a result of sweating, urinating, menses, and so on. Voluntary pollution, on the other hand, most often arises through breaking the purity rules of one's caste. The list below indicates some of the purification rites needed to deal with various degrees of voluntary pollution.

Scale of Voluntary Pollution[1]

Pollution	Purification Methods
Accidental physical contact with impure person	Bath
Sexual intercourse with a non-caste woman (for men)	Bath, feast, verbal atonement
Sexual intercourse with non-caste man (for women)	Bath, feast to caste, physical beating
Accidental killing of monkey	Bath, donation of miniature of animal to Brahman
Accidental killing of cow	Bath, feast, penalty, verbal atonement
Deliberate killing of cow	Bath, feast, heavy penalty, beating, pilgrimage, donation of miniature to Brahman
Marriage to noncaste person	Dissolution of marriage, bath, beating, feast, heavy penalty

Another way of dealing with this danger is to avoid those situations in which one may become polluted. The caste system itself provides such a mechanism. At the top of the hierarchy are the Brahmans whose ritual status is high and are therefore most liable to the polluting influences of the lower castes. At the bottom are the outcasts such as the *bhangi* (sweeper), the *dhobi* (washerman), or the *camar* (tanner). By their occupations they are continually brought into contact with impurity that would require a major purification for the Brahman, but since they are of a lower status they may deal with such impurity. Their status, however, is one of greater impurity than that of the other castes, and so they may pollute those castes by their touch.

The concept of pollution that has such a great complexity in Hinduism is found in many other societies to some degree. Evans-Pritchard writes of the Nuer, "Adultery, besides being a wrong done to the husband by infringement of his rights, is a further wrong to him in that he is polluted." The husband who discovers his wife's immorality demands not only compensation from the man but also the giving of an ox called *yang kula*. This is paid to protect the husband from the consequences of the adultery: "All three persons are polluted, but if sickness results it falls on the husband, and it is most likely to fall on him if the adultery took place in his home."[2] The *yang kula* is sacrificed to wipe out the pollution.

It is very common to find that all bodily emissions are considered polluting, and once they are discharged from the body they become dangerous as well. Rom gypsies, for example, consider all emissions from the top half of the body to be clean and curative, and all emissions from the lower half to be polluting. Saliva is considered to have curative properties especially with regard to the "evil eye." On the other hand, contact with menstrual blood, urine, feces, and semen can cause illness and result in social exile.

Other illustrations are found from the Old Testament with the concepts of ritual uncleanness. The law of Moses made a clear distinction between the clean and the unclean: "You must distinguish between the holy and the common, between the unclean and the clean" (Lev. 10:10). This ceremonial defilement was contracted in several ways, and for each, provision was made for cleansing.

The first class of defilements involves those resulting from bodily discharge: "A woman who becomes pregnant and gives birth to a son will be ceremonially unclean for seven days, just as she is unclean during her monthly period" (Lev. 12:2); a man with a bodily discharge is unclean (Lev. 15:1–15) and those things that he touches; a man who has a discharge of semen is unclean till evening (Lev. 15:16–18). Washing with water is a common purification for these pollutions.

Second, there are those forms of pollution relating to skin diseases, especially leprosy (Lev. 14). The person, his clothes, and his house are all polluted. A third form is that of touching a dead body (Num. 19:11–22). In this case a person is unclean for seven days, and he has to bathe on the third and seventh days to become ceremonially clean.

A fourth class of defilements include those of clean and unclean foods. This is one of the long-standing debates of biblical studies to which some anthropologists, such as Mary Douglas, have recently made a contribution.[3] Leviticus 11 contains an extended list of creatures that may or may not be eaten for reasons of ritual purity. The most popular theory among critical scholars is that advanced by W. Robertson Smith who considered the system to be based on Semitic tribal taboos and the worship of clan totems.[4]

Mary Douglas has proposed an alternative theory based essentially on the fact of the holiness of God, a word that she reminds the reader comes from the root meaning to "set apart." The distinction between what is of God and what is not of God is further expressed as an order within nature. Any class of creature that does not come into the following well-defined categories disturbs God's order and is therefore not clean. As God made three environments, land, sea, and air, all creatures should reflect these:

Land: animals with four legs that chew grass.
Sea: fish with scales.
Air: birds with feathers and two legs, which fly.

If the proposed interpretation of the forbidden animals is correct, the dietary laws would have been like signs which at every turn inspired meditation on the oneness, purity and completeness of God. By rules of avoidance holiness was given a physical expression in every encounter with the animal kingdom and at every meal.[5]

This theory recognizes various social boundaries. Within those boundaries things are orderly and therefore regarded as pure. However, at the boundaries there is an area of ambiguity and so the danger of pollution (see Figure 7.1). People who are in these marginal states, although they may have done nothing morally wrong, are defiled because of their status. "Take, for example,

Ambiguous
boundary zone:
"sacred" area
subject to taboo

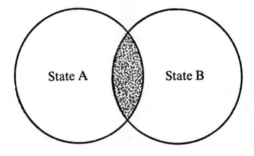

*Figure 7.1. The overlap of social boundaries producing a zone of
ambiguity and danger*

the unborn child. Its present position is ambiguous, its future
equally. For no one can say what sex it will have or whether it
will survive the hazards of infancy. It is often treated as both
vulnerable and dangerous."[6]

These concepts of clean and unclean must not be relegated to
some historical discussions with no importance for today. Many
animistic peoples on becoming Christian are concerned about
these very points. I have often been asked by those involved
with the independent churches of Africa whether a woman can
attend church during her monthly period. While Western man
tends to limit pollution to matters of hygiene, those from a
primal worldview see pollution as having an important religious
meaning.

It can be seen that the concepts of pollution merge with those
of taboo, which in turn overlap with those of sin. The relationship between pollution and morals is far from being straightfor-
ward, but pollution beliefs frequently uphold the moral code of
a people.

Concepts of Sin

Sin is frequently regarded by many as being a concept that is imposed on a primal society by Western missionaries. While this may be true in part, it is necessary to recognize that the concept of sin is universal. The offenses that are regarded as sin vary from one culture to another, but the concept is common to all.

Alan Tippett has proposed three classes of sin with regard to animistic societies.[7] These provide a useful framework for the discussion of this particular topic.

Antisocial Sins

These are offenses against the kinship group, tribe, or any member of the tribe. These rules recognize a strong sense of group solidarity and group cohesion. Incest is frequently the most serious sin, as it is among the Nuer. Failure to respect authority is a sin, especially if a son disobeys his father. Use of sorcery against one's own people is another sin.

As these sins relate to the group, they therefore do not apply to members of another group unless they are bound by some ceremonial agreement. Thus, one finds a dual moral code, one relating to insiders and another to outsiders. An offensive act against a member of another tribe may not be a sin, except insofar as it may bring reprisals for which the group as a whole is held responsible.

Theological Sins

These are offenses against tribal gods or ancestors. They may occur as a result of neglecting to perform correctly some ritual, thus causing offense to the god or ancestor. They may result from a failure to observe a taboo or offer a sacrifice. Many unexplained calamities are attributed to theological sins.

A society depends for its cohesion not only upon interpersonal relations but also upon the support of its deities and ancestors. If a person sins against the gods or ancestors, the support of these supernatural beings will be withdrawn, and the whole community will suffer. Thus, when a member of a tribe becomes a Christian, he is in fact committing a theological sin because he no longer practices the established rituals. Repercussions could come upon the whole tribe with fearful results.

Extracommunal Sins

A third class of sins includes those offenses against forces outside the normal life of the tribe. Many of these offenses are committed unwittingly because the person does not know the rules or taboos of a particular deity or even know of the existence of this "unknown god." For this reason a shrine may be built to an "unknown god" (Acts 17) and sacrifices made, just to avoid such a danger.

It is when a person is outside his home territory that he is in greatest danger. He does not know the abodes of the spirits and the taboos of the local deities. The people settled in Israel by Nebuchadnezzar were attacked by lions because they did not know the laws of the god of the land.

For this reason one finds in all societies a wide range of charms and rituals to protect the unwary traveler by land or by sea. Within folk Islam charms are common. The distinctive "Hand of Fatima" is common in North Africa and the Middle East. The Sufi orders of Islam often turned the granting of *baraka* (holiness in the form of power) to travelers into a highly profitable commercial venture with agents to collect the payment from the traveler who successfully completes his journey. In a similar way some Christians wear a St. Christopher's medallion when they are travelling.

A study of these various classes of sin can show an interesting comparison between tribal and Western views of sin. All societies tend to have an informal classification of the degree of seriousness of various sins. In Western society the worst sins are usually conceived as being murder or rape followed by theft, and much lower down the list one will find sins such as lies, lack of hospitality, and being mean. In many tribal societies the order is almost reversed. Being mean and inhospitable to your own people is a great sin because it touches the very solidarity of the group. On the other hand, murder or rape of members outside the group is of little significance.

Does this variation mean that there are no universals with regard to sin? The Bible speaks about a definite standard and says that falling short of that mark is sin (Rom. 3:23). The ideal is exemplified by the Ten Commandments, which provided a practical moral outline for Israelite society. Prohibitions against stealing, murder, and adultery tend to be almost universal, but the way in which they are actually defined varies from one culture to another. Thus, through a personal, culturally conditioned conscience, every individual has an awareness of what is right and wrong.

Wayne Dye saw the reality of this as he was doing Bible translation among the Bahinemo of Papua New Guinea:

> I tried to translate Jesus' list of sins in Mark 7. As each sin was described, they gave me the local term for it. They named other sins in their culture.
>
> "What did your ancestors tell you about these things?" I asked them.
>
> "Oh, they told us we shouldn't do any of those things."
>
> "Do you think these were good standards that your ancestors gave you?" They agreed unanimously that they were.
>
> "Well, do you keep all these rules?"
>
> "No," they responded sheepishly.
>
> One leader said, "Definitely not. Who could ever keep them all? We're people of the ground."
>
> I took this opportunity to explain that God expected them to keep their own standards for what is right, that He was angry because they hadn't. Then I pointed out that it was because they fell short of their own standards that God sent His Son to bear their punishment so that they could be reunited with him.
>
> This was a crucial step towards their conversion.[8]

The universal awareness of sin in primal societies, if understood within the context of their own culture, can provide a bridge for the presentation of the gospel.

Sacrifice

If the concepts of sin and pollution are common to all peoples, so also is the concept of how they may be cleansed, and that is by means of sacrifice. As one may expect with any universally held concept, the actual way that it is expressed and practiced will vary greatly, but one can distinguish some basic features.

First, a sacrifice is commonly regarded as a ritual in which an object is presented to a god or an ancestor. Edmund Leach considers the sacrifice as being a gift or a tribute or even a fine to the gods: "The performance is an expression of the principle of reciprocity. By making a gift to the gods, the gods are compelled to give back benefits to man."[9] In sacrifice an object passes from the profane to the sacred and shows the intentions of the sacrificer toward the spirit. By them the visible world penetrates the invisible world, and man offers something of the visible world to the invisible. Just as by death a person passes through into the invisible world, so by the killing of an animal the "metaphysical essence" is transmitted to the gods. However, as Leach further points out, "Gods do not need presents from men; they require signs of submission. The material body of the sacrificial victim may well be a serious economic cost to the giver of the sacrifice, but, at the metaphysical level, economics is not the issue. What matters is the act of sacrifice as such, which is indeed a symbol of gift giving, but gift giving as an expression of reciprocal relationship rather than material exchange."[10]

Second, the sacrifice may be a variety of objects, but in popular usage the term usually applies to an animal that is slaughtered. In Africa, the hen is a common sacrifice whereas a sheep or a goat is most prestigious. An ox or a cow is usually the greatest sacrifice, especially among herders such as the Nuer or the Karimojong. In nearly all cases the sacrifice is a domestic animal associated with man, and being valuable to man will be a loss to him.

On some occasions vegetables may be offered, but these are usually regarded as second-best. The Nuer may offer a cucumber, but the man prays asking that God will accept the *yang* (ox).[11] This is meant to be a means not of deceiving God but of correctly fulfilling the ritual and so fulfilling the correct symbolism. Vegetable offerings are frequently offered at harvest festivals. In West Africa, offerings of cooked grain and yams are made to the ancestors residing in the earth, with the fundamental intention of increasing the power of the life of the departed.

Inanimate objects may also be given to gods and ancestors. In

Ghana, before cutting down a palm tree a Krobo man needed to gain permission from his father or grandfather who planted the tree. The man would pour out a libation to the ancestor and explain the reason for which he has to cut the tree.[12] The Brahman priest would often offer a libation of water to the rising sun.

There are those cases in which images are offered to the gods. One may frequently see in this a close symbolism relationship between the image and that of the affliction. In Madras I knew of a young man who had gone blind and was advised by the priests to make two miniature golden eyes to offer to a local god. In 1 Samuel 6:1–7, one reads the story of how the ark of the Lord was captured by the Philistines, but as a result the people were affected by a plague caused by rats and resulting in unsightly tumors. The advice of the diviners was to make five golden models of rats and tumors and pay homage to the God of Israel.

No sacrifice has caused more horror to the European than that of human sacrifice. When the great temple of Huitzilopochtli was dedicated in 1486, the Aztecs amassed more than 20,000 sacrificial victims who lined up waiting their turn. Four men held the victim over a stone, and the priest cut deeply with a flint knife and pulled out the palpitating heart, which was offered to the sun god. The body of the victim was then cast down the temple stairway. The fact of such sacrifices convinced the Spanish conquerors that the Aztec gods were demons and that they as Christians were duty bound to obliterate every trace of this ritual. For the Aztec, however, sacrifice was devoid of cruelty, and death was seen as homage to the god, of whom the victim actually became the living incarnation at the moment of death.[13]

The third aspect of sacrifice is that of the actual offering, or more particularly the ritual killing of the animal. For the Nuer one may distinguish four main stages in the process. First, the animal is formally presented to the god. Then it is consecrated by having the ashes of cattle dung rubbed lightly on its back by the man who is offering the sacrifice. One can here see a close identification between the man and the animal he is offering. The invocation is the next stage in which the man stands with his spear in his hand and prays to the god, stating his intention.

Finally, the animal is speared. The aura of sacredness that surrounds this act links with the theory of the sacrifice as a marker in the boundary between this world and the "other."

The fourth point to note is the communion meal that often occurs following the sacrifice. The Nuer, after the killing, cut up the animal, cook the meat, and eat. This is not a contradiction to the aspect of offering the animal because the Nuer consider that it is the life of the animal, and not the flesh, that is offered to the god.

The parallels between their traditional sacrifices and those found in the Old Testament have been obvious to many animists. The main difference is that the Israelites were to make offerings only to the one God, while the animist may offer sacrifices to many others. Even so, the significance of sacrifice to the animist is of great importance because it is a means of relating to the unseen world and in so doing dealing with sin and pollution.

The scapegoat sacrifice recorded in Leviticus 16 provides one of the most meaningful illustrations to primal peoples. The picture of one animal being offered as a sacrifice and the other being loaded with the sin and contaminations of Israel has parallels in many societies. Don Richardson tells of one example from among the Dyaks of Borneo:

> While the entire population of Anik gathers closer, an elder selects two chickens from the village flock. Checking to make sure both chickens are healthy, he slays one chicken and sprinkles its blood along the shore. The other chicken is tethered alive to one end of the deck of the little boat, with a few grains of rice to keep it docile.
>
> Someone else brings a small lantern, ties it to the opposite end of the deck and lights it. At this point each resident of the village approaches the little boat in turn and places something else, something invisible, upon the deck, midway between the shining lantern and the living chicken.
>
> Ask a Dyak what he has placed between the shining lantern and the living, unblemished chicken and he will reply, *Dosaku!* (my sin).
>
> When every resident of Anik has placed his or her *dosa* upon the little boat, village elders raise it carefully from the ground and wade out into the river. Then they release the boat into the current. As it drifts downstream, Dyaks watching from the shore grow tense. Elders standing chest-deep in the river hold their breath. If

the little boat drifts back to shore, or hits a snag and overturns within sight of the village, the people of Anik will live under a pall of anxiety until the ceremony can be repeated next year! But if the little boat vanishes around a bend of the river, the entire assembly will raise their arms toward the sky and shout, "Selamat! Selamat! Selamat!" (We're safe! We're safe!)[14]

The New Testament reveals that no matter how perfect are the sacrificial rituals, they are never totally satisfactory, and the perfect and complete sacrifice in the personal offering of Jesus Christ was necessary: "So Christ was sacrificed once to take away the sins of many people" (Heb. 9:28).

Notes

1. K. S. Mathur, *Caste and Ritual in a Malwa Village* (Asia Publishing House: London, 1964), pp. 119–20.
2. E. E. Evans-Pritchard, *Nuer Religion* (Oxford University Press: New York, 1977), p. 185.
3. Mary Douglas, *Purity and Danger* (Routledge & Kegan Paul: London, 1966); Michael P. Carroll, "One More Time: Leviticus Revisited," in Bernhard Lang, *Anthropological Approaches to the Old Testament* (Fortress Press: Philadelphia, 1985), pp. 117–26.
4. W. Robertson Smith, *Lectures on the Religion of the Semites* (A. & C. Black: London, 1927).
5. Douglas, op. cit., p. 57.
6. Ibid., p. 95.
7. Alan R. Tippett, *Solomon Islands Christianity* (William Carey Library: Pasadena, 1967), pp. 16–19.
8. T. Wayne Dye, "Toward a Cultural Definition of Sin," *Missiology* 4, no. 1 (1976): 26–41.
9. Edmund Leach, *Culture and Communication* (Cambridge University Press: Cambridge, 1976), p. 83.
10. Ibid.
11. Evans-Pritchard, op. cit., p. 197.
12. Hugo Huber, *The Krobo* (Anthropos Institute: Bonn, 1963), p. 44.
13. Victor Wolfgang von Hagen, *The Ancient Sun Kingdoms of the Americas* (Granada Publishing: St. Albans, 1973), p. 101.

14. Don Richardson, *Eternity in Their Hearts* (Regal Books: Ventura, 1981), pp. 106–7.

8

The Power of Ritual

We have already emphasized that primal worldviews are concerned with powers and a close relationship between the visible and the invisible, the gods and man, and man with the world in which he lives. This relationship means that humankind not only is influenced by forces but is able to influence them. Rituals are visible demonstrations of the religious beliefs of a people. They enact a drama of these beliefs and aspirations and in so doing influence powers to achieve the desired ends. As a consequence of this symbolic nature, rituals show a wealth of color and form. They may range from simple actions to elaborate ceremonies. Rituals involve singing, dancing, acting, reciting incantations, praying, and making a multitude of items that are believed to give power. These are the aspects of primal religions that can lead the outsider to a deep respect and appreciation of the people or a sense of condemnation of what appears to him to be no more than a primitive ritual.

Because there is such a wealth of ritual activity within every society, it is impossible to give more than a basic introduction. Within all societies, an individual may commonly perform minor rituals before he has to face a challenging situation. The schoolboy, for example, may cross his fingers for good luck before he goes in to see the principal. Rituals, however, may develop into elaborate festivals in which thousands of people participate with zeal and devotion.

Ceremonies and rituals bring color into the life of primal societies, but they do more than that. Rituals have much in common with theatrical performances. They are a set of fixed forms that are performed on set occasions. The full meaning of rituals, like that of plays, relies on a set of shared conventions that are known to the insider. However, as La Fontaine has pointed out,

> the great distinction between ritual and drama lies in the fact that ritual, unlike a play, is purposeful activity; that is, it aims to affect the world. . . . Whether it is the material world that is to be affected, as in the rituals for rain, at harvest or when bringing new ground under cultivation, or human beings who are to be redistributed among the groups and positions that make up social life, ritual is expected to produce results.[1]

Rituals provide a means by which human beings are involved with and are able to influence the world order.

As pointed out by Sir Edmund Leach, "most ritual occasions are concerned with movement across social boundaries from one social status to another, living man to dead ancestor, maiden to wife, sick and contaminated to healthy and clean, etc."[2] As we saw in the previous chapter, these social boundaries are times of ambiguity and therefore of pollution and danger. Rituals provide the means and power by which these dangerous transitions may be overcome.

There is always a danger of oversimplification when it comes to classifying such a complex set of phenomena as religious rituals, but one may identify three broad categories: calendar rituals, rites of passage, and rites of crisis.

The division between these classes is based not on differences in the rites themselves but on how their social functions are perceived by the people.

Calendar Rituals

Calendar rituals are those that are held on a regular basis, usually, but not always, in accordance with the agricultural cycle. In general they seek to bridge the boundaries of the periods of the year. They aim to ensure success and prosperity in the future or to protect against danger and failure that could harm crops or animals. Because they are scheduled long in advance, there is a growing sense of anticipation as the days pass. This usually leads to a considerable degree of preparation that may develop over the years to make these rituals some of the most elaborate of festivals. It is important to appreciate the importance of festivals in all societies, not just those with a primal worldview.

One characteristic of such rituals is that they often enact the life of a particular god or his interaction with the life of that society. The elaborate rituals of the Old Testament clearly show this pattern, and so does the historical Christian calendar. Christmas celebrates the birth of Christ, at Easter Christ's death and resurrection are remembered, and at Pentecost the giving of power to His followers.

Within all societies one finds various overlapping sets of calendar rites. These may recognize the activity of various deities important to the people or relate to the agricultural cycle or even the business activities of the people. In many societies where one of the major world religions has been adopted, one finds both the religious festivals of the new religion and the remains of various ancient practices that are often regarded as superstitions or traditional customs. This can be seen in the following list of the major British calendar rituals. One could also describe in an additional column the many local rituals followed in particular areas of the country.

British Calendar Rituals

Month	Christian	Business	Superstitious	Children's
1.		New Year	First-footing	
2.			Valentine's Day	Pancake Day
3.	Lent			Mother's Day
4.	Easter		April Fools' Day	Easter Eggs
5.	Pentecost	May Day		
6.	Ascension		Longest Day	
7.		Holidays		Holidays
8.				
9.	Harvest			
10.			Halloween	
11.				Bonfire
12.	Christ's birth	Xmas!		Santa Claus

Calendar rituals may grow or decline in importance with a particular people. The celebration of Ascension Day was once an important festival in the Christian calendar, but it passes almost unnoticed among Christians in Britain today. In general, smaller, more isolated societies have fewer such rituals, but as a society becomes more numerous and complex, one finds an increasing complexity of such calendar rituals.

Agricultural rituals are some of the most common because they touch the very means of livelihood of the people, and so it is not surprising that one of the most common is harvest festival. Once the harvest has been gathered, people are able to relax and begin to enjoy the fruit of their labors. They dance, sing, and eat their fill. Among the Ga the great annual feast is *hummowo* (hunger-hooting). The Ga people from all over Ghana go to their homes for this feast. At this time the entire remainder of the corn from the previous year is cooked and presented by the priests at the shrines of the ancestors and gods. The spirits are asked to come to eat and drink and continue to protect them against disease and misfortune. After this the people eat the rest of the food (which may consist of massive amounts if the previous year had been a good harvest). Then before any new corn is eaten, some is offered to the ancestors and gods. There then follows a time of rejoicing and license. The new agricultural year has begun, and the people greet each other with the cry:

> Take life, take life.
> May the year's end meet us,
> May we live to be old,
> May no black cat cross between us,
> At the end of the year may we sit again.[3]

These harvest rituals are believed to be necessary to take away the dangers that could be incurred in eating the new harvest. The rituals signal to the people that they may now safely eat the crops since they are ritually clean for human consumption.

The advent of rain is usually an important event, and especially so in the Sahel region of Africa. So-called rainmaking rituals are common to people living in an area that has a long dry season. The ritual described at the beginning of chapter 1 is an example. However, it is perhaps wrong to call such ceremonies rainmaking. These rituals, which include sacrifices, allow the people to gather together and pray for rain, especially when its start seems to be delayed. The elders know the signs of the weather and carefully time the rituals to coincide with when the rains should start. It is, however, wrong to think of such rituals merely as a set of activities. The people do believe in the effectiveness of the ritual in the sense that their performance is a cooperation with the ordained pattern of nature. To neglect them would be to hinder the fulfilling of the cycle by offending the ancestors and gods.

Rites of Passage

The term *rites of passage* was popularized by van Gennep in his now classic work of that name.[4] By this term van Gennep sought to describe the wide range of transition rituals that mark the important stages in life. These include birth, puberty, marriage, and death. Life is seen as a progression from one stage of existence to the next. When a person is incorporated within a particular stage, then there are order, acceptance, and predictability. The great danger lies in the actual process of transition from one stage to the next, which entails the crossing of social boundaries. At this point a person is neither of one group nor the other, and so there is a confusion of roles and possible danger for the individual and the society as a whole. To ensure security at these points of transition, most societies have important rituals in which powers are enlisted to bring about the transformation.

These rituals also become times of celebration as they proclaim the change of status of the individual who becomes a member of the new group. A child becomes a man; a young woman becomes a married woman who will soon bear children; or an elder of the tribe dies to become an influential ancestor and will as such continue to assist his people. As with the calendar rites, so these rituals become times of festivity and a gathering together of the tribe or family for celebration.

In a broad sense all transition rites have a three-phase structure (see Figure 8.1). The first is that the person has to be

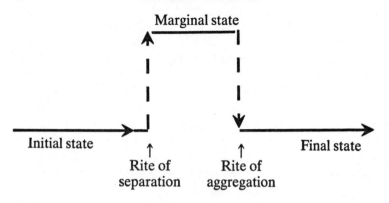

Figure 8.1.
The general three-stage scheme characteristic of most rites of passage

separated from his or her initial role. This may involve the physical removal of the person from the village, a change of clothing, or ritual washing to remove any pollution caused by the transition. Second, there is a period of transition that may last for a few moments or a few months. During this phase the person is kept apart from ordinary people, being considered in some way as polluted or dangerous. In the third phase the person is brought back into normal society and ushered into his or her new role. The actual proceedings of this stage are often similar to those of separation but in reverse.

Birth Rituals

In all societies there is great joy when a wife finds that she is expecting a child. This is essential for the continuity of the tribe, and the child that is born is thought to belong to the whole group. As soon as the woman knows she is pregnant she will start to observe various regulations and taboos. The woman may stop sexual relations with her husband, avoid certain foods, or wear charms that are believed to protect her and her baby from harm.

During the period of childbirth there are often rituals performed to give protection to the mother and baby as a new individual joins the social group. The placenta is often looked upon as a religious link between the mother and baby and therefore must be disposed of in a prescribed manner. The Krobo of Ghana have the custom that a male member of the household takes the cord and placenta on the leaves of the nyaba tree to bury it in the courtyard. While carrying it, and again when placing it in the hole, the man has to be careful that it does not turn upside down or else the woman could have no further deliveries.[5]

The Minahasa are one tribe among the many thousands in Indonesia. For them the cutting of the umbilical cord is of great importance. At that very instant the baby will gain the power of life. The witch doctor ties the cord with a thread using three knots. The husband or the father-in-law gives the child a name from one of the ancestors of the family. The witch doctor holds the child and prays, "We give you the name . . . so that you may have the attributes of him/her. O ancestor, here is your grandchild. Take care of him/her because he/she is your existence right now."[6] After the prayer he cuts the umbilical cord and gives the child to the grandmother. The placenta with the cord is then placed in a pot with the words, "I am so sorry that you have to be separated from your friends." The pot is then buried near the entrance of the house.

The Minahasa often place a mirror above the head of the baby when it is asleep. This, it is believed, will keep the ghosts away because they do not like to see their faces. Forty days after birth, another ritual is held in which the hair of the child is shaved because otherwise the baby will become sick. The witch doctor will make a charm for the child, and the grandmother will feed the baby with a small portion of liver that has been dedicated to the ancestor. In this way the child will have a long and successful life like the ancestor, and so is brought into the social life of the community.

Puberty

Initiation rites mark the transition from childhood to adulthood and as such are celebrated among all primal societies. They separate the person from one life in which the child is dependent upon its mother into another life as an adult with the opportunities of marriage and parenthood. These rituals show the characteristic three-phase structure of a rite of passage. The rituals associated with this transition often include the following:

1. Separation and seclusion from the normal life of the society.
2. Testing to show that the person is worthy to be a man or a woman. This often involves the need to respect the elders.
3. Instruction in the religious mythology of the people and in the accepted behavior of an adult.
4. Marking as a sign of adulthood. Circumcision is common, but there may also be tattooing or scarification.

Initiation rites are usually complex and full of symbolism, and there is little opportunity here to describe but the outline of one such ritual. The Karimojong call the male initiation rite *asapan*, and this usually takes place when a boy is between fourteen and eighteen years of age. The ritual was described to me by an elder when I was in Karamoja in 1983. The boy's father will usually judge when the time has come, and permission will be granted by the elders. There is no special physical trial for the candidate, but he must show himself docile and obedient to those who are already initiated. On the eve of the ceremony, all the relatives gather to feast and drink.

At sunrise, the initiates, helped by their kinsmen, are led together with the selected oxen to an appointed place (rite of separation). The boys then have their hair plaited with a band made from the tendons of the spinal cord of cattle, and this is a distinguishing mark of the initiate. Once this ritual is completed, the initiate takes his spear and approaches the ox he has brought. It is at this point he is expected to display courage and skill and strike the ox so as to kill it with a single blow so that it falls to the left side.

The animal has to be divided according to very strict rules, and at the same time the diviners will study the entrails of the animal to see if there are any ill omens (see chapter 9). When this is done, there then comes an important aspect of the ceremony in which the initiate approaches the carcass of his ox and drinks lengthily of the blood. When the Karimojong warriors are looking after the herd, they live almost entirely on milk and blood. The rest of the animal is then divided and portions given to various kinsfolk according to fixed patterns.

Once the meat is divided, the initiates stand before the elders, and for a moment there is silence. The elders then take the chyme from the stomach of the animal and smear it over the head, back, and shoulders of the boy. "Be strong! Be rich! Cherish many friends!" With these words the elders bless him. Then comes a ceremonial beating of the initiates by the elders, who order the youths to go and get wood and cook the meat. Respectfully they do this task before they move on to the next part of the ritual. Here the chosen elder moves to a sacred tree and splatters it with the chyme. This is done to propitiate the supreme being, Akuj, and to pray for the blessing of the initiates. In the evening all the men eat together, and so the day closes. This is but the first of four days that make up the period of transition. After this period the initiate will then be brought back to the homestead amid great rejoicing and recognition of the fact that he is now a man.[7]

Initiation is one of the most difficult rites of passage for Western Christians to appreciate. A major reason for this is that in Western society we lack any such distinct ritual and merely have a confusion of lesser rituals. Sexual maturity may come at fourteen, but the British law allows the possibility of marriage only when one is sixteen. Driving a car is allowed at age seventeen, and voting at eighteen, while twenty-one remains the "old-fashioned" legal age of maturity. Perhaps this is one of the reasons why our young people experience the identity crises known as "teenage." Neither they nor their parents are sure if they are children or adults.

Initiation rites could be described for both males and females from many parts of the world. Some are kept secret from outsiders, while others may be spoken of openly. Basically, initiation provides the bridge by which the child becomes an adult member of the society. The person is seen as being born again into a new social status and will often wear clothes to signify this change and receive respect as an adult.

It is necessary to state that some initiation rites include the dedication of the person to a particular spirit or deity, and in some cases this has even led to spirit possession. For this reason most missionaries have objected to initiation rites and discouraged their converts from taking part. While recognizing this danger it is also necessary to realize that if a person fails to go through such rituals, according to the tribe, that person is no longer regarded as a full member of the community. The convert is therefore a nonperson with regard to his own society and so may have little influence within the community.

This raises many questions with regard to the Christian attitude to initiation. Is there a place for the evaluation of the initiation rite to determine to what extent a Christian convert could be involved? Or what elements would make the ritual totally unacceptable? Or could a new Christian ritual be created to usher a candidate to adulthood?

Marriage

One of the primary aspects of adulthood is that the person should marry and have children. In this way human life is preserved, propagated, and perpetuated. Marriage therefore comes at the very center of human life and signifies the formal transition from single to married status. Because of the importance of the tribe and the family, marriage is not seen so much as the binding of two individuals as an association of two families.

As with the other rites of passage, the first step is the setting apart of the individual from his or her usual activities. This procedure can be seen within Western society where immediately before the wedding, the bride and the groom are separated. The groom is taken out by male friends for a stag party in which they may indulge in excessive drinking and sexual joking. It is regarded as bad luck for the bride to see the groom on the day of the wedding before she actually arrives at the church. Special clothes are worn for the ceremony, which is rich in symbolism. The bride is dressed in white, symbolic of purity and virginity. Finally, the couple must be incorporated into social life again, but this time in their new status as a married couple. In contrast to being set apart from each other, now the couple are set apart as a unit from other people during their honeymoon.[8]

Death

The rituals surrounding death are often long and complex as one might expect from a fear of the ancestors and spirits. Death is not seen as the end of existence but the initiation of the person into a new stage. Funeral rites must include the practical aspects such as the disposal of the body, but more important they must deal with any evil that has occurred as a result of this transition. As mentioned in chapter 5, the occasion of a bad death, such as that of a young person or a woman in childbirth, is the cause of much concern. The ghost of the person must be placated and any malice dealt with by sacrifice or punishment of the guilty. The varied rites aim to separate the dead person from his family and to assure his goodwill.

Rites of Crisis

The calendar rituals and the rites of passage are, in some way, predictable. However, there are many other events that are not: sickness, disease, war, accident, drought, and unexpected death. The secular worldview deals with these by giving explanations of how they have occurred. For example, a man is killed in a car accident, and the inquiry shows that it was caused by poor brakes on the car. Within a primal society the question of the cause would be taken further: "Why was it that this particular man was killed?" "Why was he walking across the road at that time?" Secular society has no real answer to this type of question apart from that of probability or coincidence. It is seen as an unfortunate situation of two pieces of material trying to occupy the same space at the same time. No real attempt is made to explain why it occurred, only how it occurred.

Primal worldviews, on the other hand, seek to address the question of why this particular man was the one killed in the accident. The answer given is that there were some supernatural powers operating that caused his harm. This may be attributed to witchcraft, sorcery, or some other antisocial activity. If this is the case, balance and harmony must once more be brought to the system, and they can be achieved only through a particular ritual. A religious specialist must be called in who is particularly proficient in handling powers in order to restore the situation. It is at this level that one finds a deep awareness of folk religion and magic in many societies. This topic will therefore be explained at greater length when the various practitioners such as the shaman and witch doctor are considered.

The Place of Ritual

Within primal societies the observance of rituals plays a major part in society. They are an important element in the very intricate and complex pattern of society that provides a particular moral order. Rituals provide traditionally approved ways by which the people are able to influence the powers that they believe control their lives.

Not only do rituals provide a way of dealing with the powers influencing the world, but they provide an enactment of the religious and magical beliefs of the people. The rituals are symbolic illustrations of the way that man relates to the gods and nature. The Australian aborigines whose totem is the locust may well perform a ritual in which they imitate the locusts as part of their ceremony to bring about an increase in the supply of this insect.

Rituals also have an important social value in providing a time of festival and celebration, which gives character to tribal life. Festivals are a necessary part of every society, whether it be a small tribe or a nation of millions. We have seen from the list on page 95 that the British calendar revolves around the great Christian festivals. Rituals are not so obviously important among Protestants of northern Europe as they are among many peoples of the world.

However, even within secular Britain, where churchgoers are less than 15 percent of the population, most people attend baptisms, church weddings, or funerals once or twice a year. Folk Christianity centers upon these rites of passage. They not only provide occasions for family gathering and celebrations, but the religious symbolism is seen as an essential part of the drama, enabling movement across a social boundary.

The fact that rituals are so important in many primal societies means that when a person is converted to Christianity and he is encouraged to reject his traditional ceremonies, he finds only a few Christian rituals to meet his need. Christianity appears somewhat colorless compared with the more dramatic rituals of his tribal religion. One popular view of the intended destination for the letter to the Hebrews is that the recipients were Jewish converts tempted to apostatize. As Donald Guthrie writes, "In place of the grandeur of the ritual of the old order was substituted a spiritual conception centered entirely in a Person and no longer in a splendid temple. It must have caused much perplexity in the minds of the recently converted Jews."[9]

In order to meet this need, many of the world religions have related to the traditional rituals of the people. Either the old festivals were transformed into a form more characteristic of the new religion, or the new religion arranged a parallel ritual that coincided with the traditional festivals. This is one way of meeting the cultural void that the new convert may feel. Christmas and Easter were originally traditional festivals, and they have become a central part of Western Christianity. Harvest festivals were held by the Angles and Saxons before the time that they were Christianized. Some aspects of this still remain, such as the corn dolls that are tied on the last sheaf of corn.[10] This is a topic to which we will return in the consideration of folk religion.

Many missionaries have realized the importance of establishing cultural substitutes within the local church. Among the Gonja of northern Ghana the new yam festival has traditionally been an important festival to celebrate the beginning of the new harvest. This has now been contextualized and made part of the life of the church. The Christians now give thanks to God for His gracious provision of a new harvest of yams.

In seeking to find suitable Christian substitutes, three factors must be preserved. First, the ritual must be an illustration of Christian truth through the use of symbols relevant both to the culture of the people and to the Scriptures. Second, although the coming of Christianity will challenge many social issues, there should be a strengthening of family and social relations as far as possible. Christian rituals should reinforce these social patterns so as to provide order within a society. Third, the rituals should allow the people to participate in Christian worship in ways that are relevant and meaningful to them.

Notes

1. Jean S. La Fontaine, *Initiation* (Penguin Books: Harmondsworth, 1985), p. 184.
2. Edmund Leach, *Culture and Communication* (Cambridge University Press: Cambridge, 1976), p. 77.
3. Personal account from Richard Foli, himself a Ga-Adangme from Ghana.
4. Arnold van Gennep, *The Rites of Passage* (Routledge & Kegan Paul: London, 1977).
5. Hugo Huber, *The Krobo* (Anthropos Institute: Bonn, 1963), p. 144.
6. Personal account from Charlotte Peleake (1984), a missionary working among the Minahasa.
7. Augusto Pazzaglia, *The Karimojong—Some Aspects* (EMI Books: Bologna, 1982), pp. 103–22.
8. Anne Sutherland, *Face Values* (BBC Publications: London, 1978), pp. 43–44.
9. Donald Guthrie, *New Testament Introduction* (Tyndale Press: London, 1966), 3:31.
10. James G. Frazer, *The Golden Bough* (Macmillan: London, 1978), pp. 588–609.

9

Divining the Unknown

The sun was beginning to climb high into the sky when I came across a young Karimojong warrior squatting on the side of a small hill overlooking a herd of cattle. In his right hand he was holding a pair of rough leather sandals that he suddenly tossed into the air. His eyes followed the path of the sandals as they fell to the sandy earth, and then I saw a broad smile spread across his face as he looked with delight at the result. This warrior had been with the herds for some weeks and was trying to decide whether it would be a good time for him to return home to his wife. The sandals had fallen in such a way as to indicate that it would indeed be a good time to return, and that his animals would be safe in the protection of his fellow warriors.

How do you make a choice between two or more options? How do you find out the cause of misfortune? What happens when something goes wrong? Making decisions is part of everyone's life, and we will all occasionally be confronted with difficult decisions that leave us perplexed and uncertain. Finally a decision must be made, and we have to bear the results whether they be good or ill.

How do people actually make decisions? First, we all use our plain common sense to deal with the multitude of little matters that confront us every day. The difference between two options may be so great that we hardly feel as though there is a decision to be made because the advantages of one are so obvious. The Westerner has refined this approach through the use of management techniques so that he has ways of differentiating between two closely similar options.

Within primal and folk worldviews, when options require

consideration, the person may feel that he needs to draw upon additional principles. His own understanding is limited, and so he needs the assistance of "supernatural" persons or powers in making the decision. Behind every unusual event, there is believed to be a cause that is frequently beyond the ordinary. Divination is the means by which a society seeks to determine the origin of a problem and then to discover the appropriate answer. The important theme within divination, as Victor Turner has shown among the Ndembu, is that of "bringing into the open what is hidden or unknown."[1] The Westerner may be able to consider some events as resulting from coincidence, but even we are sometimes pressed to supernatural explanations at times. In America, some two million citizens are devoted to astrology while millions more are curious enough about it to purchase books and to consult newspaper horoscopes with regularity. In Britain, it is claimed that more than two-thirds of the adult population read their horoscopes.

It is therefore useful to consider first the situations in which people use divination before going on to consider the actual methods of divination that are used in many societies.

The Uses of Divination

In most societies one finds various levels of divinations. At the simplest are those general methods that may be used by most people within the society, in the same way as a football referee will toss a coin to decide in which direction the teams will play. In such do-it-yourself type divination, questions are answered almost automatically with a simple yes or no. At a more advanced level one can find the specialist diviner who is renowned among the people. Such people are called in for the most important incidents, and the client will present some gift to the diviner. The diviner's reputation will increase with his successful divinations or decline if the people lose trust in him. Divination may be used to provide answers to some of the following issues.

Sickness

A primary occasion when divination is used is when a member of the family is ill. It is necessary in such a situation both to diagnose the cause of the sickness and to recommend a cure. Sickness is seen not merely as resulting from some natural process but as resulting from a wide range of antisocial and unseen powers. This is illustrated in a discussion that occurred between an African tribesman and a missionary doctor:

TRIBESMAN: This man is sick because someone worked sorcery against him.

WHITE DOCTOR: This man is sick from malaria because he was bitten by an infected mosquito!

TRIBESMAN: Yes, he was bitten by a mosquito—but *who* sent the mosquito?

In the case of sickness the diviner may pronounce the cause as being one of several different factors depending upon his particular worldview. The sickness could result from sorcery or witchcraft or an offended ghost or ancestor. As a result of the diagnosis the person would be recommended to visit a herbalist or a witch doctor or even the missionary doctor if the sickness is diagnosed as being a "white man's illness" (see Figure 9.1).

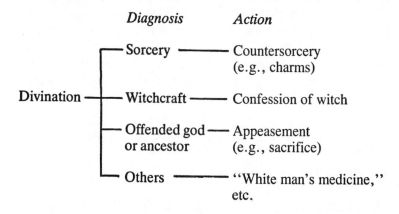

Figure 9.1. The pattern of divination, diagnosis, and action

We will look at the understanding of sorcery, witchcraft, and healing in later chapters. It is, however, necessary to realize that in almost all cases the diviner is concerned with an understanding of the total social context of the particular sickness: "He acts as a mechanism of redress and social adjustment in the field of local descent groups, since he locates areas and points of tension in their contemporary structures."[2] In this way sickness is regarded not only as a physical phenomenon but as one that has its origin within the social context and the wider unseen world.

Public Calamity

Famine, drought, and epidemics are issues of great importance to any people. Why have they occurred at that time? Has a god been offended? For a major crisis such as this the diagnosis is often that a major deity has been offended, and so only an important sacrifice will be sufficient to appease the god. The moral law of a society is most vividly demonstrated through its breach. The diviner therefore plays an important part in upholding the moral law of the society by exonerating or accusing individuals according to that law.

Social Actions

Marriage is a significant social institution for every people, and it is often difficult to know which persons should marry. Divination may provide an answer for this, even if it only results in a narrowing down of the options. Astrology is an important means of divining the future in many parts of the world and especially in India. The following advertisement in an Indian newspaper illustrates the point:

> Match for pretty virgin, B Sc, 35, accomplished, family of status, Aries. Decent marriage, owns property. Caste and province no bar. Box 73372 CH Hindustan Times.

Appointing Leaders

The Western pattern for appointing a leader is that of an election in which the decision of the majority of people is taken as binding upon all. Many societies regard such a method as being very dubious because in important matters the views of the ancestors are of equal or even greater importance. One must therefore ask the ancestors or god(s) to identify the person who is to be the leader of the people. Prayers are therefore made before using some means of divination. The story of the replacement of Judas, in Acts 1, provides a fascinating illustration of this sort of practice. The apostles first used their common sense to identify who would be likely candidates, and then after prayer "they cast lots" (Acts 1:26).

Agriculture

Especially in areas of the world where the rainfall is unpredictable, the farmer needs to know the best time for him to plant his crops. If he plants them too early and the rains fail, then he loses the seed, while if it is too late, then the rains stop before the seed has become properly rooted. Where is a good place to plant a garden? He does not want to offend a spirit or a god by planting a garden in the wrong place.

Identifying an Offender

A man is sick and fears that someone is practicing sorcery against him. In order to obtain a cure he needs to answer the questions, "Who did it?"; "Why did he do it?"; and "What means has he used?" It is not to be forgotten that more than once the British police have made use of a medium to find the whereabouts of the body of a murder victim. However, within primal societies the diviner is concerned not merely with identifying offenders but with rectifying disturbed social relations.

Methods of Divination

The methods used for divination seem almost endless. What one society may use another would regard as peculiar. However, for the people concerned the means used is taken seriously and has been passed on from generation to generation. In all cases the aim is to obtain disclosure from the unseen world outside human knowledge about a particular situation.

The various techniques that are used can be placed into three main categories: divining techniques, spirit mediumship, and ordeals.

Techniques

The theory of these methods is that by some means the non-empirical affects natural aspects of the world order. The diviner is knowledgeable in these signs and so is able to "read" them by various ritual techniques. This usually requires special knowledge that is passed on orally or in some cases is gathered into an elaborate written text.

Perhaps the most widespread of all methods is that of astrology. Here the planets, except Neptune and Pluto, are supposed to exert an influence on human lives. A person's destiny is dictated by the house (constellation of stars) that the sun was in when the person was born. The exact date of birth of the person is therefore necessary for the horoscope to be written. It is therefore obvious that astrology is mainly confined to literate societies and is not common among tribal societies. In Britain, many tens of thousands of copies of *Old Moore's Almanac* are sold every year. This booklet claims to forecast the events of the coming year and to give advice to the individual depending on the time he or she was born.

Most societies use some sort of technique that may be regarded as a chance phenomenon. For example, some English-people seek to "read" the tea leaves left at the bottom of a cup. They have some clearly defined rules by which the pattern made by the tea leaves is interpreted. The common practice among the Karimojong is the throwing of sandals in the air. The way in which the sandals land provides a "yes" or "no" answer in the same way as we may toss a coin.

The Yoruba of Nigeria have a complex system of divination dependent upon the use of a pattern of split nuts. In this method, known as *ifa* divination, the diviner lays out the nuts on the sandy ground, and the patient first of all prays to the spirits represented in the shells and then tells his problem. The diviner now calls on his own ancestors for assistance. Through a complex set of manipulation of the nuts, he is able to obtain "yes" or "no" answers to various questions, so giving an answer by a process of elimination.

Evans-Pritchard made what has now become a classic study of the poison oracle (the *benge*) in the daily life of the Azande of southern Sudan. He writes,

> The poison used is a red powder manufactured from a forest creeper and mixed with water and paste. The liquid is squeezed out of the paste into the beaks of small domestic fowls which are compelled to swallow it. Generally violent spasms follow. The doses sometimes prove fatal, but as often the fowls recover. Sometimes they are even unaffected by the poison. From the behaviour of fowls under this ordeal, especially by their death or survival, Azande receive answers to the questions they place before the oracle.[3]

The Azande rely on the *benge* oracle and would not make any important decision without consulting it.

An alternative to the yes-and-no method is that in which a map is constructed in some way. Among pastoral peoples an animal is often slaughtered and the intestines or liver cut open. From the patterns on these organs the elders are able to identify the terrain and then identify where good grazing is to be found. The Karimojong use this method seemingly quite successfully to graze their animals in the dry scrub lands of northeast Uganda.

It is interesting to see how many such methods are mentioned in the Bible: "For the king of Babylon will stop at the fork in the road, at the junction of two roads, to seek an omen: He will cast lots with arrows, he will consult his idols, he will examine the liver" (Ezek. 21:21). Egyptians tended to look for pictures in the surface of the water in the same way as a fortune-teller looks into her crystal ball. Perhaps this is the context of the incident of Joseph's silver cup in Genesis 44:5, 15: "Isn't this the cup my master drinks from and also uses for divination?" God evidently tolerated this means of divination as being a culturally appropriate method for an Egyptian ruler within the context of the degree of divine revelation given at that period of history.

Spirit Mediumship

Spirit mediums are those who claim to make contact with ghosts or spirits or gods. Frequently the medium enters into a trance during which the ghost or spirit answers questions through his body. The method by which possession occurs varies from culture to culture. Some mediums regard silence and meditation as being essential, while others use dance, rhythm, and noise. This will be considered further in chapter 15 when spiritism is discussed.

An outstanding example of this form of divination was seen in the oracle at Delphi in which a young virgin became possessed with a spirit and could thus foretell the future. This is perhaps a case similar to that of Paul in Philippi, in Acts 16, which will be discussed later relating to spirit possession.

A variation on this pattern is that in which a ghost or an ancestor is called by the medium and allowed to communicate with the living. The Ouija board is perhaps the most common form in Europe. Here the ghost is believed to be able to spell out words by moving a glass to various letter cards arranged in a circle.

In societies where ghosts are greatly feared and the need for a good death important, there are usually rituals that allow the ghost to speak. Such a case is found with the Jola of Senegal:

> The body, tied to the bier, is covered with a blue cloth. Cowhorns are tied at the head of the bier, and four men carry the bier into the crowd for interrogation. Various questions are put to the body and the spirit of the dead person propels the bearers backwards or forwards in a "yes" or "no" answer. When the cause for death is ascertained, sacrifices of chickens are made, the blood of which is sprinkled on the bier. Palm wine is also sprinkled on the bier. These things are done as offerings to the dead person so that he be pleased and rest in peace and not trouble anyone.[4]

Ordeals

Ordeals have been used by many societies in order to prove the guilt or innocence of a person. Among many peoples in West Africa the boiling water or oil test is common. If two people are in dispute, they are required to put their hands into the boiling water and pull out a stone or some similar item. The theory is that the spirits know who is the guilty person and so will punish him and allow the innocent party to remain unscathed or almost so. If one of the persons refuses to put his hand in the water, he is "obviously" guilty.

The poison cup is another variation of this form of divination by ordeal. This is a common practice in many parts of Africa and is used to detect and punish a robber, witch, or murderer. The ancient Israelites had such a practice to detect if a woman had committed adultery. Her husband could bring her before the priest who would "take some holy water in a clay jar and put some dust from the tabernacle floor into the water" (Num. 5:17). The woman is then to drink the water. If she is guilty, her abdomen will swell and her thighs waste away, and she will be accursed among her people. If she is innocent, she will not be affected, and her husband is to take her back as being blameless (Num. 5:11–31). This is another example of God using a culturally known method that was appropriate and meaningful within the particular historical context of Israel.

It is obvious that a person who is sincerely convinced of the effectiveness of these rituals and the total worldview of the society will probably confess rather than take the punishment. An innocent person, on the other hand, will be convinced that his or her innocence will be demonstrated. This method has many parallels with a lie detector (polygraph), which assumes that a person's pulse rate or blood pressure or perspiration rate increases when he is lying. These techniques do not always work, but they play an important social role. Although the polygraph is less than 100 percent accurate, in 85 to 90 percent of cases wrongdoers admit their guilt when accused of lying.[5]

Divination in a Changing World

We have seen that in primal worldviews unseen powers, whether they are personal or not, are interwoven with the lives of the people. Divination provides a person with a means of perceiving the causes of events and knowledge of how to deal with the many options that confront him. The methods used may seem strange and even primitive to an outsider, but they can be remarkably effective. Evans-Pritchard, while living among the Azande, ordered his life, for a period, according to their customary means of divination.[6] He did not find that this was more or less advantageous than his previous Western means of making decisions. In studying the Karimojong, I have been impressed by the effectiveness of their divination as a means of providing grazing for their cattle.

Three reasons may be proposed that give some explanation for this effectiveness. First, delays in making decisions can be both stressful and ineffective. Divination allows a person to actually make a decision, and this in itself is valuable. In many cases any decision is better than no decision at all. Second, professional diviners are often astute people with a wisdom born of experience and an intimate knowledge of their people. Frequently, one senses the diviner interpreting the results of a particular ritual to explain and justify a particular course of action. Third, the diviner operates in emotionally charged situations, and the symbolism of his craft strikingly restates the social norms of society. He therefore upholds tribal morality and so brings stability and healing to social tensions.

Divination provides a set of rituals, based upon the traditions of the people, to help in the making of decisions. It therefore enables the people to cope with complex situations and to avoid the nagging guilt that may result when the results would seem to show that a wrong decision was made. Divination takes the responsibility away from the individual and places it upon the unseen world.

The coming of Christianity and Western education has had some important effects on the whole concept of divination. In general, Western education has been a secularizing influence on most peoples.[7] Let us consider the various uses made of divination by primal peoples and how they are being replaced. First, the diagnosis of sickness has often been replaced by Western medical technology. Primal societies may appreciate its value, but it is essentially nonreligious. This causes a major division between healing and religion, which are usually considered inseparable. Second, appointing a leader has now become a process of election depending upon persuasion and reason. Third, social actions such as marriages have become dependent upon "love" arrangements between the parties concerned, with less regard for the views of their parents, never mind their ancestors. Fourth, agriculture has been left in the hands of college-trained experts who are able to test the soil and come to scientific conclusions. Even the identification of an offender has been left to the police and the courts. S. G. Williamson, writing about the Akan, records that a student of his once remarked, "In olden times there were no policemen and no need of them; the gods were the policemen."[8]

The role of divination has therefore to some extent been replaced primarily by a secular philosophy that looks to science for its answers. No one would question the value of intellectual inquiry, and the Bible itself places importance on the human use of reason. However, the overall process has basically been one of secularization or, as Max Weber described it, the "demystification" of society.[9]

Nevertheless, divination has not entirely been rejected, and it frequently continues in a "folk" aspect in many societies, especially among the poor who are unable to make use of scientific methods, which are expensive.

The most popular form of divination in Western society is astrology. This "folk" use of divination comes to the fore during public or personal crises, in times of fear, anxiety, and confusion. It happened in Europe in the seventeenth century after a plague of epidemics; it happened in Germany after the First World War; and it is happening today in the Western world. Astrology has arisen in our scientific age because people have found the material things failing them. Similarly they have become disillusioned with a secular form of Christianity. According to astrology, one's destiny is in the stars. Horoscopes may indicate what the stars have dictated for us, and if they do, to be forewarned is to be forearmed.

The significance of divination in most societies raises some important problems for new converts to Christianity. They need to be led to a trusting relationship with Jesus Christ and assured that there are no forces in the universe, either natural or supernatural, real or imagined, that can endanger them. How does the convert discover the will of God? Rejecting the secular option, the pastor or missionary needs to be able to present a means of Christian guidance that deals with the practical issues of daily life. What means does the Christian have? The accepted Christian answer would be the Bible, prayer, and the prompting of the Holy Spirit. These three aspects are important, and the young convert needs to become aware of how to use his Bible, pray, and sense the prompting of the Spirit. However, these often appear very abstract and intellectual for the young convert, and he remains uncertain exactly what is the will of God as opposed to his own thoughts. In addition they lack a ritual with which he is more familiar and which gave him a definite answer.

In the Old Testament we read of the following provision made by God for the people of Israel: "The nations you will dispossess listen to those who practice sorcery or divination. But as for you, the LORD your God has not permitted you to do so. The LORD your God will raise up for you a prophet like me from among your own brothers" (Deut. 18:14–15). The gift of prophecy was very common among the people of Israel. During the time of Samuel, the prophets were known as "seers" (1 Sam 9:9) and played an important role in the life of the society. Later, during the time of the classical prophets, the revelations of God were often received through visions (Isa. 6:1; Jer. 1:11–13), dreams, and even audible voices. In the book of Acts it is reported in numerous places that the members of the church had visions: Ananias (9:10ff.); Cornelius (10:3ff.); and Paul (16:9ff.).

Could it be at this level that the spiritual gifts, and especially that of prophecy, have a particular relevance for the church of a primal society? Some may ask how this varies from spirit mediumship. Two basic principles should be seen when a person is exercising a God-given gift of prophecy. First, the result will be the edification of the believers, and second, the practice should be disciplined: "For you can all prophesy in turn so that everyone may be instructed and encouraged. The spirits of the prophets are subject to the control of the prophets" (1 Cor 14:31–32). Prophecy is not, in the first instance, foretelling but rather forth telling. It is the presentation and evaluation of the situation and must be in line with the revelation of God as found in the Scriptures. Thus, the Scriptures themselves speak of the need for discernment with regard to the prophetic message (1 Cor 14:29). Further, the uncontrolled ecstatic forms of spirit possession common in mediumship are to be avoided. The Holy Spirit does not dominate the personality of the Christian prophet but works with and through his personality to achieve healing and wholeness.

Perhaps in our desire to distance the young church from the unacceptable aspects of the old culture, we have failed to appreciate the important role of divination. We have presented a God who is unable to communicate with human beings except through a Book accessible only to the literate. On the other hand, the Scriptures speak of spiritual gifts that may cause tensions with the secular worldview but become very meaningful to the young churches of Africa, Asia, and Latin America, as can be seen in the rapid growth of the Pentecostal churches in these areas.

Notes

1. Victor W. Turner, *The Drums of Affliction* (Hutchinson: London, 1981), p. 29.
2. Ibid., p. 51.
3. E. E. Evans-Pritchard, *Witchcraft, Oracles and Magic Among the Azande* (Clarendon Press: Oxford, 1976), p. 121.
4. Information from a missionary working among the Jola (1982).
5. Nigel Rapport, "A Policeman's Construction of the Truth," *Anthropology Today* 4, no. 1 (1988): 7–11.

6. Evans-Pritchard, op. cit., pp. 120–75.
7. Elmer S. Miller, "The Christian Missionary: Agent of Secularisation," *Missiology 1* (1973): 99–108.
8. J. N. Kudadjie, "How Morality Was Enforced in Ga-Adangme Society," in E. A. Ade Adegbola, *Traditional Religion in West Africa* (Asempa Publishers: Accra, 1983), p. 171.
9. Max Weber, *The Protestant Ethic and the Spirit of Capitalism* (Allen & Unwin: London, 1930).

10

Mediators Between God and Man

In a world of many powers, spirits, and gods, the ordinary person has a sense of apprehension and fear. He therefore looks for someone who may help him approach the spirit or deity. The specialist may be a king, medicine man, seer, or rainmaker, but we shall use the general term *priest* to describe this role of mediation. People can go and tell him their problems, and he in turn will approach the god(s) through prayer, sacrifice, and the interpretation of dreams. Through his knowledge of rituals, the priest is able to bridge the separation between the sacred and profane realms. This principle can be seen in the Epistle to the Hebrews, which says the Levitical high priest is "selected from among men and is appointed to represent them in matters related to God, to offer gifts and sacrifices for sins" (Heb. 5:1).

The Nature of a Priest

Like many of the concepts that we have been considering, the basic principle has many variations when one moves from one society to another. The significance and complexity of the priesthood generally correspond with the size of the community. In small societies, it is the shaman (see chapter 14) who tends to be the most important practitioner. As the community increases in size one finds a growing importance of the priesthood with elaborate rituals and costly sacrifices.

Priests may be appointed to the task in many ways. An individual may offer himself or be proposed by others. However, a more common procedure is that a person may become a priest only if he is a member of a particular family or clan. Among the Hindus it is the Brahman caste who have the particular task. The Israelites restricted the priesthood to the tribe of Levi according to the directions recorded in Numbers 8. The role is therefore one that is ascribed by birth rather than achieved by effort.

In African societies men or women may be priests. However, many societies restrict the task to men, and women have a more limited role. Often the society imposes certain restrictions on who is eligible to be a priest even within a hereditary priesthood. The Old Testament Levitical priesthood required a priest to have a minimum age of 30 and to be free from physical defects (Num. 8:23–26).

Paul Radin describes the qualifications of a Tahitian priest:

> The men set apart for the priesthood were able-bodied and most of them were tall. They were free from personal defects as the gods were supposed to reject a man with a blemish, such as having a humpback, bald head, blind eye, or eyes that squinted. They must also be deft of hand and sure-footed, so as not to be awkward in the service of the gods.[1]

Some form of training is usually required before the person may take up his task. This may range from informal instruction of a son by his father to that of elaborate training colleges attached to major temples. It is important that the candidate learns to perform rituals without fault because it is in the correct performance of the ritual that its effectiveness is found.

It is not only rituals that are to be learned but also the special knowledge that may be secret to those initiated into the priesthood. The Maori candidate is required to learn the contents of "the three baskets of knowledge," as they are called. The first contains the knowledge of peace, goodness, and love; the second contains the prayers, incantations, and rituals used by mankind; the third contains the knowledge of wars, of agriculture, of woodwork, stonework, earthwork, in fact of all things pertaining to earthly life.[2]

The priest finally has to go through some form of initiation before he, or she, is qualified and so recognized by the community. Among the Ashanti the period of training lasts for three years, which culminates in a final initiation ritual:

> A pot is set near some logs that have been placed outside the old priest's house. After dark, drummers and singers assemble and the logs are lit, the fire being kindled with a flint and steel. The new priest is dressed in a palm-fibre kilt with all his charms upon him. His hair is then cut and put into a pot and the old priest examines the new priest's head in order to take away any bad "spirits of possession," for it is these, placed there by certain fairies, that are supposed to cause a priest to do wrong. The new priest will dance all night to the accompaniment of the drums and of singing. Early the next morning this pot is placed on the head of some young boy and he is told to run off with it wherever he wishes and to place it, inverted, on the ground. Finally the new priest will "cut" a sheep for his god and pray: "God so-and-so, accept this sheep and eat; today you have completed marriage with me; this is a sheep from my hands, stand at my back with good standing." [3]

As already mentioned, the organization of the priesthood may range from the lone priest tending his small shrine in his village to a vast hierarchy of hundreds of priests. As a member of the institution of priests, he is accepted as a religious and spiritual leader in the society. In this way the priesthood is ascribed a respected position within society and often becomes allied with the secular leadership, which may be the local chief or the president of a modern state. This is illustrated within Christianity by the relationship between church and state, where the church has often been allied with the ruling classes. In Islam, there is, technically, no priesthood, though there are local community leaders who perform an important spiritual role being called *imam, mullah,* or *mufti.*

In some cases the roles of high priest and king become merged in one person. Among the Lugbara of Uganda, the elder of a lineage is also the priest of the ancestor shrines of that lineage. King Solomon clearly took this role upon himself at the inauguration of the temple in Jerusalem. Similarly the emperors of China offered public sacrifices at the great annual festivals. The Pharaoh of Egypt was regarded as a god incarnate—the sacred king. As a result of his complex personality he alone was the intermediary between humankind and the gods. He was the person who offered the sacrifices at the important ceremonies, though for all practical purposes he delegated this function to a particular priesthood. The priest therefore shared, to some degree, in the king's divinity and rule. This was one of the reasons for the stability of the ancient civilization of the Nile valley.[4]

The Role of the Priest

The primary role of the priest is to act as a mediator between humankind and the spirit world. As such he is an expert in ritual and has the knowledge of the gods and spirits. Evans-Pritchard describes the Nuer priest of the earth as being "essentially a person who sacrifices on behalf of man below to God above." [5]

Rituals

The fact that the priest has the monopoly to exercise certain rituals gives him a vital role within the society. Among the Nuer, the priest of the earth is alone able to perform certain rituals. Only he can perform the rituals essential in a case of murder, which include giving sanctuary to the killer, negotiating a settlement, and then making the sacrifices to enable normal social relations to be reestablished. A similar form of monopoly is found within the Roman Catholic church in which only a correctly ordained priest is allowed to celebrate the Mass.

The rituals performed by the priesthood are symbolic of the religious and magical beliefs of the society. Among small communities the role of the priest ranges over many areas. He may perform the functions of a diviner or a medicine man or a shaman. His rituals may range right across the spectrum from the purely magical to the purely religious. The so-called *juju* priests of West Africa still have a thriving business, even in the big cities, with the production and sale of charms. These charms are frequently called *fetishes*, but this term has a wider range of meaning, and so the term *charm* will be used here because it is more specific. The charms consist of stones, wood, or a leather pouch containing some material. No one considers these items to have any power in themselves, but it is believed that the *juju* priest is able to infuse the object with a potency to achieve the desired objective. A man may even make his own charm and then take it to the priest.[6] It has a similarity with a person taking a newly acquired rosary or statue of the Virgin Mary to the priest to have it blessed.

The charms may be worn around the neck, the waist, or the arm and are believed to give protection against sickness, danger, and even sorcery. It is possible to obtain for oneself "bad medicine" for use for vindictive purposes. The priest would normally sell such a charm only on the condition that it would be used for legitimate punishment. This would include cases where adultery, theft, or illegal business practice is suspected.

As the priesthood grows in size and order, the rituals tend to be more complex and more religious in the sense of being appeals to God rather than a manipulation of spiritual powers. The more magical class of rituals tends to be left to the shaman or medicine man and so eventually becomes the "folk" beliefs of the people rather than the "orthodox theological" beliefs of the society. The priesthood may construct elaborate temples, wear special garments, and produce special items for use in the rituals. The position of the priest therefore becomes increasingly prestigious within the society.

Taboos

Not only does the priest have to perform the rituals in the approved manner, but he is frequently required to observe certain taboos and restrictions. Levitical priests were allowed to marry only virgins or the widows of other priests. Roman Catholic priests are expected to be life-long celibates. If a Catholic priest does break the rule concerning his sex life, he may not officially perform the liturgy of the Mass. However, if he insists on celebrating the Mass, the validity and efficacy of the ritual are not questioned. The emphasis here is upon the correctness of the ritual rather than ritual purity of the practitioner. Among other priesthoods such is not the case, and the ritual impurity can make the ritual void and may even cause the death of the priest.

The Ga priests have elaborate restrictions as described by M. J. Field:

> Every priest must observe certain taboos. He must not see a dead body, and if himself about to die he must be taken from the place of his god. He must not eat salt except in the form of sea water. No one must speak to him while he is eating. He must not eat fermented food and must refrain from sexual intercourse on certain days of the week and before performing important rites. He must not eat on any day until the sun has shone. In the rainy season he fares less badly than one might fear, for some kind friend always goes outside, gazes at the streaming clouds, and shouts cheerily that the sun is shining.[7]

Formalism

The creation of a priestly class that has a monopoly of the religious ritual has the danger of losing its charisma and becoming formal and legalistic. The exclusive prerogatives of the priesthood will not remain unchallenged forever. Many societies have faced a reaction against the established monopoly of the priests. A classical example of this is the prophetic movement among the Israelites, which was a reaction against the compromise and formalism of the Levitical priesthood. A similar movement occurred against the monopoly of the Brahmans in about 600 B.C. This finally led to the formation of two new religious movements, Buddhism and Jainism. The house church movement within Western Christianity has been regarded as an illustration of the reaction against varying degrees of formalism within the established church.

Because of the close relationship between the secular leader, be he chief or king, and the priesthood, a change in the one affects the other. The traditional religious leaders of a people may therefore be the strongest opponents of a new religion and lead the persecution in alliance with the chief. Methodism first gained a footing in southern Ghana among the Fante people in the 1840s. In most cases the chiefs were friendly to the Methodists because they could see that the church was part of the bigger process of the European way of life. The priests had little more than local fame and had therefore no cause to feel their position was under threat.

There was, however, a priesthood that had grown in power, influence, and wealth. It was the Nanaam cult, which centered upon a sacred grove of trees, that was considered to be able to give guidance concerning future actions. The supposed oracle powers of the cult gave the priests influence throughout the area. When a small Christian community emerged in the locality and a junior priest of Nanaam renounced the cult and joined them, the stage was set for a clash.

The priests were then looking for an opportunity for vengeance. This came when one day the Christians were cutting wood near the sacred grove. The priests accused them of actually cutting wood from the sacred grove itself and urged the chief to punish the offenders. A company of armed men were sent to the Christian community, and they flogged the Christians and burned their houses. The British governor heard of this mistreatment and brought the case to trial. During the trial the converted priests exposed all the deceitful practices of the Nanaam cult. The chief and the people were disillusioned, and eventually the cult was destroyed and the people accepted Christianity. A school was built on the site of the sacred grove.[8]

Religious Places

Priests are normally associated with some particular shrine, sacred place, or temple. These may be divided into two classes: natural places and those that are man-made.

Natural Sacred Places

These places are usually those that produce an immediate sense of awe for the people. They may be spectacular waterfalls or an unusual cluster of trees or a mountain rising from a flat plain. These places are seen as meeting points between the visible and the invisible worlds. At these places sacrifices may be offered, rituals performed, and prayers said all with greater efficacy. They are therefore places guarded by sacred taboos and preserved from common use.

Mountains are often regarded as sacred places and even as the home of the gods. Jomo Kenyatta, describing the religious beliefs of his people, the Gikuyu, wrote,

> The mountain of brightness [Mt. Kenya] is believed by the Gikuyu to be Ngai's [supreme god] official resting-place, and in their prayers they turn toward Kere-Nyaga and, with their hands raised towards it, they offer their sacrifices, taking the mountain to be the holy earthly dwelling-place of Ngai.[9]

There is a legend in Bali that tells of a time when the island was flat and barren, but at the time that their neighbors on the island of Java were becoming Muslim, the Hindu gods entered Bali and created the mountains and made the island fertile. As the myth implies, the mountains do indeed dominate the island, positioned as they are at the center and made fertile by the volcanic soil. To the Balinese the mountains are the center of the world, the home of the gods, and as such they are the highest and most holy places. The sea, by contrast, is the lowest place, and so is unholy and the river carries the filth of the world out to the sea.[10] Sacrifices must be made to the gods on a regular basis, and especially at one great ceremony made every 100 years. In 1967, when preparations were being made for this great ceremony, the volcano erupted, which was taken to be obvious proof to the people that the gods were angry. Many sacrifices were made, but the gods were not satisfied until some 1,000 people died in the eruption.

Sacred groves and trees are common in many parts of Africa. These taboo areas are set apart for religious activities, and people will not graze their cattle near the area or cut down the trees for firewood. The Gikuyu do not build any shrines themselves but regard the huge mokoyo tree that stands boldly out from the plain as a symbol of the mountain. It is under these trees that the Gikuyu will make sacrifices to his god.[11]

Water is commonly found to have religious significance, and

so it is not surprising that the rivers, lakes, and waterfalls are frequently held in religious awe. The holy River Ganges is perhaps the most venerated river on earth. To bathe in its waters is believed by Hindus to bring cleansing from the pollution of life. Many peoples believe that there are spirits who inhabit rivers, lakes, or waterfalls, and it may be necessary to offer a prayer or sacrifice before crossing the water in question.

Man-Made Sacred Places

Frequently, people tend to build some sort of structure as a symbolic focus of their worship. This may be on the banks of a river or on a sacred mountain. The construction may be a small pile of irregular stones or a mighty temple.

Altars are often no more than a natural stone standing out of the earth. Its unusual color or shape seems to give it a particular significance. For the pre-Islamic Arabs, black stones such as meteors were of special religious importance.[12] Many of the wayside shrines of India are erected stones, which may be painted and garlanded with flowers by a devotee.

Shrines are simple structures that are often built to protect a particular ceremonial item or to act as a house for the deity. The household shrines to the ancestors are common in many Oriental homes. In Africa, family shrines are constructed in the form of a small hut in the homestead. These are used for pouring libations for the ancestors and offering food and sacrifices. They are often the center of the religious life of the family.

In some places a shrine may be constructed over the grave of an important person. Sacrifices, libations, and prayers are offered to the departed in request for assistance with some problem. Within the Sufi orders often the grave of the founding "saint" becomes the center of pilgrimage and prayer. The *baraka* (spiritual power) of the saint is conceived as being passed on to his followers and can give protection from the *jinn* and the evil eye This *baraka* movement in Islam spread through most of North Africa in the fifteenth century and was a major factor in the conversion of many of African peoples to Islam.[13] This movement is generally known as *maraboutism*, a term originating from the Arabic word *rabit* meaning "a man who has gone into ascetic retreat." The *marabout* would gain an increasing reputation in an area and become known as a worker of miracles. When he died, a whitewashed tomb was built as a mausoleum. The immediate area around the tomb became sacred and one of asylum and blessing.[14]

The preservation of relics of a saint became an important aspect of most of the world religions. The temple of the tooth in Kandy, Sri Lanka, was an important feature of the movement of Buddhism to that country. Relics of notable Christian saints and even portions of the cross have been transported through many parts of the world.

As the particular cult becomes more influential, the center of religious ritual takes on a more important function. This is usually encouraged by the king who sees the priesthood as a means of consolidating his own political power. When the northern kingdom of Israel separated itself from Judah, Jeroboam realized the problem he faced since the temple was situated in Jerusalem. He therefore made two golden calves at Bethel and Dan and appointed a priesthood to offer sacrifices to them (1 Kings 12:25–33).

Religious temples have come to be some of the most impressive of all human constructions. Their very form and decoration reveal something of the beliefs of the particular culture. The Taoist temples of Hong Kong are not separate entities but are built as part of the gardens in which they are set, so demonstrating their very oneness and harmony with nature. The imposing Muslim minarets rise above the clamor of ordinary human life almost as if they are pointing to the transcendence of Allah. Inside, the mosque has a simplicity of line and avoidance of any imagery to ensure that nothing is compared to Allah.

In the New Testament, it is the writer of Hebrews who takes up the issue of the Old Testament priesthood in the most direct way. This letter persistently presents Jesus Christ as a priest who surpasses Aaron (Heb. 7:11) and who offers a perfect sacrifice, not here on earth, but before the very presence of God the Father (Heb. 8:1–7). Thus, it is no longer necessary to offer sacrifices to God because the perfect and adequate offering has already been made. The imagery of the priest and the sacrifice is well understood by primal societies. This provides a very meaningful bridge in the presentation of the gospel.

The church in its role of the body of Christ is anointed to a priesthood in the world. However, the Christian is required to offer not animal sacrifices but "spiritual sacrifices acceptable to God through Jesus Christ" (1 Pet. 2:5). In other words the Christian is to live a holy life pleasing to God: "But you are a chosen people, a royal priesthood, a holy nation, a people belonging to God, that you may declare the praises of him who called you out of darkness into his wonderful light" (1 Pet 2:9).

Notes

1. Paul Radin, *Primitive Religion* (Dover Publications: New York, 1957), p. 130.
2. Ibid., p. 152.
3. Ibid., pp. 129–30.
4. E. A. Wallis Budge, *Egyptian Religion* (Routledge & Kegan Paul: London, 1979).
5. E. E. Evans-Pritchard, *Nuer Religion* (Oxford University Press: New York, 1977), p. 292.
6. John Onaiyekan, "The Priesthood in Owe Traditional Religion," in E. A. Ade Adegbola, *Traditional Religion in West Africa* (Asempa Publishers: Accra, 1983), p. 48.
7. M. J. Field, *Religion and Medicine of the Ga People* (Oxford University Press: London, 1961), p. 8.
8. F. L. Bartels, *The Roots of Ghana Methodism* (Cambridge University Press: London, 1965), pp. 54–61.
9. Jomo Kenyatta, *Facing Mount Kenya* (Heinemann: Nairobi, 1982), p. 234.
10. Anne Sutherland, *Face Values* (BBC Publications: London, 1978), p. 62.
11. Kenyatta, op. cit., p. 236.
12. Willard G. Oxtoby, "Arabian Religions," in *Encyclopaedia Britannica*, 15th ed. (Encyclopaedia Britannica, Inc.: Chicago, 1981), 1:1058.
13. Spencer Trimmingham, *The Sufi Orders in Islam* (Oxford University Press: New York, 1973), p. 84.

14. H. A. R. Gibb and J. H. Kramers, *Shorter Encyclopaedia of Islam* (E. J. Brill: Leiden, 1974), p. 326.

11

Witchcraft

Witchcraft for most Western people is associated with black cats, evil sabbaths, and blood pacts with the devil. The mere mention of the word *witch* causes a strong emotive reaction with most people, and yet this very response can cloud our appreciation of what is truth and what is fiction. Witchcraft is a phenomenon that seems to be universal in all societies, and yet the secrecy that covers the subject seems only to produce a strange mixture of fear and fascination.

In all societies withcraft is believed to be evil by the vast majority of the people. This particular concept seems to some extent to provide an answer to such perplexing problems as "What causes sickness, suffering, and death?" "Why did this misfortune have to happen to this particular person?" These are fundamental questions that all religions try to answer in their own ways, and yet for the individual in the midst of a particular crisis the usual answers provided seem remote from his own situation. He is concerned with the immediate situation: "Why was it that *my* crops failed?" "Why was it that *my* child died?" Often the answer given is that the event was caused by the activation of evil powers by a person with whom the individual has had bad social relations. Jealousy, spite, and envy within individuals are seen to be the root causes of the suffering and hurt that have been experienced.

Two basically different ways have been identified in which people may harness and activate supernatural power to achieve their evil desires. After his study of the Azande of southern Sudan, Evans-Pritchard commented, "There is much loose discussion about witchcraft. We must distinguish between bad magic (or sorcery) and witchcraft. Many African people distin-

133

guish clearly between the two and for ethnological purposes we must do the same."[1] It is often difficult for an outsider to distinguish between these two aspects, and in many cases the two overlap. However, for simplicity and clarity we shall designate these two by the same terms used by Evans-Pritchard: *sorcery* and *witchcraft*.

Sorcery, which will be further investigated in the next chapter, we shall define as a deliberate, conscious act of an individual to harm another by use of "supernatural" forces. This usually requires the manipulation of particular objects and the performance of rituals believed to generate a potency that is often used for selfish purposes. On the other hand, *witchcraft* is essentially the result of an unconscious response of a person toward another that causes harm. This concept is more difficult for the Westerner to understand and so will need to be more fully expounded. However, it may be useful at this point to list the essential differences between these two phenomena:

Sorcery	*Witchcraft*
Conscious act	Unconscious act
Deliberate act	Involuntary act
Uses some technique	Uses no technique
External	Internal to the person

In both cases harm is caused to a person by another without recourse to any direct physical assault. The persons concerned would have no hesitation in believing that it results from the manipulation of supernatural powers.

Witchcraft—the African Tradition

There can be no doubt that the fear and hate of witches are common throughout much of Africa. Colonial governments have legislated against witchcraft, and missionaries have condemned it as evil, but even so its presence in the continent is still known. In previous generations witchcraft was regarded as the cause of all mysterious deaths (bad deaths) and disease. On occasions the fear of witches spread across large areas of the continent:

After the Second World War, a movement of witch hunters came from Ghana, across Togo and Dahomey, and into Nigeria. Known as *nana tongo*, or *antinga*, these men spread excitement into many villages, enriched themselves and their initiates, and yet were supported by a large body of public opinion, even among the educated, as doing good work in checking the harmful deeds of witches. Their activities were only checked, publicly at least, by prohibitive legislation in 1951.[2]

Today most Western-educated Africans are reluctant to speak about this subject to Westerners because they know that they will be misunderstood and even ridiculed for what will be called "primitive ideas." Even so the fear of witchcraft is known to many peoples in Africa today.

Among the Azande, for example, if a man is careful to take all the normal precautions but still wounds himself with his machete while clearing a field, he assumes that this must be the result of witchcraft. As we have said in earlier chapters, the notion of coincidence, or probability, is not sufficient for the primal worldview. There must be an answer to why it has happened to this individual, and witchcraft is the "obvious" answer for the Azande.

Becoming a Witch

The Azande believe that witchcraft is inherited from one's parents. A man who is a witch will pass on the substance to his sons and likewise a mother to her daughters. The witchcraft substance (*mangu*) is considered to be a definite physical part of the body, which resides near the liver or gallbladder of the person. This substance can be discovered by autopsy, and a postmortem may be performed on a person accused of witchcraft. With the relatives in attendance, the blood brother of the dead man cuts open the abdominal cavity to expose the intestines. If no witchcraft substance is found, the family rejoice and put the intestines back into the corpse, which is then buried. If, however, the substance is found, the intestines with the witchcraft substance may be hung on a tree for all to see.[3]

One may ask the question, What would happen if a father was known not to be a witch, and yet his son is proven to be one? This can be answered in a logical way: the son was illegitimate.

Although inheritance is a common way by which people are believed to become witches in many parts of Africa, other peoples believe in alternative means. The Ibo of Nigeria believe that witches can infect innocent people by putting a special medicine into their food. The person is then open to the influence of the witch and often develops a craving for human flesh.[4] The Nupe of Nigeria are now essentially an Islamized people and believe that a person may become a witch by having an ointment rubbed into the body or eyes. In most cases, it is believed, a person is reluctant to become a witch and would not seek to become one, as in the case of sorcery.

Witchcraft Activities

Some of the common activities attributed to witches are night flying, nocturnal gatherings, and cannibalism. Some horrific stories are told about the activities of witches, but when one seeks to understand how this can occur, one meets a perplexing observation. If one asks if a witch actually flies to her nocturnal meetings, one would be given a strong affirmative answer. However, if one asks if the person still remains asleep on the bed, once again the answer is in the affirmative. It is the "soul," or witchcraft essence of the person, that is believed to leave the body when the person is asleep and perform these various activities.

This can be illustrated by an actual case reported to the author from among the Ga people. A man awoke in the night to find his wife in a deep sleep. Concerned about her condition he tried to waken her but to no avail. In desperation he cut her skin with a knife, but she remained asleep, and no blood flowed from the wound. Finally, he rubbed pepper in the wound but still to no avail. When morning came, the woman suddenly woke in great pain from the wound. Her husband was then convinced she was a witch.[5]

This ambiguity concerning the nature of witchcraft has led some Western writers to speak of it as being unreal: "Witchcraft . . . is an imaginary offence because it is impossible. A witch cannot do what he is supposed to do and has in fact no real existence."[6] However, in talking to Africans, one is impressed by the fact that they stress that such things do happen. In some way the soul, or witchcraft essence, does leave the body and does cause harm to others. One must here again recognize the difference between Western and African worldviews in their understanding of the intrinsic nature of man. As stated earlier, the secular worldview considers human nature to be a total entity, like an integrated machine. On the other hand, primal worldviews see the possibility of various parts of the immaterial aspect of human nature leaving the body. Thus in African terms it is quite logical for the witchcraft essence to leave the body and do its own will.

Many different activities are attributed to witches. First, they are believed to fly at night. Often when they fly, they are believed to give off light like a firefly. The Ubangi tribes of Zaire believe that the witchcraft essence, called *ndoki*, can be seen as a light coming from the mouth of the person. The light gets brighter or duller as the person opens or closes his mouth.[7] It is also believed that they fly on the backs of birds and animals or even become these animals. Bats, owls, jackals, dogs, and cats moving around at night are often believed to be witches. This belief in the night flying of witches is found almost universally. Second, witches are believed to gather in groups in order to achieve their evil aims. The Yoruba believe that the initiation into these organizations, called *egbe*, is achieved by eating human flesh.[8] The witch is thought to be able to enter the house of a sleeping person and "eat" the body of the victim, although to other people there will seem to be no change in the person's body until the person starts to become ill. Third, witches are thought to have an insatiable appetite for sex and indulge in gross immorality.

When one seeks to obtain an answer to the question, Are witches conscious agents when performing these activities? the answer is given in the affirmative. Most peoples would believe that these activities are taking place in the spiritual realm, but this does not mean that the activities are illusory. The activities are performed, it is believed, and there is resulting harm. However, for those holding a secular worldview there is a problem of whether the acts are real or imaginary. Within this context, witchcraft is regarded as imaginary and unreal.

Dealing with Witchcraft

A number of measures can be taken to deal with the power of witches. First, there are "medicines" or charms prescribed by a diviner. These may be worn by the individual or placed at the door of his house and are supposed to give protection from witches.

Second, there is the activity of the witch doctor. Most Western people tend to associate the witch doctor with being the chief of the witches. Even colonial governments have legislated against him while leaving worse people unmolested. The witch doctor is in fact the specialist doctor to whom one goes when one is suffering harm from witches. He is the chief enemy of witches and is both a respected and a feared member of the community. He uses his supernatural powers to identify and defeat the powers of witches. However, it is necessary to appreciate that the presence of a witch doctor in a community heightens the belief in witchcraft as a whole.

Parrinder has described him in the following way: "The witch-doctor is not a practising witch, but it is true that he may well have certain affinities with witches. He has something of the same spirit. He has to be like witches so that he may overcome them by his more powerful spirit."[9] As Evans-Pritchard described it, "Only by Beelzebub can one cast out Beelzebub."[10]

The witch doctor seeks to identify the witch in the community who is causing the particular sickness or harm. Wearing clothes or barkcloth or leaves, the witch doctor will often dance to the beat of drums and rattles until his spirit identifies the witch to him. Almost always those who are identified as witches are women, in contrast to the fact that witch doctors are almost always men. The witch is also frequently a close relative of the afflicted person; for example, the accusations are often made between cowives of a polygamous marriage or between wives of different men living in the same compound. Jealousy is the heart of the matter, and in a small community the witch doctor is usually aware of any anger or jealousy toward the victim.

Although witches are believed to be "conscious agents," most people accused of such activities are surprised. However, the line between wishing ill of a person or dreaming that one is hurting a person and that of consciously being aware of witch-craft activities can be very blurred. If a wife has been angry with a cowife, and the latter becomes ill, when the first wife is then identified by the witch doctor as being a witch, does it not seem logical that the witch doctor is right even in the mind of the accused herself?

The witch doctor will then prescribe some means by which the accused person may correct the harm. Among the Azande they may be required to spit water. In this act, the accused takes a mouthful of water and spits it onto the ground. This is supposed to "cool" the witchcraft essence within the person so that it is no longer operative.

Another common requirement is for the accused to confess her sins. Some of the confessions can be very explicit as seen from these gathered from the Ga people:

"I have killed fifty people including my own brother." "I have taken the womb of another woman."[11]

Why do people make such confessions? First, because once they have been accused of witchcraft, they are considered to remain a danger to society until they have confessed. However, once a confession has been made and the appropriate actions taken, the person will be accepted back into society, and the sick person is believed to get well. Thus it is frequently easier to accept the diagnosis than remain under suspicion. Second, in all communities there are those people who live on the margin of the society such as elderly widows and those with mental illnesses. Often such marginalized people become the scapegoat in a society when problems occur, and they may confess out of fear. Third, there are also those people obsessed with the fear of becoming witches, and so they readily confess when diagnosed as such by the witch doctor. A comparable attitude is found in most societies in which certain people, out of a neurotic fear of becoming sick, cling to the healer.

A third means by which witches may be dealt with is by witch-finding cults, and one may place in this category the activities of some of the African independent churches. About 1934, there was a major witch hunt in Malawi by a group called *bamucapi*. In every village they visited, the people were made to stand in rows according to their sex. Everyone then had to pass in turn behind the witch hunters who tried to catch their reflections in a mirror. A suspect was asked to submit her or his horn of witchcraft.[12] These witchcraft crazes have arisen periodically in various parts of the world, including the Western world, as will be seen later.

Most Western missionaries have tended to regard witchcraft as being merely an illusion of the devil, which would be answered by Christian education. However, the independent churches have had a more practical attitude toward those believing that they have been afflicted by witches. They have accepted the belief that witches may cause illness and pray against such harm:

> The other day, I heard a woman confessor in one of our most renowned indigenous churches claim that a witch hit her right wrist with a heavy stick in her dream. On waking she began to feel a biting pain in her wrist upon which she came to the local prophet for help. She concluded that her pain was cured after the prophet and the rest of the faithful members had prayed fervently for her.[13]

It is necessary to reiterate the fact that witchcraft and sorcery are considered to be two overlapping systems by which evil is caused. Although most African peoples have a clear distinction between the two concepts and two words to describe them, the two are not mutually exclusive. One can sometimes hear of events that include aspects coming under both the categories of witchcraft and sorcery. This is illustrated by the story of a man in Zaire who bought special magic from Ethiopia, i.e., sorcery. This enabled him to change into the form of a rat and enter houses without the occupants knowing in order to steal from them, i.e., witchcraft.[14]

Witchcraft—the European Tradition

Although the concept of witchcraft has a major place in the societies of Africa, it is not limited to that continent. Witchcraft may be regarded as a universal primal belief and one that continues within many societies even after they have become Christian, Muslim, or Hindu by allegiance. The previous description of African witchcraft concepts provides a framework in which the beliefs of other peoples may be considered.

One can see the similarities between the beliefs of the Tetum people of Indonesia and those previously discussed:

> Witches are persons credited with the talent to propel their souls through the air and penetrate the bodies of fellow villagers. A witch's soul, like that of an ordinary mortal, is normally invisible. It can change shape and size, so is capable of entering a victim's mouth, nose or ear. Invasions occur at night while the victim is sleeping.[15]

Flying beliefs are common in many parts of the world. In Hindu mythology, stories of magical flight are known, as with the tales of flying carpets among many Middle Eastern peoples.

In Europe the concept of witchcraft has been known from earliest times. In ancient Greece and Rome only those magical practices that were intended to do harm were condemned and punished. These activities were often ascribed to the gods themselves, and certain goddesses, such as Diana and Selene, were particularly associated with the performance of malevolent magic that took place at night. The Germanic peoples who spread throughout Europe during the decline and fall of the Roman Empire were known to believe in witches and sorcery. These powers were especially attributed to women, and the old-woman witch type that was to become central to European tradition has its origin at this period.[16]

With the coming of Christianity to the Germanic peoples from the fourth century onward, all other religions together with every class of magic were condemned. In A.D. 690 Theodore of Canterbury legislated against those who sacrificed to demons or used divinations.[17] Witches, diviners, and adulteresses were to be driven out of the land by the laws of Edward (A.D. 901). Charlemagne condemned witchcraft as evil and passed the death penalty for those who practiced such. The position of the church was stated at the little-known Council of Ancyra in the ninth century:

> Some wicked women, reverting to Satan, and seduced by the illusions and phantasms of demons, believe and profess that they ride at night with Diana on certain beasts, and with an innumerable company of women, passing over immense distances, obeying her commands, as their mistress, and evoked by her on certain nights. . . . Therefore, priests everywhere should preach that they

know this to be false, and that such phantasms are sent by the Evil Spirit, who deludes them in dreams. Who is there who is not led out of himself in dreams, seeing much in sleeping that he never saw waking? And who is such a fool that he believes that to happen in the body which is done only in the spirit?[18]

The parallel notion of night flying to cause harm in both African witchcraft and in the European tradition is apparent. However, this statement of the church that night flying is illusory did not stop the belief in such events. Folk belief in witchcraft, nocturnal gatherings, and werewolves persisted and even grew stronger in the minds of the ordinary people.

Contact with Arabic culture as a result of the Crusades introduced studies such as alchemy and astrology and produced a new interest in what has been called "natural magic." This resulted in many new ideas at the time of the Renaissance. However, it was also to lead to a reaction against heretics, and it was this that eventually caused the church to change her views about witchcraft. This is carefully analyzed by Keith Thomas in his important work, *Religion and the Decline of Magic*. He concludes,

It was only in the late Middle Ages that a new element was added to the European concept of witchcraft which was to distinguish it from the witch-beliefs of other primitive peoples. This was the notion that the witch owed her powers to having made a deliberate pact with the Devil.[19]

In 1417, a strange dark-complexioned people suddenly appeared on the eastern frontier of Germany. They were dressed in exotic and colorful clothes and claimed to be exiles from the country they called "Little Egypt," probably northern India. These nomadic people gradually spread throughout Europe and became known as the gypsies. With them they brought a multitude of folk beliefs characteristic of India: fortune-telling, charms, and sorcery. E. B. Trigg argues that this was probably one of the events that led to the sudden revival of belief in witchcraft and sorcery in the fifteenth century.[20] Even today the gypsy is known as a fortune-teller or a seller of "lucky white heather." Their beliefs have added much to the folk beliefs of the Christianized peoples of Europe.

It was a decree of Pope Innocent VIII in 1484 that opened the door to the change of position and was to lead to witch crazes throughout Europe. This decree allowed two Dominican friars, Heinrich Kraemer and Johann Sprenger, to attempt to purge witchcraft from Germany. Two years later these men produced the text *Malleus Maleficarum* (The Witches' Hammer). This was an encyclopedia of demonology in which witches were condemned not for the harm they may cause to others but because they were devil worshipers—the greatest of all heresies.

It is difficult to chart the developments of the beliefs through the next four centuries. However, the pact with the devil came to be a central issue, and this has led to the definition of a witch that is still held by English law today. It originates from Sir Edward Coke who defined a witch as "a person that hath conference with the Devil to consult with him or to do some act."[21]

Witch crazes had arisen in various parts of Europe prior to the decree, especially when people were faced with some notable disaster. The Black Death, which spread across Europe from 1346 to 1351 and which killed at least a quarter of the population, led many to look for scapegoats. Jews were commonly blamed, along with those branded as witches. Following the decree of 1484 the Inquisition spread through many parts of Europe, and it is estimated that some nine million people died in Europe accused of witchcraft in a little over 100 years.

Britain was saved from the worst of the persecution by the Reformation, but one of the greatest English witch finders was Matthew Hopkins who was most influential between 1642 and 1649 (see Figure 11.1). His method of ascertaining guilt was by "pricking," which meant that a person was pricked with a needle all over the body to find the insensitive spot produced by being touched by the devil. Accusations of night flying, practice of the Black Mass at nocturnal gatherings, and sexual perversions were common. Animal familiars were another common feature of this period. The British Museum posseses etchings from this period in which an accused witch is pointing out the names of the various animals in her house.[22]

Confessions were an essential part of witch finding, in the same way as we noticed in Africa. Torture was common during the witch crazes, and people were subject to the rack, thumb-

Figure 11.1. Frontispiece to The Discovery of Witches, *a pamphlet by Matthew Hopkins, 1647. Hopkins is shown accusing a woman who admits to possessing certain familiar spirits depicted as animals. On the left is Sir John Holt, Chief Justice of England, who opposed the conviction of witches.*

screws, and branding. Trial by ordeal was also known, for instance using the ducking-stool. Trickery was also used in which people were promised a light pilgrimage if they confessed, and they died burned at the stake still professing their innocence. At the height of such panics, people were executed on the testimony of a single person who claimed that they had bewitched him. The last execution for witchcraft in England was at Exeter in 1648, but in Scotland and in other parts of Europe the executions continued into the following century. This is one of the aspects of European history that tends to be forgotten: "The vast majority of those tried and convicted during the witch persecutions were innocent—which few would now dispute."[23] Evil can destroy and harm in many ways—through the accuser or the accused.

The famous Salem witch trials of 1692 are usually regarded as the end of the period of witch crazes in the West. The discovery of trade routes to the New World and to Asia opened up new opportunities. Technological developments began to occur, which were to result in the modern secular worldview. Witchcraft was rejected as mere superstition, and the notion of the witch became a figure of fun—an old woman with a black pointed hat riding on a broomstick with her black cat.

During the twentieth century many have questioned the validity of the secular worldview and have sought for religious and magical powers. Often Christianity has been rejected, and people have sought for more exotic religions or magical practices. The general tolerance of other beliefs within the pluralistic societies of Europe has allowed people to explore and practice a wide range of teachings including witchcraft. These persons claim to be adherents of the ancient pagan religions, which were persecuted by the church of the Middle Ages as being counterreligion. These practitioners now seek to secure public recognition and respectability by appealing to the modern attitude of religious tolerance.

The contributor to the *Encyclopaedia Britannica* III on the subject of witchcraft makes some important observations:

> These practitioners usually turn out to be entirely sincere but misguided people who have been directly or indirectly influenced by Margaret Murray's article "Witchcraft", in the Fourteenth Edition of Encyclopaedia Britannica (1929), which puts forth in its

most popular form her theory that the witches of western Europe were the lingering adherents of a once general pagan religion that has been displaced, though not completely, by Christianity. This highly imaginative but now discredited theory gave a new respectability to witchcraft and, along with the more practical influence of such modern satanists as Aleister Crowley and Gerald Gardner, contributed to the emergence of do-it-yourself prescriptions that have done much to encourage the unashamed emergence of the self-styled witches that are sometimes featured in the Sunday newspapers. The author of this article has sobering visions of the antics he may be prescribing for the "witches" of the twenty-first century.[24]

African witchcraft has relevance only within the primal worldview. To the secular man, it is no more than an imaginary offense, as stated by Evans-Pritchard. However, the issues of evil that it seeks to answer and the jealousy that is so often at the center of witchcraft accusations are part of the fallen nature of man. These aspects do not disappear with Western education but are only transformed and appear in other forms. The seeking of power for selfish purposes leads some in every community to follow the path that is known to be evil. The Bible portrays the picture of Satan and his demonic host who are all too anxious to lead humankind further down such an evil path.

Notes

1. Geoffrey Parrinder, *Witchcraft: European and African* (Faber & Faber: London, 1970), p. 13.
2. Ibid., p. 130.
3. E. E. Evans-Pritchard, *Witchcraft, Oracles and Magic Among the Azande* (Clarendon Press: Oxford, 1976), p. 16.
4. Parrinder, op. cit., p. 141.
5. Personal informant of the author, 1984.
6. Parrinder, op. cit., p. 13.
7. Henry Griffiths, "Animism Remains Strong in Nominally Christian Zaire," *EMIS Pulse* 19, no. 11 (1984): 2–4.
8. J. S. Eades, *The Yoruba Today* (Cambridge University Press: Cambridge, 1980), p. 125.
9. Parrinder, op. cit., p. 182.

10. Ibid.
11. M. J. Field, *Religion and Medicine of the Ga People* (Oxford University Press: London, 1961), pp. 139–43.
12. J. Akim Omoyajowo, "What Is Witchcraft?" in E. A. Ade Adegbola, *Traditional Religion of West Africa* (Asempa Publishers: Accra, 1983), pp. 323–24.
13. Ibid., p. 334.
14. Griffiths, op. cit., p. 3.
15. David Hicks, *Tetum Ghosts and Kin* (Mayfield Publishing Company: Los Angeles, 1976), p. 110.
16. Maxwell G. Marwick, "Witchcraft," in *Encyclopaedia Britannica* III, 15th ed. (Encyclopaedia Britannica: Chicago, 1981), 19:898.
17. Parrinder, op. cit., p. 17.
18. Ibid., p. 19.
19. Keith Thomas, *Religion and the Decline of Magic* (Penguin Books: Harmondsworth, 1978), p. 521.
20. E. B. Trigg, *Gypsy Demons and Divinities* (Sheldon Press: London, 1973), p. 4.
21. Thomas, op. cit., pp. 523–24.
22. Matthew Hopkins, *The Discovery of Witches* (1647), pamphlet in British Museum.
23. "Witchcraft in Europe," in *Family of Man* (Marshall Cavendish: London, 1975), 3:1031.
24. Marwick, op. cit., p. 899.

12

Sorcery and Black Magic

"You know," said Bob, "we've just had a bit of trouble with that worker, Toto. Died, you know."

"No, I didn't. He was the kid who came to you from Dar-es-Salaam?"

"Yes, but he was the sole support of his lazy large family there, and they put a curse on him. You know, he wasn't here more than a month before he began to go into a sort of Victorian decline, fatigue. He grew tireder and tireder, and I took him to the clinic finally. It was a modern one completely screened, bug-proof. I went to see him in the ward a few days later. He looked pretty bad, particularly with that thick ring of black flies that had settled on his mouth. How they had gotten into the room, the nurses didn't know. The other patients had no flies near them. I swished them away from Toto, and killed them easily. We checked the screens; there wasn't a hole.

"I went out to talk with the doctor, and when we returned together there were the flies again, a thick, horrible ring around Toto's mouth—and no others in the room. Again we swished them off and killed them. Toto's pulse was failing.

"I went back to the house and talked to my head boy. Sure, he knew all about it. Toto's father had employed a witch doctor to put a curse upon his son.

"The next morning I came to the hospital early and walked through the ward where the native patients were sleeping peacefully. So was Toto, for he was dead. The black nurse was standing beside him.

"His last words, she said, were, *'Mama, yangu niwie rathie*—Mama, forgive me. . . .'

"I bent down to close his eyes and brush off that obscene

148

thick beard of flies around his mouth. They too were dead.''[1]

This conversation took place between two Englishmen who were living and working at that time in East Africa. A multitude of similar stories could be recounted from all around the world. They leave even the secular Westerner with a sense of awe and a multitude of unexplained questions. They illustrate what we will define as *sorcery*, or black magic. This differs from witchcraft in that it is a deliberate, conscious act of an individual, or group of individuals, to harm another by supernatural means. However, as stated in the previous chapter, these two phenomena may well overlap in their actual form and nature.

Jealousy, hatred, revenge, and greed are the motives for the practice of sorcery. Whereas in Western society an individual may resort to physical violence, in primal societies sorcery may be used as an alternative means of causing hurt. Sorcery consists of techniques, rituals, or various manipulations that are deliberately aimed at causing harm to others. As such there is always a secrecy about such matters and a reluctance to talk about the methods. There are, however, many stories about the effects of sorcery, and it is often difficult to distinguish fact from fiction. Either way, in primal societies the fear of sorcery is very real and evident. This means that the psychological effect upon the people concerned is great, but the consequences of sorcery cannot be analyzed simply as psychosomatic.

Because sorcery is a technique, it is possible for anyone with some knowledge to use the method to harm another. Most people, however, have only a vague idea of the rituals, but everyone is aware of the need to perform correctly such rituals if they are to be effective. For this reason, a person would make use of an individual recognized as being skilled in the arts of black magic. The actual identity of such a person is not publicly recognized, but most people in an African society would know of some such person. For a price, the practitioner will perform the necessary rituals. Success will enhance his reputation within the community, while failure will usually go unnoticed.

The Evil Eye

All over the Muslim world the evil eye (*nazar*) is considered to
be a frequent cause of misfortune. According to Moorish
proverbs, "The evil eye empties the house and fills the graves";
"One half of mankind die from the evil eye"; "The evil eye
owns two-thirds of the graveyard."[2] So firmly is the belief held
in North Africa that if a person looks at another's animal and
shortly afterward it dies, he is held responsible for the loss.

The belief in the evil eye comes from the uncanniness of a
particular look that is regarded as showing envy and covetous-
ness. The eye is regarded not only as an instrument for transmit-
ting evil wishes but also as an originating source of injurious
power. This power need not be a voluntary act but can work
automatically from a person desiring something of another.
Thus, a man blind in one eye is assumed to be envious of
another man with two good eyes, and a barren woman would be
envious of a woman with many children. The danger is considered to be even greater if it is accompanied with speech that
expresses admiration or envy. A mother would feel great fear if
a European woman were to smile at her baby and compliment
the mother on a lovely baby. This may be normal practice in
Europe, but in North Africa it could be regarded as the exercise
of the evil eye.

Not everybody has the power of the evil eye, and some
people may have it in higher degrees than others. Persons with
deep-set eyes and eyebrows meeting over the nose are regarded
as particularly dangerous. Fair eyes are uncommon in the
Muslim world and so often leave an uneasy impression. Among
the Berbers of North Africa, a person would not eat in the
presence of another who did not have food. The envious look of
the hungry person may mean that the eater would take poison
into his body as he eats. Even a dog present when a person is
eating would be given a morsel to prevent its covetously
looking at him.

The methods that are used to protect a person from the
influence of the evil eye are many. One type of approach is to
use some manner of ruse to counteract the influence. A child
may be left unwashed or may be dressed in rags, or a baby boy
may be dressed in girl's clothing.[3] Among the Pukhtun of

Pakistan a black spot made of kohl powder is placed upon the child's face.[4] All these things will make the child less attractive, less open to envy, and so divert the evil eye.

Another means by which protection may be afforded is by the use of charms, which are known in the Muslim world as *tawidh*. There are a great many charms that are put to many uses. Charms made of iron or the claws of tiger or bear are thought to be able to resist the influence of the evil eye by some inherent property of the material itself. Other objects, such as bones or cowrie shells, are of no value in themselves but serve to catch the eye and avert the covetous look.

One of the quickest methods of protection is the hand itself, the fingers outstretched, which is considered an effective means of protection. The number five, as signified with the spread fingers, is also a common symbol to protect against the evil eye. Muslim women will often wear charms that in some way use the symbol of five. The Hand of Fatima (see Figure 12.1) is common, as are amulets patterned in five conspicuous knobs. The symbol of the eye itself is regarded as having great power in throwing back evil, and it is often used in patterns and designs.

Yet another important means of protection is the Qur'an itself. The Qur'an recognizes the effects of the evil eye as seen in sura 113:

> Say: I seek refuge in the Lord of Daybreak
> From the evil of that which He created;
> From the evil of the darkness when it is intense,
> And from the evil of malignant witchcraft,
> And from the evil of the envier when he envieth.[5]

A charm may be made by writing words from the Qur'an on some material, which is then kept in a locket or leather bag.

The belief in the evil eye was the heritage of pre-Islamic folk belief, which the Arabs had in common with other Semitic peoples.[6] However, the belief in the evil eye has been found to occur among many societies outside the Muslim world. For example, among the Mexican migrants into Texas one finds the belief in *mal ojo*—evil eye. Children are believed to be especially susceptible to this misfortune, for they lack the spiritual strength of an adult. If a child's illness is diagnosed as being due to the evil eye, the parents will review those who have admired the child during the day and decide which one sent the affliction. That person is then sought out and asked to touch the child on the head. This action is believed to remove the power that the admiring look sent into the child and returns the patient's body to its normal state.[7]

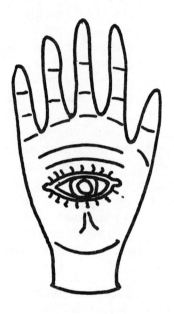

Figure 12.1. A common Muslim charm known as the "Hand of Fatima"

The Spell

The concept of uttering of a spell is universal among human societies. It takes on many forms, but the basic elements are the same. A spell may be conceived to be of one of two forms. First, it may be a deliberate way of causing harm by the uttering of a series of evil words, which express the desires of the speaker. In this form it is often known as a curse. Second, the spell may take the form of words that give protection against evil spirits and powers. It may even take the form of a blessing upon a person or an object.

To appreciate the concept of the spell it is necessary to realize that in primal worldviews words are not merely viewed as vibrations in the air. Words that are said deliberately with intention can take upon themselves a reality of their own, which can bring about the desires of the speaker. This can be for the good of a person as with a blessing or for harm as with a curse. The effectiveness of the spell is dependent upon several factors: the intensity of the desire, the manner of its expression, and the personality of the curser.

Behind the spoken word stands the personality of the one who created the words. The greater the personality of the speaker, the greater will be the effectiveness of the spell. Thus, if a god utters a curse, then the effect will be very great indeed. This is reflected in the Old Testament passages in which God says to Adam, "Cursed is the ground because of you" (Gen. 3:17). The curse here is God's judgment against sin. The potency of the word is seen in many of the healing miracles of Jesus and in the cursing of the barren fig tree (Mark 11:14, 20, 21).

For this reason a spell is often strengthened by calling upon the name of a spiritual being. These spells may consist of pleas, commands, and threats designed to persuade or coerce the spirit to do the speaker's bidding. They may also make use of certain traditional secret words and phrases considered to be of great power. The following spell has been recorded among the Muslims of Malaysia and was recited while a person buried a wax image of an enemy:

> Peace be to you! Ho, Prophet 'Tap, in whose charge the earth is,
> Lo, I am burying the corpse of somebody,
> I am bidden (to do so) by the Prophet Muhammad,
> Because he (the corpse) was a rebel to God.
> Do you assist in killing him or making him sick:
> If you do not make him sick, if you do not kill him,
> You shall be a rebel against God,
> A rebel against Muhammad.
> It is not I who am burying him,
> It is Gabriel who is burying him.
> Do you too grant my prayer and petition, this very day that has
>   appeared,
> Grant it by the grace of my petition within the fold of the Creed La
>   ilaha.[8]

A curse may also be increased in its effectiveness by some simple ritual. A common practice in West Africa is the licking of certain medicines prior to the utterance. These are often contained in an animal horn, and most sorcerers would have such a horn. Among the Yoruba of Nigeria the curse (called *epe*) is one of the commonest causes of psychiatric disorder. The results may be immediate or may not appear for several days, depending upon the power of the medicine used and the defenses of the victim:

> With *epe*, the man does what he is told to do. He may hang himself or run about the market showing his penis (or her vagina), or he may lay hold of a machete, and run about attacking people. He doesn't talk irrationally or see spirits; he does what he is told to do. *Epe* may take nine days to work...*epe* is like a slow poison.[9]

The relationship of the curser to the cursed is also an important factor in the effectiveness of the curse. In many societies the curse of a parent upon a child is considered the worst form of curse. Among the Karimojong, the curse of an elder upon a young warrior is considered to be of greatest force. In both these cases the possibility of cursing strengthens the authority structures within the society. This results in a stabilizing of the traditional social structure and values.

The effectiveness of a curse may be removed in many ways. Charms may offer protection, but if the curse is stronger, they will be overcome, and the person will need to go to a healer who himself may be a sorcerer. Raymond Prince described such a Yoruba healer:

> One healer showed me his pair of horns, both filled with a solid black medicine that protruded from the top of the horn; one was a cow's horn and showed evidence of constant use, for the black medicine was worn away in the shape of his mouth; the other was a twisted antelope horn, and thrust into the medicine were a cobra fang and a pin, made he said of copper and lead. To use it, he pulls out the pin and rubs it over the tip of his tongue; then whatever he says will come to pass. I have reason to believe that the former horn is the one he uses for patients, and that the latter is for *epe* (curse), but the healer vehemently denied it.[10]

The efficacy of a curse is also commonly believed to be

influenced by the guilt or innocence of the person on whom it is pronounced. A North African proverb illustrates this: "A curse without a cause does not pass through the door." Many societies even believe that if a curse is undeserved, it may recoil onto the curser himself. A blameless life is the greatest protection against the power of the curse: "Like a fluttering sparrow or a darting swallow, an undeserved curse does not come to rest" (Prov. 26:2.).

Magic Rites

In most primal societies, an unusual death, sickness, or misfortune is believed to be the result of black magic or sorcery. Black magic frequently makes use of spells, but these are usually accompanied by some magical rite. There are several elements that are common to sorcery in most societies.

The first is the need to "label" the victim. The sorcerer will often use a substance that has been in contact with the victim, such as hair, excrement, or clothing. He may also name the person so that there is no error in identity. This is considered as a way of opening a passage through his defenses. Janice Reid describes the importance of this aspect among the Yolngu, an Australian aboriginal people:

> When the victim goes to the toilet someone may take his excrement and put it in the fire. His stomach will blow up like a football. Occasionally a person may take another's soiled clothes or underpants—particularly those soiled by his sweat or urine—make a fire inside a hollow log, put these inside and seal it. The victim's body will swell until the flesh inside is soft. When the skin is touched it leaves an impression. The victim is hot. He can't bear clothes. He will soon die.[12]

This illustrates a second principle: the sorcerer will carry out a ritual that tends to demonstrate the effect he wishes to cause. These rituals are usually models or pictures of the desired effects. The voodoo doll is one of the most commonly known examples of this form of magic. In this case a wax image of the victim is made by the sorcerer. Then, with the recitation of certain curses, pins are pushed into the image. As the pins are pressed into the image, it is believed that a similar hurt will affect the victim himself.

Finally, the power is believed to be derived, either from certain spirits who are summoned or from certain powerful medicinal substances. An example described by Raymond Prince from the Yoruba illustrates this:

> You take the hair of a man's head. You prepare medicine and put it with the hair and put them both in an ant hill. As the ants are circulating about the medicine, so the victim will feel it inside his head or you may put the medicine and the man's hair under an anvil, and every time the blacksmith strikes the anvil so he will feel it inside his head.[13]

Among the Azande the sorcerer would make use of certain objects fashioned from trees and plants that Evans-Pritchard has called "medicines." These would include what Europeans call homeopathic medicines. Important magical rites are accompanied by spells in which the sorcerer tells the medicines what he wants them to do. These are carefully chosen words spoken in a "normal matter-of-fact voice" as in dispatching a boy on some errand.[14]

Magic is essentially a technique by which rituals are performed according to certain socially established patterns and taboos. For this reason magic may be classified by the society as being either good or evil. The use of magic for evil we have tended to call sorcery. However, magic may be used for socially approved ends, such as combating witchcraft, dealing with sorcery, or even harming an enemy army. Both use the same methods, but the difference lies in the moral value placed by the society on the desired aims of the magic.

A healer will use methods similar to those of the sorcerer who caused the victim's sickness. The healer only succeeds in obtaining a cure by the use of his powers and knowledge because they are greater than those of the sorcerer. Writing of the Yolngu people, Webb expresses this dichotomy:

> In East Arnhem Land there are two classes of magicians or medicine-men. Members of the one, whose operations are wholly of an evil character, are known as *ragalk*, while members of the other, whose operations are always of a benign character are known as *marrngit*.[15]

A kind of warfare exists between the forces that do good and those that do harm to man.

Ritual magic must not be considered as being limited to isolated tribal societies. It is this form of magic that has grown most rapidly in Western societies during this century and has been called *wicca*. These rituals consist of a numerous and complex series of rites requiring many objects and elaborate symbolism. A magician or witch would make use of various instruments known as "weapons." Aleister Crowley's list of weapons includes swastika, crown, wand, crook, sword, spear, scourge, lamp, sandals, dagger, tripod, cup, cross, and sickle.[16] These instruments should be made by the magician himself, and detailed directions are given concerning their manufacture and "consecration." Robes and special clothing are often worn for the rituals, which are held in secluded places. These items are believed to be linked to natural forces that heighten the magician's powers.

Sorcery—Real or Imaginary?

Most Western people, when they are confronted by magic, ask whether it really works. Secular anthropologists tend to view the phenomenon of sorcery as objectively as possible while still holding to a secular worldview. Janice Reid writes after her years of studying Yolngu sorcery: "An axiom of the ethnographic enterprise is that sorcery is not 'real' in any empirical sense, or, if it is performed, . . . it does not actually harm the intended victim."[17] However, even she is not free from the perplexity raised from the study of this phenomenon. She realizes that she was brought up with one set of assumptions about the nature of reality, and the Yolngu with another. She writes, "My short answer to the question, 'Do you believe in sorcery?' is usually, 'Not when I'm in Sydney.'" It must be admitted that the actual threat of a curse or sorcery has a great psychological effect on a person living in a society that believes in these phenomena. The power of suggestion alone is often enough to make a curse self-fulfilling. Often the subject is told either directly or indirectly that a curse has been placed upon him. The Christian, however, cannot leave the discussion at this point, and neither does the Bible.

First, one must note that the use of sorcery is explicitly
forbidden among the people of Israel: "Let no one be found
among you who sacrifices his son or daughter in the fire, who
practices divination or sorcery, interprets omens, engages in
witchcraft, or casts spells" (Deut. 18:10–11); "Do not allow a
sorceress to live" (Exod. 22:18). The Old Testament uses a
variety of words to describe various magical practices. Today it
is not possible to know exactly the original forms of magic
employed, but the use of so many terms demonstrates the fact
that all forms of magic were forbidden for the people of Israel.

In the former passages the Hebrew word translated "sorcerer" is *ksp*, which comes from the root meaning "to cut." It
probably refers to herbs cut for the making of charms and
spells.[18] The Hebrew term translated "casts spells" has the idea
of binding in the sense of making amulets. The most striking
reference to this form of sorcery in the Old Testament is found
in Ezekiel 13:18, 20:

> Woe to the women who sew magic charms on all their wrists and
> make veils of various lengths for their heads in order to ensnare
> people. . . . I am against your magic charms with which you en-
> snare people like birds and I will tear them from your arms; I will
> set free the people that you ensnare like birds.

This would suggest that a form of ritual magic was being
employed in which the sorceress was symbolically binding the
victim in a knot with a result that he would become sick and die.
This form of practice using knots is still found in many areas of
the world.

Second, although the Bible takes sorcery seriously and regards it as having power and reality, it is not something that
should cause the Christian fear. The power of God is continually seen to be greater than that of the sorcerer. This is seen in
the case of Moses and the Egyptian magicians (Hebrew *hrtm*
meaning "chief priest," the title borne by the greatest magicians). The Exodus record says that the magicians copied
Moses in turning their rods into serpents, in turning water into
blood, and in producing frogs (Exod. 7:11—8:20). They failed,
however, to perform any of the other acts.

Numbers 22—23 records the incident in which Balak com-
missions Balaam to curse the people of Israel: "Now come and

put a curse on these people, because they are too powerful for me'' (Num. 22:6). This is a typical form of malevolent magic. Balaam, however, was not able to curse effectively those whom God had blessed: ''How can I curse those whom God has not cursed?'' (Num. 23:8). Balaam was able to bless or curse only according to the will of God.

Third, those involved in magic are required to destroy their devices on becoming Christians. An outstanding example of this is seen during Paul's visit to Ephesus. The Ephesian sorcerers were famous for a particular form of charms, which were known as the ''Ephesian letters.'' These were scrolls on which certain magic phrases were written, and these were believed to provide the owner with safety in his travels, bring children to barren women, and guarantee success in love. Similar charms are found in much of the Muslim world where verses from the Qur'an are made into charms. Of the Ephesians, it is written; ''Many of those who believed now came and openly confessed their evil deeds. A number who had practiced sorcery brought their scrolls together and burned them publicly'' (Acts 19:18–19).

Fourth, for a person who believes that a curse has been placed upon him, it is insufficient to dismiss the matter as being either imaginary or without consequence. The individual needs to be reassured that the God to whom he has committed his life has all the resources to overcome the powers of evil. He no longer needs to depend upon charms and other forms of magic to protect him because now he has the indwelling person of the Holy Spirit within him: ''The one who is in you is greater than the one who is in the world'' (1 John 4:4). I have found that two illustrations have proved to be useful when praying with such people. The first is that of building a wall of God's protection around them, and the second is the severing of any bonds of evil that may be holding them. Witchcraft, sorcery, and the evil eye all stem from envy, jealousy, and hatred. All these things are the very antipathy of what God desires from humankind whom He created. No wonder these acts are condemned as evil.

The fifth factor that should be understood by the Christian is the social context of witchcraft and sorcery. It has already been mentioned that frequently those accused of being witches were people at the edge of society, such as an elderly widow living on

her own. Clyde Kluckhohn in his study of the Navaho speaks of
how hostile impulses may find a socially acceptable way of
expression through witchcraft accusations.[19] The accused, who
are usually minority groups or those marginal to the society,
thus become a "scapegoat" for the social tensions. This has a
complementary function in that members of the main society do
not seek to draw attention to themselves as being agitators or
overly ambitious. These unsocial attitudes would bring only
jealousy and hostility with the possibility of witchcraft accusations, or sorcery. Thus, witchcraft has a latent function within
the society of being a means of social control and encourages a
leveling of economic resources. If such beliefs are removed,
there is the danger of selfishness and materialism being given
full expression.

Notes

1. Hassoldt Davis, *Sorcerer's Village* (George G. Harrap:
   London, 1956), pp. 247–48.
2. W. Westermarck, *Pagan Survivals in Mohammedan Civilization* (Macmillan: London, 1933), p. 24.
3. V. R. and L. Bevan Jones, *Woman in Islam* (Lucknow
   Publishing House: Lucknow, 1941), p. 359.
4. Akbar S. Ahmed and David M. Hart, *Islam in Tribal
   Societies* (Routledge & Kegan Paul: London, 1984), p.
   315.
5. M. M. Pickthall, *The Meaning of the Glorious Koran* (Men-
   tor Books: New York), p. 455.
6. Westermarck, op. cit., pp. 56–57.
7. William Madsen, "Value Conflicts and Folk Psychother-
   apy in South Texas," in Ari Kiev, *Magic, Faith and
   Healing* (Free Press: New York, 1974), p. 426.
8. Kirk M. Endicott, *An Analysis of Malay Magic* (Clarendon
   Press: Oxford, 1970), p. 130.
9. Raymond Prince, "Indigenous Yoruba Psychiatry," in Ari
   Kiev, *Magic, Faith and Healing* (Free Press: New York,
   1974), p. 91.
10. Ibid., pp. 99–100.
11. Bevan Jones, op. cit., p. 320.

12. Janice Reid, *Sorcerers and Healing Spirits* (Australian National University Press: Canberra, 1983), p. 43.
13. Prince, op. cit., p. 90.
14. E. E. Evans-Pritchard, *Witchcraft, Oracles and Magic Among the Azande* (Clarendon Press: Oxford, 1976), pp. 177–78.
15. Reid, op. cit., p. 57.
16. *Mystical Rites and Rituals* (Octopus Books: London, 1975), p. 107.
17. Reid, op. cit., p. xix.
18. J. D. Douglas, *New Bible Dictionary* (IVP: London, 1968), p. 766.
19. Clyde Kluckhohn, *Navaho Witchcraft* (Beacon Press: Boston, 1967), pp. 76–128.

13

Spirit Possession

Most Western books dealing with the subject of spirit possession usually commence with the question: Can spirit possession
actually occur? However, anthropologists have shown that over
90 percent of all the societies in the world have some concept of
spirit possession. Almost all primal societies believe in the
possibility of an individual's being possessed by an external
spiritual being. This is a natural consequence of primal
worldviews that allow the interrelationship between the natural
world and that of the spirits and gods. The secular worldview,
on the other hand, tends to exclude such a relationship, and so it
questions the whole concept of spirit possession. It therefore
seeks to describe these phenomena in physical, psychological,
and nonreligious terms.

The main difficulty in a study of the subject of spirit possession is the lack of any clear analysis. Books that have been
written on the subject focus upon the descriptive elements,
which frequently result in the details of the practice obscuring
the major issues involved. This is especially true when one is
living and working in a cross-cultural situation. Exotic and
bizarre behavior can be misinterpreted by the outsider. It is the
aim of this chapter and the three following to examine the
fundamental nature and characteristics of possession and then to
consider the Christian response.

When studying possession across many different cultures,
one begins to see various patterns depending upon how the
person believes he relates to the spirit or group of spirits. Four
particular aspects may usefully be identified, and an understanding of these provides an initial framework for any study of
this subject.

The first aspect of the possession phenomenon is *medium-ship*, in which the person claims to act as an intermediary between human beings and spirits or ghosts. The emphasis here is one of communication between the spirit and the world of humankind. The second aspect is *shamanism*, which has been widely studied by anthropologists. Here the practitioner claims to work in cooperation with spirits with the aim of achieving healing within the community. The third aspect may be called *trance*, or the *mystic quest*. Here the person seeks to enter into a mystic relationship with a god or spirit, with resulting ecstatic emotions. The final class is called *possession* and occurs when a society claims that a person is under the control of a spiritual being. Often this is described by the people as having been "ridden" or "mounted" by a god or spirit in an analogous way to a person riding a horse.

Classification of Spirit-Human Relations

Class	Role of Person	Aim of Activity
Mediumship	Intermediary	Communication
Shamanism	Cooperation	Healing
Mysticism	Identification	Communion
Possession	Subservience	Control by spirit

These phenomena should not be considered to be mutually exclusive. They often overlap. The outsider in particular may have difficulty in identifying which one he is actually witnessing, but the individual and the society concerned are usually quite convinced of the particular form. For the Christian to dismiss all these as being simply of the devil is to fail to appreciate either the role of the phenomena within the society or how to approach the situation in a way that will be meaningful to the society as a whole. In this chapter we want to look at the question of possession.

Sickness and Spirit Possession

Primal societies recognize that when a foreign spirit intrudes into a human body, various manifestations may occur. For purposes of analysis these may be placed into two classes. The first class are those manifestations that must be considered in terms of sickness. The second are those in which the spirit manifests its control over an individual's body and so acts in a way characteristic of the spirit rather than that of the normal person. However, between these two classes come the illnesses that Western medicine would describe as psychiatric. One may therefore prefer to see the two classes of manifestations as the two extremes of a line.

In the first case, the society believes that the intrusion of the spirit is the cause of a particular sickness afflicting an individual. The healer will usually diagnose the cause of sickness by divination, and healing will then be attempted by the identification of the spirit and its exorcism from the person. A cultural outsider may well identify and describe the sickness in terms of the medical categories of his own society. However, this does not take away the fact that people of the particular society are convinced that the sickness is caused by spirit possession and not by germs or psychological problems.

In the villages of India, for example, it is commonly believed that a person may be possessed by a *bhootha*, or wandering spirit (see chapter 5). These ghosts haunt deserted houses, isolated fields, cremation grounds, or dark clusters of trees. The ghost may take hold of any passerby who unwittingly defiles its place or trespasses within its domain. The person will become depressed or exhibit some particular physical ailment. Healing, it is believed, can be achieved only through the exorcism of the *bhootha*.[1]

The Shona people of southern Africa believe that any spirit can bring about any physical or mental illness. The two most important groups of spirits are those of ancestors and witches. However, they also believe that diseases may be due to other causes such as worry, incorrect use of magical medicines, and improper development of the brain.[2]

Jane Murphy gives an example from the Inuit of Alaska:

An Eskimo woman . . . was diagnosed as having stolen from someone else a fox, which was causing her illness, and she later came to believe that a fox was living inside her. Her voice became hoarse from barking, and she clawed a fester inside her mouth where she thought a fox hair was coming out.[3]

This story begins to show the overlap between physical illnesses and those that Western medicine would class as psychological.

In the second class of manifestations, or the other end of the line, the spirit is seen as wanting to exhibit certain behavior patterns through the person. In this case the individual is not considered to be sick but as being the vehicle through whom the spirit is manifesting itself. Possession in these cases requires that the individual "self" be removed from the position of control. Possession here leads to observable changes of behavior depending upon the nature of the possessing spirit.

Animal Spirits

Among the Iroquois, persons who suffered from impulses to walk on all fours, grunting like a bear, were regarded as being possessed by the spirit of the bear. Kleptomaniacs, by analogous reasoning, were regarded as being possessed by the spirit of a chipmunk.[4]

An Old Testament example of this is seen in the story of Nebuchadnezzar. According to a tradition preserved by Eusebius, the king was "possessed by some god or other."[5] "He was driven away from people and given the mind of an animal; he lived with the wild donkeys and ate grass like cattle; and his body was drenched with the dew of heaven, until he acknowledged the most High God" (Dan. 5:21).

Local Deities

Priests are often considered as being possessed by the particular deity that they serve. Frequently, during religious rituals, the priest will wear the mask representing the deity and take on the behavior of the deity. In this case the priest willingly acts out the role of the god and so becomes possessed by the deity. The realm between acting and actual possession by the god thus becomes vague.

Haitian voodooism provides a classical case of possession in which a *loa* (spirit) mounts the participant during the ritual. Then, for several hours or so, the person dramatically acts out the role of the god or goddess.

Ancestor Spirits

The possession of a person by the ghost of a particularly noted ancestor is another common form of possession. In this way the individual is believed to exhibit the gifts and abilities of that ancestor.

Evil Spirits

These are those spirits that the society regards as being harmful for both the individual and the society as a whole. Several examples of this form of possession are found in the New Testament: "Teacher, I brought you my son, who is possessed by a spirit that has robbed him of speech. Whenever it seizes him, it throws him to the ground. He foams at the mouth, gnashes his teeth and becomes rigid" (Mark 9:17–18). The Greek text uses the term *echonta pneuma alalon*, "having a dumb spirit." Another case is that of the Gerasene demoniac who terrorized the district: "This man lived in the tombs, and no one could bind him any more, not even with a chain. For he had often been chained hand and foot, but he tore the chains apart and broke the irons on his feet" (Mark 5:3–4).

The parallels of these accounts with those of some of the worst aspects of voodoo possession are obvious:

> A seizure appears somewhat like an epileptic fit. The individual loses control of his muscles, and often collapses and becomes rigid. His eyes turn up so that they may appear to be white with none of the iris showing, and the heart-beat fluctuates wildly. He may roll about and foam at the mouth, and in this state of dissociation may even cause himself serious injury—for example, by falling into a fire . . . If the seizure has been induced by bad magic, a voodoo priest will have to be called in for help in diagnosis and treatment.[6]

During periods of possession, the victim may demonstrate

outstanding abilities. These include unnatural strength and even uncontrolled violence. Acts 19:13–16 tells the story of seven Jewish exorcists who tried to drive evil spirits out of a man in Ephesus: "Then the man who had the evil spirit jumped on them and overpowered them all. He gave them such a beating that they ran out of the house naked and bleeding." In other cases, victims may handle burning tapers, set fire to gunpowder on their bare hands, or even slash themselves with knives with no aftereffects. The uttering of all kinds of vile obscenities is also common.

Exorcism and Healing

If a particular society believes that a sickness is caused by spirit intrusion, then the assumed cure is the expulsion of the spirit by the process of exorcism. Therefore, in primal societies one will find healers who exercise this particular ministry. This requires two features: the use of defined rituals, and the endowment of the exorcist by a more powerful spirit.

Among the Shona a popular method for the exorcism of a spirit is that in which the spirit is transferred from the patient to an animal such as a sheep or a fowl. The animal is then driven into the woods, taking with it the curse that has caused the sickness. This "scapegoat" approach is one that is common in many forms of exorcism. Another method used by the Shona is that in which the patient is taken to a crossroads where the spirit is exorcised by pronouncing a spell. The evil spirit leaves the mad person and remains at the crossroads to afflict some other passerby.[7]

A similar form of exorcism has been described as occurring among the Yemenite Jews in Israel. Spirits, it is believed, can be exorcised only by the most powerful healers (*mori*) who have in their possession the sacred books (*sifre heftz*).

> Another method used to exorcise the spirits is to take a sheep, dove, or chicken and revolve it three times around the patient. The *mori* then whispers to the spirits, "Masters, please have mercy upon the patient and take the sheep instead." Immediately afterward the sheep is slaughtered. One of the following phenomena should then be observable as a sign that the spirit has left the

patient: 1. The sign of the broken cup. If a cup containing fluid should break during the exorcistic ritual, it means that the spirit has left the body of the patient and entered the cup, which breaks as a result of this invasion. 2. The sign of the fire. A light or a fire where it has not previously been indicates that the spirit has left the patient and ignited the flame.[8]

Among the Chinese, prolonged sickness often causes people to consult a medium. Frena Bloomfield recounts the story of an elderly lady who had been suffering badly from aches and pains in her joints for a long time. Although she had been taking medicine prescribed by her doctor, it seldom helped. Finally her family took her to see a medium famed for his healing powers. The medium became possessed by the god, Eldest Wang Yeh, who revealed that

> the illness was originally caused by five minor demons who could be persuaded to leave her body if she burned hell money for them and left an offering of food outside her house the next day to convince them to go. Grandmother Huang began to feel better from then onwards and regained considerable mobility in her limbs.[9]

These stories show some similarities with the account of the Gerasene demoniac recorded in chapter 5 of Mark. Jesus recognizes, as did the local people, that this man's sickness was due to spirit possession. The spirits clearly recognized the greater power present in the person of Christ, but it is notable that the spirits were not merely dismissed from the man. A process of artful bargaining then ensued. As Duncan Derrett, an anthropologist, remarks, "Without the bargaining we should not have known whether the man was a lunatic, fanatic, etc, as opposed to a subject of possession."[10] He goes on to stress the fact that many similar events have occurred in exorcisms recorded by anthropologists throughout the world. The spirits are finally transferred to the herd of pigs, and the deaths of the pigs confirm the complete deliverance of the man from the power of the spirits. It is notable that no blood is shed, and so this cannot be regarded as a sacrifice to appease the spirits. Neither does Jesus make any capital out of the successful exorcism.

In many societies where possession is a well-known phenomenon the symptoms will often recur. This is frequently the case where the "sickness" in Western terms would be classed as psychosomatic. An example would be a woman who is unhappily married or is barren or feels socially deprived for one reason or another. Exorcism may provide relief from the affliction for a period, but eventually the bouts become chronic and the woman needs to be treated in another way. An alternative treatment is what is often known as "possession cults," which are found in many primal societies.

Possession Cults

In possession cults the individual comes into a working relationship with the afflicting spirit. The individual remains free from the recurring sickness so long as she takes part in the periodic cult festivals. During these festivals she becomes possessed by the spirit, which acts out its particular character; first the person has to be initiated into the cult. In the course of time the person may graduate to a position in which she is in full control of her own spirit and is capable of controlling and healing others with similar afflictions.

An example of this type of cult is that of *sopono*. *Sopono* is a Yoruba name for a family of smallpox spirits, which include a range of sickness far wider than that implied by the word *smallpox*: fevers, boils, rashes, and psychoses. The initiation, which is secret, is reported to take twenty-one days. The initiate is taken to the shrine dressed in a white cloth. She enters the shrine backward, and after calling the *sopono* spirits the woman will finally become possessed by the spirit that has "borne her." For the next three weeks the woman remains at the shrine, and every morning she is washed; sacrifices are made on the third, seventh, fourteenth, and twenty-first days.

During the annual festival the members of the cult become possessed by the particular spirits that "chose" them on the first days of their initiation. These rituals have a festive mood, with most of the village in attendance. Raymond Prince vividly describes the actual possession:

> They placed one of the sacrificial bowls upon the girl's head, and the (cult) women began to sing louder, calling upon the spirit of the particular *sopono* that habitually possessed this girl. The girl's face

became vacant, and her eyes focused upon a distant place. Suddenly she fell forward in a kind of swoon; the "mother" supported her; someone else seized the calabash so that it wouldn't fall; others threw water on her feet. In a few seconds she revived a little; they guided her fingers up over the rim of the calabash, and she was drawn to one side, where she stood, somewhat dazed, the "wife" of the god.[11]

Voodooism initially derived from the Fon people of West Africa who were taken as slaves to the West Indies. For this reason one finds in the West Indies a number of characteristics similar to the cults of Africa. The marital theme is even more developed in the voodoo cults of Haiti. The person who wishes to secure the permanent protection of one of the *loa* (spirits) may make a formal proposal of marriage through the voodoo priest. Once the marriage has been agreed, the *loa*'s duty is to watch over his wife, but he must be given presents in return. Some human spouses make up a separate bed for their spirit and sleep on it on the allotted night.[12]

In Sudan, it is believed that spirits may possess a person causing a form of sickness and melancholia that particularly afflicts Muslim women. When a spirit has possessed the woman, she is not considered responsible for her actions, and she may smoke, drink heavily, or act in some other antisocial manner. Once the possession manifests itself, a day is arranged for what is called the *zar* ceremony. Here female friends gather at the patient's home where food and drink are served in an atmosphere that more resembles a party. A medium presides over the activities and determines which spirit has possessed the woman. Drumming accompanies the sick woman as she dances out her feelings and frustrations in the midst of the gathering. Laid on the floor around the dancing woman are placed mattresses onto which she finally faints at the climax of the ceremony, indicating that she is released from the spirit and the sickness.[13]

Many of these cults relate to the religious beliefs of the people before the coming of the world religion to which they would now acknowledge allegiance. The Hausa of Nigeria, for example, are Muslim, and yet the *bori* cult is an important one among the women. The primal religion of the Hausa was displaced from the public realm of society, which is dominated by men: "Women became possessed by the old gods which their men had discarded."[14]

Characteristics of Possession

The phenomenon of possession is far more complex than most people imagine, and it is therefore useful to recognize a number of particular characteristics. These may be considered as sets of opposites.

Helpful or Harmful

It may seem surprising to an outsider that possession may be regarded as anything but harmful. However, most societies in which possession is common make a clear distinction between these categories. Possession that causes sickness is regarded as harmful, but that experienced by the priest or healer is considered to be for the general help and well-being of the society as a whole.

The Bible, on the other hand, condemns all forms of possession. This is illustrated in the account of Paul's stay in Philippi:

> Once when we were going to the place of prayer, we were met by a slave girl who had a spirit by which she predicted the future. She earned a great deal of money for her owners by fortune-telling. This girl followed Paul and the rest of us, shouting, "These men are servants of the Most High God, who are telling you the way to be saved." She kept this up for many days. Finally Paul became so troubled that he turned around and said to the spirit, "In the name of Jesus Christ I command you to come out of her!" At that moment the spirit left her (Acts 16:16–18).

The girl was literally described as having a "python spirit." "Pythons" were people who were believed to be inspired by Apollo, the "Python" god, who is embodied as a snake. The chief shrine was originally at Delphi, but others existed throughout the Roman world. Young virgins were attached to these shrines and were believed to become possessed by these spirits who were able to give advice and foretell the future. Thus, in the eyes of the local people this form of possession provided a valuable service. Not only did the owners of the girl lose the source of finance, but the local people lost a means of divining the future. No wonder Paul and Silas were attacked by the crowds.

Voluntary or Spontaneous

From the previous point it can be seen that possession may be something that is either sought or unsought by the person concerned. A priest, for example, may seek to become possessed by the god of which he is a devotee. On the other hand, a traveler who violates a taboo area may be seized by a spirit who causes him to become sick.

A person who is seeking to become possessed by a spirit may use a variety of different methods that are recognized by the particular society. Rhythmic music and dancing with a strong beat are common practices. Drums are commonly used in Africa, as they are among the shamans in many parts of the world. The North American healers make use of rattles for a similar purpose. Drugs, smoke, perfumes, and incense are also used to stimulate possession. These aspects will be considered further in following chapters.

It is, however, necessary to appreciate that even a priest or healer who voluntarily seeks to become possessed may do this only for the general good of the community. The members of a possession cult participate only because they know of no other way to be free from their affliction and to have their felt-needs met. In some cases Western medicine may offer a physical cure, but it fails to meet the individual's emotional and religious needs. Christianity must be demonstrated to be able to meet an individual's deepest spiritual needs.

Individual or Communal

In the case of a priest, healer, or shaman, possession is always individual, as it is with many cases of sickness. However, it is possible at religious rituals for a whole group of people to become possessed during a prolonged period of dancing and singing. This is usually only a temporary event and lasts until the ceremony is completed. During such a communal ceremony some may be particularly possessed and be mounted by the spirit to do some particular activities.

Although it is true that in such rituals there is always some degree of acting on the part of the participants, these rituals cannot just be regarded as interesting cultural ceremonies. Possession contradicts the very dignity of humankind as created by God and robs the people concerned of their integrity and a true self-respect. Possession and allied rituals must therefore be condemned by Christians. The church must be willing not only to acknowledge the reality of spirit possession in its various forms but should be able to minister to those afflicted in this way. As one Ghanaian pastor said to me, "We want missionaries who are both educated in the Bible and who have power to deal with the spirit world." The Appendix of this book gives a few practical guidelines for those who find themselves in such situations.

Notes

1. Uma Anand, "Ritual Arts at Wayside Shrines," in *Gods of the Byways* (Museum of Modern Art: Oxford, 1982), p. 11.
2. Michael Gelfand, "Psychiatric Disorders as Recognized by the Shona," in Ari Kiev, *Magic, Faith and Healing* (Free Press: New York, 1974), p. 163.
3. Jane M. Murphy, "Psychotherapeutic Aspects of Shamanism on St. Lawrence Island, Alaska," in Ari Kiev, *Magic, Faith and Healing* (Free Press: New York, 1974), p. 68.
4. Anthony F. C. Wallace, *Religion: An Anthropological View* (Random House: New York, 1966), p. 141.
5. R. K. Harrison, *Introduction to the Old Testament* (Tyndale Press: London, 1970), pp. 1114–16.
6. "Voodoo," in *Family of Man* (Marshall Cavendish: London, 1975), 3:1059–60.
7. Gelfand, op. cit., p. 163.
8. Jozef Ph. Hes, "The Changing Social Role of the Yemenite Mori," in Ari Kiev, *Magic, Faith, and Healing* (Free Press: New York, 1974), pp. 375–76.

9. Frena Bloomfield, *The Book of Chinese Beliefs* (Arrow Books: London, 1983), pp. 107–8.
10. J. Duncan M. Derrett, "Spirit-possession and the Gerasene Demonic," *MAN* 14, no. 2 (1979): 288.
11. Raymond Prince, "Indigenous Yoruba Psychiatry," in Ari Kiev, *Magic, Faith, and Healing* (Free Press: New York, 1974), pp. 107–8.
12. I. M. Lewis, *Ecstatic Religion* (Penguin Books: Harmondsworth, 1971), p. 63.
13. Marjorie Hall and Bakhita Amin Ismail, *Sisters Under the Sun* (Longman: London, 1981), pp. 190–197.
14. Lewis, op. cit., p. 96.

14

Shamanism

The second category of possession phenomena that will be considered is that known as shamanism. This is a strange exotic institution that has fascinated explorers and anthropologists. In the previous chapter the shaman was distinguished from other forms of possession phenomena by defining his role by two particular features. First, he considers that he works in cooperation with the spirits. Raymond Firth has called the shaman a "master of spirits," with the implication that he can control the spirits and cause them to be manifest.[1] Second, his role in society is that of a healer and protector of the people from spiritual powers.

The word *shaman* comes from the Tungus people of Siberia and has been applied by anthropologists to a wide category of related observations. In its classical form it particularly relates to the polar-Siberian peoples, but the term has been applied to practitioners within other societies. In Korea, for example, the shaman is known as the *mudong*, but she (most *mudong* are women) exhibits some marked differences from the classical polar forms of shamanism. Likewise with the *belian* of Malaysia and the *inyanga* of the Shona people of Africa, one can observe particular cultural differences. For this reason the term *shaman* will be regarded as consisting of two overlapping categories: circumpolar and nonpolar (see Figure 14.1).

The Making of a Shaman

The many powers of the shaman are the result of his initiatory experience that radically affects his life. One may become a

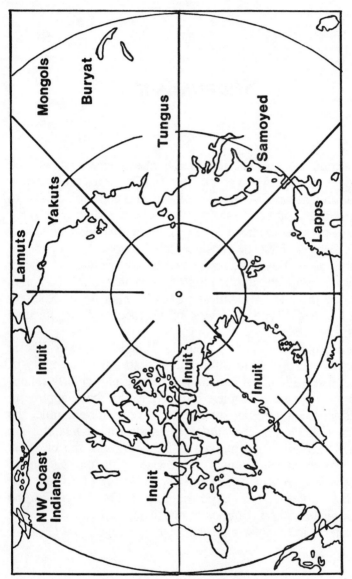

Figure 14.1. Circumpolar perspective showing some of the major polar peoples

shaman by one of three means: by a "calling" or "election" by a spirit; by the hereditary transmission of the shamanistic profession; or (most rarely) by a personal decision.

An Inuit (Eskimo), for example, would say that a person would never choose to become a shaman of his own free will.[2] He is a person very much aware of having been called by the spirits to this particular ministry. This initial calling is related to physical or mental sickness. The procedure of becoming a shaman is intended both to cure the initiate and to produce a valuable healer in the society. These people are often described as being "out of their minds," but this is distinguished from being "crazy."[3] The period of disturbance required by custom in order for a person to become a shaman is five days. Often during this period these people will not eat or drink, yet they become increasingly strong so that several men are unable to restrain them.

Among the Zulu, the potential shaman may be occasionally ill over a long period of time. Canon Henry Callaway, a missionary to the Zulu in 1870, recounts the following:

> The condition of a man who is about to be an *inyanga* is this: at first he is apparently robust; but in process of time he begins to be delicate, not having any real disease, but being very delicate. He begins to be particular about food and abstains from some kinds, and requests his friends not to give him that food, because it makes him ill. He habitually avoids certain kinds of food, choosing what he likes, and he does not eat much of that; and he is continually complaining of pains in different parts of his body. And he tells them he has dreamt that he was being carried away by a river. He dreams of many things, and his body is muddled and he becomes a house of dreams . . . on awaking says to his friends, "My body is muddled today; I dreamt many men were killing me; I escaped I know not how. And on waking one part of my body felt different from other parts; it was no longer alike all over." At last the man is very ill, and they go to the diviners to enquire.[4]

The man becomes progressively worse until he is no more than skin and bones and on the point of death. Finally, he starts to relate to the spirits, and although he continues to show marked personality changes, he begins to eat again.

Although not all potential shamans go through such a marked period of crisis, the general process of becoming a shaman is remarkably similar throughout the world. First there is a period of suffering that is interpreted as an assault by a spirit. While this is considered an experience that may happen to any person, in the case of the shaman it is merely the first indication of his future vocation. By overcoming this spirit assault, a new relationship is established between the shaman and the spirit. With the support of his friends the person manages to establish a new identity, that of a shaman. Even when the ministry is hereditary, the election of the future shaman is preceded by a change of behavior. The Akawaio of South America have the saying, "A man must die before he becomes a shaman."[5]

Often a novice will join himself to an experienced shaman and begin what may be a long and arduous apprenticeship. Some may even apprentice themselves directly to a spirit. In this way the novice learns how to perform the shamanistic rites and so call the spirits. During this time he may abstain from food, sex, or sleep. Through this arduous process he learns how to control and even master the spirits. Fantastic stories are recounted by the shaman of journeys to the underworld in which he has had to do battle with all kinds of strange and horrific spiritual opponents:

> According to the Yakuts, the spirits carry the future shaman to Hell and imprison him there for three years in a house. It is there that he undergoes his initiation: the spirits cut off his head, which they put aside (because the novice must look on with his own eyes as he is torn apart), and they cut him into little pieces, which they then distribute to the spirits of diverse illnesses. It is only by experiencing this condition that the future shaman will obtain the power of healing. His bones are then covered over again with new flesh, and in certain cases he is also supplied with new blood.[6]

To help him in this task the shaman must have the aid of particular spirits. The Inuit word for these spirits is *tornaq*, often translated into English as "familiar spirits." The shaman is not considered to be dominated by these spirits but to be at least on an equal footing with his spirit helpers. Many South American shamans refer to their spirit helpers as their "pets."[7]

A Malay shaman gets possession of a spirit familiar by inheritance from another shaman, usually a father, uncle, or grandfather. He may wait beside the grave of the ancestor in a trancelike state waiting for the gift of the spirit. He may alternatively wait in the dark forest for the coming of a tiger spirit. Endicott thinks that the form taken by the ghost of a shaman is that of the tiger spirit.[8] This spirit gives him *ilmu*, power in the form of knowledge.

The Warrior Healer

The striking imagery of the spiritual adventures of the shamans highlights their role as the champions of the people who combat the forces of evil. They must fight against not only evil spirits but illnesses and even black magic. Among the polar shamans the imagery of the warrior is even more distinct with the use of bows, lances, and swords in their rites. He is seen as the champion who through his ability to travel into supernatural worlds and to "see" spiritual beings is able to defend the community.

As a result of these special powers the shaman is able to act as a healer within his community. In order to appreciate how he can operate it is necessary to consider the ways in which his society thinks of sickness. Most shamanistic societies tend to believe that sickness comes from five major causes.

Soul Loss

The essential belief is that a person's soul may leave his body on certain occasions such as when he sleeps or is startled. This concept of the "external soul" was discussed in chapter 4. While the soul or one of the multiple souls is away from the body, it may be captured by one of the many evil, predatory spirits that exist in the world. Until the soul is returned to the patient's body the person continues to be ill.

According to the worldview of such shamanistic societies the task of the shaman is to send out his own soul to find the one that is lost. During the curing rite the shaman goes into a trance as a result of his soul leaving his body, and then with the aid of his spirit familiars he searches the supernatural worlds for the lost soul of the patient.

The son of St Lawrence Island's famous shamans said that his father's spirit familiar would undertake such an errand and could travel the eighty miles to and from Indian Point or Savoonga in less than five minutes—"just like electricity," he said—and would come back with information important to the search for the lost soul.[9]

The recounting of such stories plays an important part of the polar shamanistic rites, and the shaman may have even to fight with the evil spirit who does not want to return the patient's soul.

Various methods are used by the shaman to induce trancelike states. The polar shaman uses the consistent beat of a single drum and may also use rattles or smoke. The shaman from the Akawaio Indians of the Amazon consumes greater and greater quantities of hallucinogenic herbal preparations until he is able to induce a trance state by drinking enormous amounts of tobacco juice.[10]

Spirit Intrusion

As discussed in the previous chapter on possession, spirit intrusion may be considered as being of two forms: sickness or total behavior change. Among the circumpolar peoples, spirit intrusion is believed to account for insanity or hysteria, and exorcism is required. This does not appear to be such an important cause of sickness among nonpolar peoples.

Object Intrusion

Not only is it believed that spirits can intrude into a person's body, but so can various foreign objects. This object may have been shot into the patient's body by a spirit or sorcerer. The object must be removed if a cure is to be achieved. Various techniques may be used, but nearly all are performed to the beating of the drum. Among the polar peoples a common practice is for the shaman to suck the afflicted part of the patient's body. The spirit familiar of the shaman in this way draws the object until it is finally sucked out. The shaman will often take from his mouth a small stone, a worm, or piece of bone that he shows to those who have gathered for the healing ritual.

Jane Murphy has described such a ritual from among the Inuit of the St. Lawrence Isles:

During the singing and drumming of the seance, he [the shaman] would appear to thrust his own drum-stick into the stomach of the patient. When the stick was removed, there would be a writhing black thing—"something like a worm"—attached to the end of it. in the dimly lit room, the shaman would show the stick about and then eat the worm-like thing, demonstrating by this final act that the disease had been consumed by the spirit-familiar and was no longer noxious to the human patient.[11]

The Breaking of a Taboo

In chapter 2 we discussed the importance of taboo in primal societies. In many such societies the breach of taboo is seen as the cause of various sicknesses. Incest, sexual perversions, and offending a god are often regarded as disease-provoking transgressions. This may affect not only the individual but the family and even the community.

The shaman in this case uses his powers to find out what transgression has been committed and to discover what atonement is necessary in order to expiate the sin. In many cases public confession of the transgression plays an important part in the healing ritual.

Sorcery

Polar societies make a clear distinction between the healing magic of the shaman and the black magic of the sorcerer. Only the most powerful shaman would deal with those sicknesses requiring countersorcery.

A description of such a ritual among the Tetum of Indonesia has been described by David Hicks:

After the advance payment has been made, the shaman escorts the invalid into the womb of his house. Here a sleeping mat lies spread out near the fire blazing in the hearth. Both sit on it. The shaman takes a betel leaf, a few pieces of areca and lime, places them in his mouth and chews. A couple of seconds later he spits a gob of the areca blood onto the floor. The spittle represents a mystic bridge between the two worlds. He must throw this bridge across to make connection with the spiritual power causing the trouble. The shape of the gob of spittle and its shade of red tell the shaman what sort of spiritual attacker he is up against. If he decides an ancestral ghost is the invader, the shaman can only suggest what gift must be sacrificed by the victim to persuade the ghost to leave him in peace. But if the culprit is a witch, he can grapple with him mentally on the spot. . . . If the shaman's willpower proves stronger than that of the witch, he will sooner or later thrust the alien soul out. So the shaman sits night after night on the same mat as the victim, to protect him and prevent the evil soul from re-entering his body. When the witch realises the hopelessness of its evil ambition, the shaman's nightly visits end and the sick person recovers. . . . Should the shaman prove weaker than the witch, however, the victim's health deteriorates until death claims his body.[12]

The shaman's role is not limited to curing the sick. He may often use his powers to obtain information such as which is the best direction to go on a hunting party or if a fight with an enemy group will be successful. He may even have a legal role and deal with social disputes.

The Ambiguity of the Shaman

The shaman is a person who goes into trances, "sees" strange visions, and shows many of the behavior patterns of what a Western doctor would diagnose as schizophrenia. In the West such a person may be placed in a mental hospital as being in need of psychiatric help. However, within shamanistic societies he is held in honor and is regarded as a useful member of society.

To understand the role of the shaman, one must realize that he is functioning according to the worldview of his society. The things that he does and says may seem to be totally strange to another society, but to his own society they seem normal and completely reasonable within the context of how the people perceive the universe. As Lewis colorfully expresses it: "In the society of the mad, the normal mentally healthy person will be condemned as a lunatic."[13]

It is difficult for the secular man to appreciate the value of the shaman in primal societies. The shaman is considered to battle with the unseen forces of evil, even at the risk of his own life.

His role as healer is confirmed to his people through the demonstrations of his powers, which leave the people in awe and a sense of confidence in his healing abilities. W. F. Doty, a missionary on St. Lawrence Island in 1898, was present during a rite when the shaman was supposed to sink slowly into the ground until only the hair of his head remained visible. In his diary, Doty described putting his hand on the shaman's head and feeling it sink lower.[14] Although many shamans are known to be experts at conjuring tricks and ventriloquism, in ecstasy the shamans can do more than they themselves understand as they come in contact with unseen powers.

Because of the shaman's supposed ability to move about between the natural and spirit worlds, there are some aspects of his behavior that are different from those of the local culture. His ambiguous role means that he does not conform to some of the expected modes of behavior. One of the most surprising aspects of this is that the shamans of many polar societies are homosexual or transvestite:

> According to Bogoras, among the shamans of the Chukchi, various degrees of transformation are recognised. In the first, the shaman changes only the manner of braiding and arranging his hair; in the second, he adopts female dress; in the third, he leaves off all the pursuits and manners of his own sex and takes on those of a woman. Even his pronunciation changes from the male to the female mode. At the same time his body alters, if not in its outward appearance, at least in its faculties and forces. . . . He seeks to win the good graces of men, and succeeds easily with the aid of "spirits." . . . From these he chooses his lover and after a time takes a husband.[15]

The ambiguity of the role is further compounded by the fact that he may also have a "spirit" husband or wife!

When one considers that in most polar societies homosexuality is condemned as taboo, it can be seen that the shaman is functioning in an ambiguous sexual role within his own society. The acceptance of this role by the general populace illustrates the symbolic nature of his ministry between the natural and supernatural worlds.

Although some anthropologists have questioned the sanity of the shamans, many others have recognized that most are mentally healthy. The Soviet ethnographer Anisimov reports of

Evenk shamans that "although some revealed hysterical neurotic characteristics, there were also many who were extremely
sober individuals."[16] To disregard the shaman as being neurotic
is to miss an important aspect of his society. The shaman may
be a farsighted and ambitious member of society pursuing the
only avenue of specialization open to him. In a more technological society his talents may make him an inventor or artist, but
within the limits of his own society he seeks for new horizons
through shamanizing the spirits.

Jesus and Beelzebub

The role of the shaman as an exorcist raises some questions
concerning the difference between his function and what we see
in the ministry of Jesus Christ. Within the synoptic Gospels the
accounts of the many exorcisms of Jesus are important not only
in their own right but because they show that these exorcisms
were questioned by the people of His own day. In the so-called
Beelzebub controversy, Jesus is accused of being spirit possessed, and by this spirit He is able to cast out spirits in a way
similar to that of a shaman. The story is recounted in Mark
3:22–30, and with some additions in Matthew 12:22–37 and
Luke 11:14–22. The accusation comes as the watershed in
Christ's ministry, for it is here that His rejection begins.

In the Matthew and Luke accounts, the controversy com-
mences not with an accusation of insanity as in Mark but with a
specific exorcism. On the one hand, the people wondered if
Jesus was indeed the Son of David, while on the other the
Pharisees charged Him with performing the exorcism by
Beelzebub, "the prince of demons."

Jesus answers the charge in two parts. First, He shows the
absurdity of the charge by asking a rhetorical question: "If
Satan drives out Satan, he is divided against himself. How then
can his kingdom stand?" (Matt. 12:26). If Satan's kingdom is
divided, then it will soon fall, and so God's purposes will be
achieved anyway.

In the second part of His reply, Jesus again poses a question:
If exorcism means that one is in league with Beelzebub, by
what means do the Pharisees perform their exorcisms? This is

the only reference in the Gospels to the fact that the Pharisees performed exorcisms. Logically there can only be one of two answers, either by Satan or by God. If it is the latter, then the conclusion must be that in Christ, the kingdom of God has come. Jesus once again poses a question: "Or again, how can anyone enter a strong man's house and carry off his possessions unless he first ties up the strong man? Then he can rob his house" (Matt. 12:29). This merely reinforces the point that the many remarkable exorcisms of Jesus are a sign of the presence of the kingdom of God.

Both Matthew and Luke conclude the discourse with strong words of warning against the Pharisees. These people who were asking for "a miraculous sign" (Matt. 12:39) were in danger of the worst kind of demonic activity. They were in danger of spiritual blindness, which does not see the Spirit of God in the work of Jesus Christ.

The parallels between the Beelzebub controversy and the role of the shaman are apparent, but the application to the present-day situation is not so obvious. It is first necessary to note a major distinction between the New Testament teaching concerning the spirit world and that of most primal societies. The New Testament sees the world of evil spirits as being highly organized and uses terms such as *kingdoms*, while primal worldviews portray them as disorganized and competitive. Even the shaman would realize that he is operating with dangerous powers, but he believes that he is able to cooperate with some in order to oppose and defeat other evil spirits. Jesus, on the other hand, claimed to operate by the power and authority of the Creator God. He was therefore able to overcome the spirits that dominate humankind and release people from their bondage and fear.

Fear is a major fact in much of life in primal societies. How fear is caused and how it can be overcome can be seen in the following illustrations:

We fear the weather spirit of earth that we must fight against to wrestle our food from land and sea. We fear Sila (the weather spirit). We fear death and hunger in the cold snow huts. We fear Takankapsaluk, the Great Woman down at the bottom of the sea that rules over all the beasts of the sea. We fear the sickness that we meet with daily around us; not death, but the suffering. We fear the evil spirits of life; those of the air, of the sea, and of the earth that can help wicked shamans to harm their fellow men. We fear the souls of dead human beings and of the animals we have killed.[17]

The first missionary to the Yahgans of Tierra del Fuego, who were a shamanistic people, had been a young clergyman who arrived on the *Beagle* with Charles Darwin. He had been so threatened, mauled and even stoned that he was immediately withdrawn. The second mission occurred in the winter of 1850–51 and consisted of a mission of seven, who had to flee for their lives into the wilderness, where they perished. A third attempt, in 1859, got as far as the building of a chapel; but on Sunday morning, November 6, in the middle of the first verse of the first hymn of their opening service, the little group of four was set upon, clubbed, speared, and stoned to extinction. Finally, in 1871, when the Rev. Thomas Bridges disembarked there with his wife and infant daughter to inherit the mission and take charge, he found that there was a change of attitude among the people.[18] They now realized that the missionaries had come to tell them of the Supreme Creator whom they had previously thought was distant and unknown. The Yahgans realized that the Creator God must be more powerful than the familiar spirits of the shaman, and so they turned to the new religion.

Daniel Shaw tells a similar story of the Samo of Papua New Guinea. The Samo Christians asked God's protection over their garden rather than invoke the assistance of benevolent spirits. Shaw writes,

Christians, using their relationship with God, can accomplish for their kin through prayer what non-Christians accomplish through their interaction with the spirits. The concept of interaction is the same—only the power source has shifted. . . . They know the spirits are real, but if necessity calls for interaction with them, they pray for God's protection and step out in faith, believing that he has greater power than the spirits and will take care of them. . . . This is not a missionary's message distorted by local beliefs. Rather it is an internalisation of Christian concepts by people who have applied them to their daily living. . . . Each Samo Christian is no longer a shaman but rather attains to the royal priesthood, ordained by God and set apart to apply his power to the vital task of living for the one who gives "new life."[19]

Notes

1. I. M. Lewis, *Ecstatic Religion* (Pelican Books: London, 1971), p. 56.
2. Kaj Birket-Smith, *The Eskimos* (Methuen: London, 1959), p. 171.
3. Jane M. Murphy, "Psychotherapeutic Aspects of Shamanism on St. Lawrence Island, Alaska," in Ari Kiev, *Magic, Faith, and Healing* (Free Press: New York, 1974), p. 58.
4. Anthony F. C. Wallace, *Religion: An Anthropological View* (Random House: New York, 1966), pp. 145–46.
5. Lewis, op. cit., p. 70.
6. Mircea Eliade, *A History of Religious Ideas* (University of Chicago Press: Chicago, 1985), 3:13–14.
7. "Shamanism", in *Family of Man* (Marshall Cavendish: London, 1975), 2:693–96.
8. Kirk M. Endicott, *An Analysis of Malay Magic* (Clarendon Press: Oxford, 1970), p. 17.
9. Murphy, op. cit., p. 62.
10. "Shamanism," op. cit., p. 696.
11. Murphy, op. cit., p. 67.
12. David Hicks, *Tetum Ghosts and Kin* (Mayfield Publishing Company: Palo Alto, 1976), p. 112.
13. Lewis, op. cit., p. 180.
14. Murphy, op. cit., p. 59.
15. Joseph Campbell, *The Way of Animal Powers* (Times Books: London, 1984), p. 174.
16. Lewis, op. cit., p. 182.
17. Ibid., p. 163.
18. Campbell, op. cit., pp. 159–60.
19. R. Daniel Shaw, "Every Person a Shaman," *Missiology* 9, no. 3 (1981): 363–65.

15

Mediumship: Consulting the Spirits

In 1848, in a small village in western New York, two girls, Margaret and Kate Fox, heard strange knockings in the cottage where they lived. After this there were vibrations great enough to shake their beds. Kate challenged the unseen power to repeat the snaps of her fingers. The challenge was accepted, and each snap was answered instantly by a knock, much to the surprise of her parents (who were nominal Methodists). They believed that the knockings were caused by spirits using a code, and by interpreting the code they began to receive messages. Evidence was received that these spirits claimed to be ghosts of the dead, and news of the event quickly spread around the whole village and beyond. The Fox sisters provided the impetus for a new interest in spiritualism in Western society.

Spiritualists claim that spiritualist organizations have been formed in over forty countries, and the U.S. alone has over half a million followers. Among the members of the various spiritualist organizations have been some very notable figures such as Sir Arthur Conan Doyle[1] and the Frenchman Leon Denizard Rivail who claimed to be the reincarnation of the Celtic poet Allan Kardec.

The belief that a person may communicate with those who have died is not new but has been common to many societies for centuries. The Old Testament makes direct reference to it on several occasions: "When you enter the land the LORD your God is giving you, do not learn to imitate the detestable ways of the nations there. Let no one be found among you . . . who is a medium or spiritist or who consults the dead" (Deut. 18:9-11); "Do not turn to mediums or seek out spiritists, for you will be

defiled by them. I am the LORD your God" (Lev. 19:31). There
is also the outstanding record of King Saul's visit to the woman
at Endor, which resulted in the departed Samuel speaking to
him (1 Sam 28).

Spirit Mediumship

In a previous chapter we have already sought to make the
distinction between various classes of spirit-human manifestations. Spirit mediumship, the third aspect of possession phenomena, is distinguished from spirit possession even though
there is a phenomenological similarity. The spirit medium is
concerned with the function of communication, either one way
or two way, which invariably involves speech utterance of
some form. In spirit possession there is not necessarily any
communication of a message but a domination of the person by
a spirit.

Spiritualism cannot be regarded as just one standardized
system of belief because it manifests itself within many religious systems. Not only are there spiritualists within the primal
religions, but there are also Christian spirtualists, Jewish spiritualists, Buddhist spiritualists, and even atheistic spiritualists.[2]
In discussing this phenomenon we shall use the term *spiritualism* and not *spiritism*, which is regarded by many Western
mediums as being abusive. Although several varieties can be
recognized within the phenomenon, nevertheless, the many
forms of spirit mediumship have a number of factors in
common.

1. At death the body of the individual dies, but some aspect
of the immaterial part of the individual lives on. In Western
spiritualism, a human is assumed to be made up of three
elements: body, soul, and spirit. The body encases the soul,
and the soul encases the spirit. The soul duplicates the body
in structure, and at death the soul serves the spirit as the body
has served both the soul and the spirit in life. Animals are
believed to have souls and not spirits. In the chapter on
ghosts and ancestors we have used the term *ghosts* to
describe the nature of the surviving element of human beings.

However, because of the wide use of the term *spirit* within spiritualism we shall use the term *spirit* in this case.

2. The spirits of the dead are believed to enter a spiritual world for the dead. This is conceived of in many forms, but most Western spiritualists speak of the seven spheres that surround the earth. The lowest sphere is occupied by those who lived wicked lives on earth and were dominated by material desires. Most people are believed to enter the third sphere called "Summerland." It is very similar to life on earth but is free from evil and sorrow. The spirits in Summerland are said to wear clothes, live in houses, and even marry their soul mate. However, marriage in the heavenly sphere is considered to be wholly platonic.

Many spiritualists have regarded the so-called proofs of communication with the spirit world to be a message of good news to humankind. They claim that there is life after death, and one does not have to fear any condemnation either to heaven or to hell. Some spiritualists even claim the possibility of reincarnation and refer to the previous lives that they have lived.

3. The third assumption is the possibility of communication with the spirit world. This possibility of communicating with a recently deceased loved one has drawn many to spiritualism. However, this communication may occur only through the mediumship of a person on earth who is sensitive to the "vibrations" from the spirit world and so is able to convey messages to the living. Many different kinds of people are mediums, but they tend to share some characteristics. They often become aware of their powers while they are quite young and are frequently reluctant to become mediums. Many mediums find their powers come after a serious illness or accident. Writing of Chinese mediums, Frena Bloomfield says,

> Some people think that they have been spared death, which their accident or illness threatened them with, while others feel that the event was actually sent to them by the spirits in order to, as it were, bring them to heel.... If a potential medium tries to resist the advances of the spirits and their demands that the medium should be a voice for them, he or she is often afflicted with continuing

illnesses until submitting to them. Then the spirits allow the medium to become well and stay that way as long as he continues to work for them. If he tries to give it up, the spirits will continue to punish him.[3]

The Ga priests of Ghana are accompanied by female devotees, who are mediums bringing messages from the gods. These women are taken to be called by a god and during the excitement of dancing at the religious rituals become possessed by him. These mediums normally undergo two or three years of training at the hands of the priests.[4]

4. The medium enters into some form of trance in which he is believed to enter into a close relationship with the spirits. The trance may vary from a deep concentration to that of a genuine possession by a spirit of which the medium later has no knowledge. When a medium is about to go into trance, he will begin to breathe deeply, and even Western mediums speak about the medium's own spirit leaving his body to be taken over by a controlling spirit. Raphael Gasson in his biography tells of his own "spirit guide" who claimed to be an African witch doctor who had been in the spirit world for 600 years.[5] His spirit claimed to be Gasson's "door-keeper" to keep out evil spirits from his body. While in such trance states, mediums have been known to speak in other voices, give prophecies, write books, and offer medical advice.

5. Another assumption common to most forms of spiritualism is the need for some set pattern of rituals that occur in the seance. The meeting centers about the medium, and the numbers attending may vary from one to a dozen or more. In the West, the setting is usually the sitting room of a house, which has been deliberately darkened to help the spiritualist in his communication. This practice has often been criticized, but mediums answer that just as radio transmissions are clearer at night, so communications with the spirits are better in the dark. Hands are usually linked into a circle, and the spirits are alleged to communicate in various ways depending upon the medium. This may be by rappings, visible manifestations, voices, automatic writing, or the Ouija board.

6. A major practice in spiritualism is that of spiritual healing. John Beattie has made a study of the ghost cult among the

Banyoro of Uganda.[6] Here the sick person is the one who often becomes the medium for the ghost (spirit), but this requires the assistance of a *mufumu*, a healer who is initiated into a spirit-mediumship cult.

> When the time for the possession has come, usually at night, the people sit around the hearth, where a fire is glowing. The *mufumu* begins to shake his gourd rattle rhythmically, and everyone present begins to sing special songs. . . . (In time) the patient falls forward on his face—he has been in a sitting position. Then the *mufumu* addresses the ghost, which is now in the patient's head: "What would you like to eat?" The ghost answers through the sick person "meat". But he uses the special vocabulary used by ghosts and calls it *kanunka* instead of the usual Nyoro word *nyama*. The *mufumu* also asks the ghost who it is. The ghost may give the name of someone who has died long ago.
>
> Then the *mufumu* goes on to ask, "And what was it that annoyed you?" The ghost replies: "They refused to give me meat," or "They killed me," or "They didn't take proper care of me so I died," or gives some other reason.
>
> If the ghost asks for a goat, they bring a black one and present it to the ghost. And the *mufumu* says, "The matter is finished; here is your goat. Now leave off killing people." Then they cut the goat's throat, and they cause blood to flow into a new winnowing basket, which is sound and without holes. They order the patient to drink some of the blood. He drinks as well as he is able. Then the goat is skinned and divided up, a small part of it is cooked; most of the meat is taken home by the *mufumu*.

Spiritualist healing meetings have drawn crowds in many Western countries. The healer without asking any questions will lay his "healing hands" on the patient and seek to transmit power from himself to the sufferer. The other people in the meeting are asked to cooperate by concentrating upon the patient and sending out "healing thought rays" to assist the medium in his task. The healing is believed to have been done by the spirits who are working through the vessel of the medium. Following the meeting, the medium will feel physically tired and conscious of a loss of power.

7. Although mediumship is primarily concerned with communication with the spirit world, this often leads to an interest in

various physical manifestations. Levitation is a phenomenon claimed to have been performed by some mediums. Here a person is caused to float above the ground as if weightless. Another form is telekinesis, which is the movement of objects around the room. Western mediums speak about the forming of ectoplasm. This is described as

> a semi-luminous thick vapour which oozes from the medium's mouth, ears, nose, eyes, or from the stomach and is dimly visible in the gloom. This mist gradually becomes solid, as it eventually makes contact with the natural surroundings of the seance room. ... When touched it will move back into the body and if suddenly seized the medium will scream out or be caused to be violently sick.[7]

Chinese mediums have been known to walk on fire when in trance possession and even climb ladders made of swords as Frena Bloomfield describes:

> Finally the master medium began to ascend the ladder, pausing on each sword to rock the ladder slowly backwards and forwards. At the top of the ladder, he stood and hoisted up all kinds of personal objects which the crowd passed him, since they believed that they will gain protection for their house if they have in it some possession which has received the blessing of contact with the sacred ladder of swords during the ceremonies. Once the medium had obliged the worshippers in this way, he made his way down again, winding his body through the swords and backwards and forwards, like a contortionist, finally touching ground again, uncut.[8]

The Umbanda of Brazil

Although spiritualism is found in many countries in one form or another, the particular case of the Umbanda movement in Brazil provides an important illustration. The movement has been called by various names such as Macumba, Candomble, or Afro-Brazilian cults. In May 1975, there were recorded to be 14,000 spiritualist centers in action in Brazil guided by 420,000 mediums. Spiritualist leaders themselves say, and they are probably correct in this, that there are some 15 million Brazilians who are openly confessed followers of these cults, and some 50 million other people are to some degree involved with it at one time or another, out of a total population of 105 million.[9]

Origin

The origin of the Umbanda movement provides an important illustration of the interaction and development of religious beliefs and practices. It is especially important in showing how primal beliefs may take on new forms within a developing country such as Brazil.

Four main strands can be identified in the formation of the movement. The first comes from the African slaves taken to South America to work on the sugar plantations in the seventeenth century. The slaves tended to be sold in groups, unlike in the U.S. where they were generally sold as individuals. This caused some continuation of the traditional beliefs and practices of West Africa, and especially those of the Yoruba of Nigeria. Even today there is major trade in Brazil of African fetishes and herbs.

Because the Portuguese masters were Roman Catholic, they required their slaves to have at least the appearance of being Catholics, and this gave the second influence to the movement. Little real religious instruction was given, but the slaves did become familiar with the Roman Catholic rituals and saints. Many of the Yoruba gods thus became associated with particular Catholic saints. For example, the Virgin Mary became associated with Yemanja, the Yoruba goddess of the sea. Shango, the god of thunder and lightning, was identified with St. Jerome because of the fact that he dwelt in the desert with lions. Ogun, the Yoruba god of war, was identified with St. George, and Jesus with Olorun the chief god.[10] Eshu, the master of divination, had already been associated by missionaries in Africa with Satan, and this idea was carried to Brazil. Umbanda also has included, with modifications, many of the Roman Catholic rituals.

The third influence came from the writings of a French professor, Denizard Rivail, who wrote under the pseudonym of Allan Kardec. His book *The Book of Spirits* was first taken to

Brazil in 1858 in the luggage of a Portuguese nobleman.[11] Kardecism has always claimed to be a science as well as a religion. He proposed the standard spiritualist teaching that human beings are considered to be spirits that take up a temporary abode in physical bodies. However, he also wrote of the possibility of successive reincarnations, depending upon the moral choices made in life. The first spiritualist center was opened in Salvador in 1865, and the movement quickly spread throughout the country.

The final contribution to Umbanda was that of the traditional beliefs of the American Indians who originally lived in the country. Together these elements have produced an exotic variety of practices, which range from modified Yoruba religion to modified Western spiritualism.

Beliefs

The emphasis in Umbanda is on experience rather than doctrine, and so one cannot find any fixed creed, only a variety of religious ideas. Most Umbandists accept the Roman Catholic teaching on heaven and believe that it is some remote and distant place where God lives together with the Virgin Mary, Jesus, and the saints. Closer to humankind are the spirits, which are of diverse origin and are believed to live in the earth, sea, or other aspects of nature.

The whole belief system centers on possession. Every person is thought to be a potential medium, and by means of divination one can find out which spirit is the potential possessor. However, not all spirits initiate such a relationship, but those who do may suddenly seize their donor. The relationship between the person and the spirit is simple and direct: the person makes his body available periodically to the spirit so that the spirit may come to the earth and take part in ceremonies, and in return the spirit provides various kinds of assistance. The relationship is very intimate, but with time the medium can become possessed against his will.

In general, the Umbanda accept the Kardecist view of reincarnation. Hell is not believed to exist, and heaven is virtually impossible for them to attain. Thus, after death they expect to wait in a shadowy existence before being reassigned to another physical life. The ghosts of certain people who have lived good lives are considered to be allowed to manifest themselves at seances to give information and comfort the living.

Practices

The center of the practice of Umbanda is the ceremonies held in buildings, which may range from small living rooms to large halls. Here the mediums become possessed by their spirit, and others come to see the activity and ask for healing and help.

When a person is first seized by a spirit, this may result in a fall, or he may stagger around the room making incoherent sounds. However, with the assistance of an experienced medium the person is helped to gain control of his movements and to allow the spirit to manifest its own particular character through his body. The mediums are aware when they are possessed or when they are what they would call "pure" —that is, unpossessed. When the medium is possessed, the spirit will manipulate the medium's body in its own particular ways. An upper-class spirit would behave in a dignified way while a lower-class spirit may drink, sing, and play the fool. An *eshu* (devil) spirit may dance in a frenzied way with staring eyes.

During the ceremony, many of the experienced mediums will become possessed and will offer help and healing to the living. A common practice is for the medium to lay hands upon the patient. This is thought to be good for any sort of sickness and as a protection against bad luck. Alternatively the spirit may prescribe medicine or a herbal bath. It may even blow tobacco smoke upon the sick person in a way reminiscent of the traditional American Indian *shaman*.

Rituals

Umbanda has many rituals similar to those of the Roman Catholic church. The ritual of baptism of infants follows that of the Catholic church quite closely. The leader will recite the Christian formula. "I baptise you in the name of the Father, and of the Son, and of the Holy Spirit" and everyone present shouts, "Baptised, baptised!"[12] Infants are baptized only in such a way if it is felt that because of illness or some other reason the child is in need of special protection, and in such cases spirits act as godparents.

In many Umbanda meetings there are displays of power. In some cases gunpowder is ignited on the bare hand of the possessed medium, and another may pass a candle flame slowly over his body. On some occasions the medium is dressed in elaborate costumes to suit the personality of the spirit. Many groups have marches around the area, and some even have the offering of sacrifices for the spirits.

Why Spiritualism Has Grown

In seeking to present a reason for the growth of spiritualism during the last 150 years, it is necessary first to recognize that it has appealed to two classes of people. The first includes the prosperous communities of the Western world who have reacted against the secular view and in response to the loss of a loved one have sought comfort from the spirit world. To the wealthy classes of the Victorian era, spiritualism was considered as a novel game.

The second class of people to be attracted to spiritualism is the poor, and this is especially true among the Umbanda of Brazil. Extreme poverty and inadequate medical services lead many to seek help from the mediums. Mental illness and marital problems are common problems brought to the Umbanda for the assistance of the spirits.

In both the Western nations and Brazil, spiritualism has grown in the midst of a strong Christian presence. This clearly shows that the church has failed to meet the felt-needs of the people. For the wealthy, the church has provided an intellectual, materialistic theology, which fails to meet the spiritual aspirations of people. For the poor, Christianity has failed to meet their physical needs. The people of Brazil are looking for a religion that will meet their bodily needs, pray for healing of the sick, and show an exuberance in worship. Peter Wagner writes,

> It is no wonder that non-Pentecostal churches are winning so few people from spiritism in Brazil, relatively speaking. Spiritism is not simply ignorance, superstition, and chicanery. A Christianity which does not recognise it as a manifestation of the powers of darkness will continue to be impotent in this particular field of evangelism.
>
> The Pentecostal churches in Brazil go to the heart of the matter and recognise spiritism for what it is—supernatural, demonic activity. They believe that the miracles worked by spirits are real, but that they can be traced to Satan. Consequently, their evangelistic approach to spiritists stresses the power encounter, and they are not afraid to pit the power of God against the power of Satan any more than Elijah was when he faced the priests of Baal on Mount Carmel. Their message is that of "Christ the Victor", and a common theme in preaching is deliverance from the powers of Satan. This is the kind of message that spiritists understand and respond to.[13]

Notes

1. Oswald Sanders and J. Stafford Wright, *Some Modern Religions* (IVP: Leicester, 1969), pp. 36-40.
2. *Psychic News*, May 15, 1948.
3. Frena Bloomfield, *The Book of Chinese Beliefs* (Arrow Books: London, 1983), pp. 61-62.
4. Geoffrey Parrinder, *West African Religion* (Epworth Press: London, 1949), pp. 89-90.
5. Raphael Gasson, *The Challenging Counterfeit* (Logos Books: New Jersey, 1970), p. 83.
6. John Beattie, "The Ghost Cult in Bunyoro," in John Middleton, *Gods and Rituals* (University of Texas Press: Austin, 1967), pp. 262-63.
7. Gasson, op. cit., pp. 129-30.
8. Bloomfield, op. cit., p. 87.
9. Betty Bacon, *Spiritism in Brazil* (Latin American Group of EMA: London, 1979), p. 2.
10. Pedro McGregor, *The Moon and Two Mountains* (Souvenir Press: London, 1966), pp. 57-58, 187-92.
11. Ibid., p. 89.

12. Seth and Ruth Leacock, *Spirits of the Deep* (Anchor Press: New York, 1975), p. 298.

13. Peter Wagner, *Look Out! The Pentecostals Are Coming* (Coverdale House Publishers: London, 1974), pp. 134–35.

16

The Mystic Experience

Mysticism shares a common world with magic and religion, and although it is not always easy to distinguish it from these, its emphasis is different. Prayer and worship may form part of mysticism, but they are considered to be only the means and not the essence of the experience. Unlike mediumship, the aim is not for communication with the supernatural. Unlike possession, mysticism is not the phenomenon of being controlled by some dominating spirit or god. The goal of mysticism is union with the divine or sacred.

The relationship between mysticism and religion is an ambiguous one. A mystic may be an adherent of a particular religious system, but this need not always be the case. However, no deeply religious person can be without the touch of mysticism, and no mystic can be without some element of religion. To most people, the mystic experience is the very heart of religion, which takes it from the area of mere ritual into one of being a personal relationship with divinity. The mystical experience takes us beyond the normally accepted boundary of what is considered to be the study of primal religions, but there is an overlap that must be investigated.[1] Added to this is the fact that mystical techniques are being increasingly used in Western societies.

Characteristics of Mysticism

Within all the major religions of the world one finds a few people who have developed a means by which they are able to relate to the divine in a very personal way. They have found the external ritual practices of religion inadequate, and they have sought for some vision or direct revelation of the supernatural. Such experiences resemble the call of the shaman, medium, or prophet, and yet have their own particular distinctiveness.

The major feature of this distinctiveness is that mysticism is found in those religions that are either monotheistic or monist. Thus, mysticism is found in Christianity, Islam, and Judaism, as well as in Hinduism and Buddhism. There are some primal religions, such as those of the American Indians, that also stress the need of a quest for a vision of a supernatural spirit. However, for the most part, primal religions are concerned with the practical issues of daily life in a world considered to be inhabited by often dangerous spiritual beings and powers. Thus, mysticism tends to be the prerogative of the major world religions.

It is the fact of a single universal reality, be it conceived of as a person or not, that captures the interest of the mystic. If there is but one reality, then the aim of the mystic is to know and experience that reality. Here lies the ultimate objective of all human life and, in fact, all creation. All else in life is therefore secondary and pales into insignificance compared with the one reality. Mysticism tends, therefore, to monism: the belief that there is only one absolute reality. The desire is to establish a conscious relationship with the absolute.

Even within a religion such as Islam, which marks a clear distinction between the creator and his creation, the Sufi mystics show all the characteristics of monism. As one of the early Sufis wrote:

> I am He whom I love, and He whom I love is I:
> We are two spirits dwelling in one body.
> If thou seest me, thou seest Him,
> And if thou seest Him, thou seest us both.
>
> —al Hallaj

Al Hallaj was stoned to death by the orthodox Muslims for this blasphemy.

Mysticism by its very nature is beyond academic analysis. It is subjective and therefore cannot be interpreted into theological or philosophical language. Mysticism uses the language of poetry and symbolism to describe what is beyond definition. Often the imagery seems exotic and beyond imagination to the nonmystic. This is illustrated with the visions of Ezekiel and his descriptions of strange animals and wheels within wheels. Constantly, we find Ezekiel and the equally mystic John having to speak of the likeness or the appearance of some earthly item in order to convey what they perceived.

Second, mysticism believes not only in states of experience, but that in and through these experiences one may come to new states of knowledge. They are illuminations and revelations that are beyond the processes of the intellect. They cannot be described to those who have not experienced them except in symbolic terms, but to those who have had such feelings, there comes a mutual understanding. How can one explain sight to someone who is blind? However, to one who is also sighted, the common experience leads to easy communication.

Third, mystics of all faiths have spoken of two approaches to the ultimate reality. The first is what may be called the outward, the positive, or *via affirmativa*. This approach is through the positive assertion of the reality of the world. The mystic thinks of love, goodness, justice, and wisdom as attributes of the ultimate and then seeks to expand this to ultimate terms. Love is expanded to infinite love; purity to the sublime.

The second approach of the mystic is the inward, or *via negativa*. No predicate is considered sufficient to be attached to the ultimate, and no word may legitimately be used to describe God. He is "not this, not that!" This approach is essentially world denying, and the mystic seeks to discover reality within his own being. This is sometimes called introspective or introverted mysticism: "Only when all the images of earth are hushed and the clamour of the senses is stilled and the soul has passed beyond thought of self can the Eternal Wisdom be revealed to the mystic who seeks that high communion with the Unseen."[2]

Fourth, the stages of the mystic way are described differently by the religions of East and West. However, Underhill has attempted to identify a universal classification of the mystic way based upon the subjective experiences of the mystic. She describes the stages in the following way:

1. The awakening—this experience is usually a clear call, which is accompanied by a sense of exhilaration born of joy and apprehension. This is a conversion experience of the mystic who now has a new goal in life and sets himself the task of knowing the absolute.

2. Purgation—the awareness of one's own imperfection and finiteness. This results in the need for repentance and mortification of all that stands between the person and union with reality. To many mystics the way of asceticism has seemed the only way by which they could be purified from the desires of sin, sensuality, and selfishness.

3. Illumination—the joy of knowing the acceptance by the supreme reality. During this period the mystic may experience ecstasies that are short definite periods of rapturous trance. Many mystics never go beyond this state of bliss. It is, however, only a step toward the ultimate goal.

4. "Dark night of the soul"—after the exhilarating period of joy and communion comes the sudden loss of the divine presence. It has been called the "mystic death," "the dark night of the soul," and "spiritual crucifixion." It is a period of desolation in which the person seems abandoned by the ultimate. The person is required to surrender all, even the presence of the divine.

5. Union—this is the true goal of the mystic. Here self is of no more importance. All is the absolute. Here the language of love seems to be all that can be used by the mystic.[3]

Underhill would add that in Oriental mysticism there is considered to be a further stage beyond that of union, and that is total annihilation of the individual self in the infinite.

Mysticism holds to the quest of the absolute, the one supernatural reality, and as such the mystic seeks for union with this one. That union can be achieved only through certain personal disciplines that enable the mystic to enter into an experience of the supernatural.

Pathways to Enlightenment

The pathways of the mystic are many and varied, ranging from the passive to the active, the simple to the complex. They differ from the meditative pursuits of "high" religions to the active techniques of those from "folk" religions. The lives and spiritual quests of Christian saints, such as St. Teresa (1515–82) and St. John of the Cross (1542–91), contrast with those of the Sufis of Islam and gurus of Hinduism. In theory, the ecstatic trace is involuntary, although certain conditions are recognized as being especially favorable for its occurrence. Mystics have therefore used a variety of methods to induce the ecstatic state.

Meditation

Prayer and meditation have been important aspects of Christian mysticism throughout history. The aim has been the withdrawal from the distraction of the world and the focus of one's attention upon the absolute. This technique has been taken to an extreme within Hindu mysticism with the use of Yoga. The word *Yoga* is now well known in the West, where as a rule it is taken to mean physical manipulations of the body as a way of increasing health and efficiency. *Yoga* comes from *yug*, meaning "to join," and refers to the process by which the individual can be united with the absolute. This is accomplished by becoming a master of all of one's thoughts, feelings, and activities.

In the system of Yoga there are eight stages. The first two are ethical preparation, and the last six are contemplative (*askesis*). The first two stress importance of truthfulness, sexual purity, and nonviolence. The latter encompass the positive virtues of seeking after the absolute and include the practice of postures to aid meditation. The aim is to achieve *samadhi*, which can be likened to "sleepless sleep." As Zaehner has described it, *samadhi* "is the state of pure isolation in which there is no sense of 'I' or 'mine', a consciousness of pure detachment both from the world and from other souls. This is the highest state the Yogin can reach: detached both from the world and from God he abides in his own essence alone.''[4]

Breathing Control and Chanting

Meditation naturally leads to an awareness of breathing, which goes unnoticed in ordinary life. It is therefore not unexpected that the use of breathing control has proved common with many mystics. In Sufism, ways were developed for pronouncing the divine name, Allah, in a controlled pattern of breathing. The vigorous chanting of the name Allah is repeated until the mind is filled only with that name, and every sensory image fades. One tradition from Central Asian origin is that *Hā* (Arabic, "Him") is expired very deeply, then *Hī* is aspired as low as possible. The resulting sound is much like that of sawing.[5] In both cases the chanting is performed with the vigorous shaking of the head forward and backward.

The Hare Krishna movement (ISKCON) spread to the West in 1965 at the direction of His Grace A. C. Bhaktivedanta Swami Prabhupada. It was initially popularized in the West by the Beatles who were its most famous adherents. The central teaching of the movement is that enlightenment (Krishna-consciousness) is best realized through chanting the name of the god Krishna. This practice of using a sacred word or group of words, called *mantra*, has long been used in Hinduism. The *mantra* can be expressed through the body in seven ways: spoken aloud; as a whisper; by movement of the mouth without sound; as a mental image of the sound when spoken aloud; as an image of the sound whispered; as an image of movement without sound; as a stream of pure meaning without any image. It was Prabhupada who wrote,

> The transcendental vibration established by chanting Hare Krishna is a sublime method for reviving our transcendental consciousness.... This chanting of the Hare Krishna *mantra* is enacted from the spiritual platform, and thus the sound vibration surpasses all lower strata of consciousness namely sensual, mental and intellectual. There is no need, therefore, to understand the language of the *mantra*, nor is there any need for mental speculation.... In the beginning there may not be the presence of all transcendental

ecstasies. These are eight in number: 1. being stopped as dumb;
2. perspiration; 3. standing up of hairs on body; 4. dislocation of
voice; 5. trembling; 6. fading of the body; 7. crying in ecstasy;
8. trance.[6]

Zaehner makes an important observation concerning Yoga and
breathing control as found in Hinduism, and it may well be
applied to other schools of mysticism: "The Yoga postures and
techniques of breath-control, and the mental training that goes
with them, may lead to quite unforeseen and disturbing results
such as mental disequilibrium and nervous breakdown."[7]

Music and Dance

Although music has no place in orthodox Islam, it plays an
important role within the Sufi tradition. The *sama* (spiritual
concert) became an important feature of early Sufi practice, and
perhaps the most well-known example is the whirling der-
vishes. The three basic actions of the dervish dance (dance,
whirl, and jump) have symbolic meaning:

> The dancing is a reference to the circling of the spirit round
> the cycle of existing things on account of receiving the effects of the
> unveilings and revelations; and this is the state of gnostic. The
> whirling is a reference to the spirit's standing with Allah in its inner
> nature (*sirr*) and being (*wujud*), the circling of its look and
> thought, and its penetrating the ranks of existing things; and
> this is the state of the assured one. And his leaping up is a
> reference to his being drawn from the human to the unitive
> station.[8]

Many mystic orders have come to realize that the trance state
can be achieved more rapidly by a "mechanization" of the
technique. Rhythmical exercises involving posture, controlled
breathing, and repeated movements and sounds are now thought
to produce endorphins in the body that can cause a state of
well-being and a lack of awareness of pain or discomfort.

Hypersensations

To seek yet further ways of achieving the trance state, some
have sought to use external means such as colors and smells,

incense and perfumes, and even alcohol and drugs. The so-called psychedelic drugs, such as mescaline and lysergic acid diethylamide (LSD), and natural derivatives as found in peyote cactus and various mushrooms have also been used to produce intensely gratifying experiences and hallucinations.

These various mystic techniques have, on some occasions, led to their followers demonstrating the degree of their devotion in outstanding ways. Among the Dervish of Kurdistan, some, while in the ecstatic state, would press a skewer through their cheeks so that it passes from one side of their face to the other. Even so, there is no bleeding, and when after a few minutes the skewer is withdrawn, the wound is healed. Others may show their devotion and trust in the power of Allah by eating broken glass or taking high-voltage electricity through their bodies. All these practices would be strongly condemned by the orthodox Muslim, but nevertheless they have a marked impression upon the uneducated Muslim.

The Holy Man

The phenomenon of sainthood or holy man is one that is common among most religions of the world. Among the Hindus they would be called *sadhus* (good ones); in Buddhism, *arhats*; in Taoism, *chen jen* (true men); and in folk Islam, *wali* (friend of God) or *marabout*. These people are believed to be related in a special way to the supernatural powers. This relationship is not automatically obtained by other members of the religious cult, but it is based upon real or alleged deeds and qualities of life that they are considered to manifest. Although we are here defining this person in terms of his or her mystic experience, it must not be forgotten that the role of a saint may overlap markedly with that of the prophet, which will be considered in chapter 18.

The Man of God

The great desire in primal and folk religion, as we have seen, is for a relationship with the unseen that will help people deal with the basic issues of life. How can this be achieved when the spiritual seems distant, and one cannot be certain whether one's communication has been effective? However, if one is able to perceive something of the character of the divine within a living human being, then it may be possible for that person to act as an intermediary with the divine.

In Roman Catholicism a distinction is made between veneration (*douleia*) and worship (*latreia*). Veneration is regarded as a proper attitude toward saints, whereas worship is applicable only to God. In practice, supplications directed toward the saints can hardly be distinguished from prayers to God, even though the saints are considered theologically to be only intercessors having special access to God.[9]

The nature of the mystic experience may even lead the person to claim unity with the divine. This has been illustrated in recent years with a number of Asian movements. The Divine Light Mission is a Vedantist Hindu movement centered on devotion to the Guru Maharaj Ji, who, his followers claim, is an incarnation of ''god'' and so able to give enlightenment to his disciples.

The Miracle Worker

Another important characteristic of a saint is that he is believed to manifest the power of the spiritual world in some outstanding way. Spiritual power is considered to issue from the saint. This, it may be believed, can be acquired by veneration or touch. In this way the power or *baraka* is communicated to those in need. Miracles, especially those of healing, are frequently sought from such people. A person may go to a saint to request the blessing of the divine and leaves believing that he has made him well. News of such happenings quickly spreads, and so the reputation of the saint grows, and with it, so does his following.

The cult of the saint may continue even after his death in that some point of contact remains in a material object. It may be some relic of the saint that is viewed as containing some supernatural power that may be acquired by touching or kissing. In Sri Lanka, for instance, the tooth of the Buddha is venerated at the temple in Kandy. In the Muslim world the tombs of the *wali* can become a center for pilgrimage and the source of *baraka* (power). Another indirect form of veneration is that of the image of the saint himself or herself. Through the medium of this material object, a magical connection is believed to exist, which enables the desired blessing to be acquired.

The danger of the mystic experience is that its subjective emphasis may lead to a neglect of the natural world. It is almost the very opposite of the secular worldview, which is preoccupied with the material universe. The Hindu would say that the natural world is *maya*, or illusion. Thus, the follower of the mystic way reacts against a preoccupation with the rational and logical. Knowledge acquired by the use of sensory observation is therefore considered of lesser value than that particular kind of knowledge obtained only as a result of one's own inner psychic experience.

Most Christian mystics have always been conscious of this danger and have insisted that a moral character is of more importance than subjective experiences in assessing spiritual progress. They have therefore recognized the need for a worldview that does justice both to life in the material world and to the personal relationship with God, which may sometimes lead to deep devotion or ecstasy. The apostle Paul writes,

> If I speak in the tongues of men and of angels, but have not love, I am only a resounding gong or a clanging cymbal. If I have the gift of prophecy and can fathom all mysteries and all knowledge, and if I have a faith that can move mountains, but have not love, I am nothing (1 Cor 13:1–2).

Notes

1. William James, *The Varieties of Religious Experience* (Longmans, Green: London, 1910), p. 380.
2. Margaret Smith, *An Introduction to the History of Mysticism* (SPCK: London, 1930), p. 5.
3. Evelyn Underhill, *Mysticism: A Study in the Nature and Development of Man's Spiritual Consciousness* (Noonday Press: New York, 1955).
4. R. C. Zaehner, *Hinduism* (Oxford University Press: Oxford, 1966), p. 72.

5. Spencer Trimmingham, *The Sufi Orders in Islam* (Oxford University Press: New York, 1973), p. 197.
6. R. D. Clements, *Gods and the Gurus* (IVP: London, 1974), pp. 32–33.
7. Zaehner, op. cit., p. 72.
8. Trimmingham, op. cit., p. 195.
9. Norbert Greinacher and Norbert Mette, *Popular Religion* (T. & T. Clark: Edinburgh, 1986).

17

Folk Religion

The religious beliefs of all peoples are constantly changing in response to internal social pressures and environmental changes. However, the major factor that usually causes change is the spread of ideas and practices from one society to another. This process is generally called "diffusion" and applies to any aspect of a culture.[1] For example, paper making was first invented in China, and from there it was passed on to Mongolia, then to the Middle East, and finally to Europe.

The Old Testament provides many examples in which the religious practices of the people around Israel were seen to diffuse into Israelite religion. King Solomon provides an obvious example: "On a hill east of Jerusalem, Solomon built a high place for Chemosh the detestable god of Moab, and for Molech the detestable god of the Ammonites. He did the same for all his foreign wives, who burned incense and offered sacrifices to their gods" (1 Kings 11:7–8). This process led to marked changes in the religious beliefs and practices of the Israelites, which were condemned by Yahweh, their God, and finally led to judgment.

The Diffusion of the World Religions

It was noted earlier that primal religions are not essentially of a missionary nature. Various beliefs and practices may often spill over to neighboring peoples through intermarriage between the peoples, as was the case with Solomon. A society may also adopt a neighboring deity into their own pantheon of gods because it has a reputation of being a powerful deity. If one people defeats another in war, it is often thought that the gods of the defeated people have similarly been defeated by the god(s) of the conqueror. King Nebuchadnezzar of Babylon, for example, took captive the idols of the gods of the people he conquered.

During human history, a few religions have arisen that have been particularly missionary minded. These have had a significant impact upon world history and have frequently led to extensive changes among tribal societies. The first such movement was the spread of Hindu beliefs from India by traders throughout the area of the islands of the Indian Ocean.

The second movement was that of Buddhism, which originated in India, about 500 B.C., partly in reaction to the strong priestly role of the Brahmans. From its beginning Buddhism has had a strong missionary element in its teaching, but it was not until the time of King Asoka, ca. 250 B.C., that Buddhism spread out of India, going first to Sri Lanka. By A.D. 65 Buddhism had entered China and possibly Burma. From China it spread to Korea in the fourth century A.D. and then to Japan in about A.D. 552.

The third major movement has been that of Christianity, which quickly spread throughout the Roman Empire. It was only after the fall of the western Roman Empire that Christianity began to spread throughout northern Europe. However, in the seventh century Christianity became essentially locked into Europe with the spread of a new missionary religion, Islam. It was not until the discovery of the sea routes by the Europeans in the seventeenth century that there was further significant expansion of Christianity. The spread of European culture and colonial power during the nineteenth century has had a major impact upon tribal societies, as will be discussed in the next chapter.

Islam, the fourth major missionary world religion, spread rapidly as the new religion gave to the Arab people a new zeal and purpose. By the time that Muhammad died in A.D. 632 the Arab tribes had been united and were established as the powerful military force that under the rule of Umar conquered Palestine, Syria, Egypt, Libya, and Iraq. Within a period of only 100 years Islam stretched from North Africa eastward to

India. In following years, Islam was to be conveyed further by Arab traders reaching across the Sahara to the peoples of West Africa and by sea to the peoples of Indonesia.

It is notable that these so-called world religions developed out of what were essentially tribal religions. Hinduism emerged from the Hindu peoples, as did Buddhism. Christianity developed from Judaism, which, although a tribal religion, did already have a missionary dimension. Islam developed from the Arabs and still retains many aspects of the culture of that people. In all cases these missionary movements gained their biggest response in primal societies. This has certainly been the case with the Christian missionary movement of recent years. Once a people have accepted a world religion, they are much less likely to change their religion once again.

The Adoption of a World Religion

The response of a people to what is for them a foreign religion is not a simple process of merely accepting new ideas and rituals. A people may respond in different ways, ranging from complete acceptance to total rejection. Usually technological items are accepted more rapidly than are religious ideas. The worldwide spread of Coca-Cola is an obvious illustration of this fact. The reason for this, in part, is that religious change touches the basic ideas and values of a people in their worldview. Three main patterns of change can be identified:

1. Acculturation—the process of being converted to the new religion with its different worldview and life-style.
2. Syncretism—the selective adoption of items from the new religion and culture and reinterpreting them in terms of the old culture.
3. Demoralization—a society becomes overwhelmed by the dominant foreign culture and religion. The people feel a sense of the total inadequacy of their traditional religions, and yet at the same time are conscious of their inability to adopt the foreign religion.

Within the general area of syncretism one may observe a wide variety of differing developments of which we shall consider two in more detail. The first is that in which the society suffers stress and demoralization but then is revitalized around a prophetic figure. This will be considered in chapters 18 and 19. The second development relates to the conversion to the new religion and culture but only by a reworking of the new ideas and rituals.

As a world religion enters a primal society, the new ideas and practices are seen and interpreted by the people in the only way they are able, and that is according to their traditional worldview. Thus, what tend to be first accepted by a people are the outward forms of the new religion.

The name of the new god, or prophet, would usually be the first aspect with which they will have contact. Initially they will be able to perceive the new god only in terms of their traditional understanding of deity. With a monotheistic religion this god will almost automatically be related to any notion of a supreme being that they may have. Only later will people begin to realize any differences between the new deity and those with which they are familiar. Such differences may seem small to the people but may appear of great importance to the missionary of the new religion. An example of this was seen in chapter 15 with the Umbanda movement in Brazil. Here the names for the Roman Catholic saints have been interpreted in terms of the West African gods.

Rituals will also be aspects that are adopted early by the society. The people are able to see how these rituals are performed and even copy their performance, but to understand the actual meaning of the rituals is a different matter. In an Islamized society, for example, a people may practice the *salat* prayers with the prior washing. The washing ritual may be performed in the correct way, but the new adherent perceives the act in terms of his traditional worldview. Washing is not so much a matter of cleansing from bodily impurity before worshiping Allah, but the removal of pollution caused by the spirits or ghosts. Similarly, the confession in Islam is regarded as a proof that one is a true Muslim, but to the new adherent it may be conceived of as a magical spell to keep away evil.

Not only will the rituals be adopted, but so will the symbols of the new religion. The image of the Lord Buddha has in many parts of Asia become the focus for the prayers of the people. An image of the Buddha is believed to keep away evil spirits. Likewise, the cross in Christianity may be regarded as an especially powerful symbol to dispel evil.

The four major missionary religions all have their own holy books. For the Hindu it is the Vedas; the Buddhist, the Scriptures; the Christian, the Bible; and the Muslim, the Qur'an. The impact of a book-centered religion on a preliterate society naturally makes a great impression on the people concerning the inherent power of the book itself.

The respect shown for the holy book by the missionary only goes to heighten the awe with which the book is regarded by the people. This is especially the case in Islam, which regards the very words of the Qur'an as being those actually given by Allah to Muhammad. The people may therefore regard the book as containing an especially powerful magic to keep away evil spirits. In many parts of West Africa verses from the Qur'an are written onto a wooden board, and then the ink is washed off with water. This water is collected into a drinking vessel, which may then be sweetened with sugar before being administered as a medicine.

The continuing exposure to the new religion leads to a greater awareness of its beliefs and practices. In most cases, however, what is communicated is the academic understanding of the new religion rather than a direct relevance to those issues relating to daily life. Thus, what tends to occur is that the new religion becomes like a veneer over the traditional primal beliefs. The person will claim to be a Muslim, or Christian, but he will still retain many of his traditional beliefs and practices. However, these traditional beliefs will be modified as illustrated by the incorporation of the use of the Qur'an as an important source of healing within a traditional ritual. A convenient way of describing these two levels of religious belief is to designate them as "high religion" and "low religion." Robert Redfield has preferred to call the two "greater tradition" and "little tradition." However, it must be remembered that these are only convenient demarcations for discussion and have no clear distinction. These concepts are the creation of Western thought, and although they are helpful, care must be taken not to force the notion into a fixed mold.

High and Low Religion

Norman Allison has proposed the following useful characteristics of "high" and "low" religion.[2]

High Religion	*Low Religion*
Answers cosmic questions: origin of universe, meaning of life.	Answers everyday issues: sickness, drought, war.
Written texts with fixed system of beliefs.	No written text. Myths and rituals.
Specialist leadership roles.	Informal, no specialists.
Central institutions: church, mosque, temple. Formal training.	Few institutions. Apprenticeship type of training.
Formalized moral teaching.	Amoral system, pragmatic.

Allison brought together the views of both Redfield and Horton[3] in Figure 17.1. The figure provides a useful model in the understanding of the low religion or what may be called the folk beliefs of people.

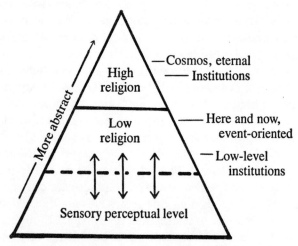

Figure 17.1. General scheme of comparison of "high" and "low" religious systems, after Allison

At the folk level there may exist a range of associated ideas, superstitions, beliefs, and rituals. An example of such can be seen in the British practices at Christmas. If one were to ask a British theologian the meaning of Christmas, one might obtain a theological understanding of the incarnation of the second person of the Christian Trinity. However, at a popular level one finds mythical characters such as Father Christmas, flying reindeer, and the fairy at the top of the Christmas tree. One also finds rituals associated with the decorating of trees, the singing of special songs, and the placing of presents in stockings hung at the bottom of the beds of sleeping children. A stranger could easily be forgiven for making the mistake that he was observing two totally different religious traditions.

However, it needs to be noted that within the secular tradition, this folk level of Christianity has been reduced to the level of custom where it is considered to have no real power or significance. One frequently finds a process occurring within a society in which formal religion is reduced to the level of folk religion, then to superstitions, until finally it is stripped of its meaning and is merely a quaint custom.

This is further illustrated by the annual fertility rites associated with the coming of new life in spring, which were common in Britain from pre-Christian times. This usually included a time of austerity followed by rejoicing at the end of winter. The church festivals superimposed themselves on this pattern, with the Lent abstinence followed by the Easter celebrations. Many pre-Christian symbols were adopted, such as Easter eggs and maypoles, symbolic of new life.

A growing awareness of the nature of high religion comes only through a process of education. The role of the priest of the new religion then takes on the additional role of teacher. Without such an awareness, the person will continue to seek to make sense of the nature of the new religion in terms of his traditional worldview. Often, however, it is the wealthier people who are better educated and are therefore more instructed in the new religion. For this reason one frequently finds that in a society there is a stratification based upon knowledge of the high religion. For example, in many African and Asian countries the wealthier (and so more educated) people are less concerned about folk beliefs. The poor, on the other hand, have never had the opportunity of learning the high religion, and so the folk aspect is of greater importance to them. The poor cannot afford to visit the Western doctor, and they feel inferior because they cannot read, and so they continue to attend their traditional healers. The Umbanda cults of Brazil provide a clear example of this fact.

Similarly, in Muslim Africa one finds that the men are more knowledgeable in the teaching of Islam than are the women. The women are also more involved with the everyday issues of sick children, problems with pregnancy, and feeding the family. They have not been instructed to find the answers to these issues in high Islam, and so they continue to be concerned about the evil eye, curses, and possession cults.

The Western Missionary Approach

In the light of the foregoing discussion it is now valuable to consider the approach of the Western missionary movement. Our heritage of Western thought has been a consideration of abstract philosophy, and so we have been concerned with ideas rather than practice. This has therefore led to a preoccupation with high religion and an almost total neglect of folk religion. Missionaries have tended to regard mission as being a debate in which they are seeking to prove their cosmology to be superior to that of the other religion. This accounts for the multitude of books on high Islam and the great scarcity of such on folk Islam. Hiebert has called this the "excluded middle," by which he indicates that Western mission has been preoccupied with high religion at one level and technology at another but has completely neglected the everyday application of religion.[4]

Thus, when primal man inquires of the Western missionary concerning his fear of ghosts or spirits, the missionary has no answer and tends to deny their existence as if they were no more than Western fairy stories. However, it is frequently at this level that people have the greatest concerns. What will his totem do to him if he becomes a Christian? How will he know when to plant his crops if he can no longer consult the diviner? How will rain come to his fields if he does not participate in the rainmaking ceremony? Does the white doctor know how to deal with witches? All these and many other questions remain unanswered. The result, as Lesslie Newbigin has pointed out, is that Western Christian missions have been one of the greatest secularizing forces in history.[5]

What is necessary is a holistic approach to mission that is able to deal with all areas of life. As pointed out by Hiebert there is a need at the level of high religion for a gospel of a Creator God who is concerned with the purpose and destiny of His creation and who has been active in the redemption of humankind.[6] It is at this level that questions relating to the origin of the universe and the meaning of life are to be found—a "truth encounter" (see Figure 17.2).

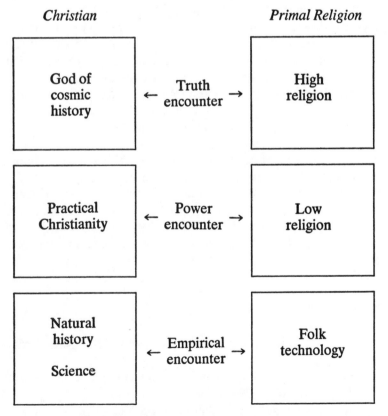

Figure 17.2. A holistic theology requires an encounter at three levels

At the middle or folk level must come an answer to the everyday needs of a people. The concern here is for healing, deliverance from the demonic, protection from the invisible powers of this world, and an answer to pollution. This involves a visible demonstration of the power of God in the world of powers. It requires a "power encounter"!

On the technological level must come an awareness of God in the natural world—an "empirical encounter." All too often Western culture glorifies scientific laws rather than the One who made the world according to those laws. The assumption of the closed universe has removed the Creator from His creation, and it will only be as God is brought back into our appreciation of science that the tide of secularization of Western philosophy will be halted.

When considering the ministry of Jesus Christ, one is impressed by His concern for the ordinary person. He was not so concerned about theological debates with the scholars of His day but with meeting the needs of the people about Him. As Bill Musk has said, "Christ, in his dealings with the ordinary people around him, tended to free them from the 'ideal' religion of the professionals."[7] Jesus related to people where they hurt—Jesus met their felt-needs. The same is seen in the early church. As Peter and John were entering the temple they met a man crippled from birth begging at the gate. The passage almost cries out with the question, What good is religious ritual if it does not meet people's primary needs? Then Peter said, " 'Silver or gold I do not have, but what I have I give you. In the name of Jesus Christ of Nazareth, walk.' Taking him by the right hand, he helped him up, and instantly the man's feet and ankles became strong" (Acts 3:6–7).

Notes

1. H. G. Barnett, *Innovation* (McGraw-Hill: New York, 1953), p. 291.
2. Norman Allison, "Make Sure You're Getting Through," *EMQ* 20, no. 2 (1984): 167–68.
3. Robin Horton, "The Kalabari World-View: An Outline and Interpretation," *Africa* 32 (1962): 197–220.

4. Paul G. Hiebert, "The Flaw of the Excluded Middle," *Missiology* 10, no. 1 (1982): 35–47.
5. Lesslie Newbigin, *Honest Religion for Secular Man* (Westminster Press: Philadelphia, 1966).
6. Paul G. Hiebert, *Anthropological Insights for Missionaries* (Baker: Grand Rapids, 1985), pp. 222–24.
7. Bill A. Musk, "Popular Islam: The Hunger of the Heart," in Don McCurry, *The Gospel and Islam: a 1978 compendium* (MARC: Monrovia, 1979), p. 214.

18

Prophecy: the Word of the Lord

The contact of a primal society with a dominant world culture and religion causes cataclysmic changes for the small community. The choice between the new ways and the traditional ways produces great tension and out of this situation may come a new figure—the prophet bringing with him the word of the Lord. The prophet figure is one of great importance among primal societies, and one whose role and place in the society need to be considered.

When the World Falls Apart

The social stress that occurs within a primal society as it comes in contact with a dominant culture shows itself in various ways. The first is a basic sense of confusion with regard to the whole concept of the universe and the people themselves. Primal societies frequently consider themselves to be the center of human existence. This is often shown in the names they use for themselves: by translation they are equivalent to the term *people*, implying that they are particularly human while others are not. This is illustrated with the Auca people of Ecuador who became internationally known as a result of the book *Through Gates of Splendour.*[1] *Aucas* means "savages" or "wild ones" and is the name used for them by their neighbors, but the name they use for themselves is *wagrani*, which means "we, the people."[2] Such a people consider themselves as being the center of humanity and their land as the center of the world. The shock of becoming aware that they are only a small and frequently insignificant part of global human society is immense. It is equivalent to the shock that occurred in Western society in realizing that the earth was not the center of the universe.

Second has come the technological shock resulting from contact with societies that are materially much more sophisticated. It causes primal societies some major questions. How can one make something like a motor car? It is obvious that the surface has not been made by chipping with an axe or by weaving or even by using the skin of an animal. Where do these strange and powerful objects come from? The old craftsmen cannot compare with the new technology and so lose respect in the eyes of their society. The new objects bring new desires to acquire these items, and this in turn leads to significant social tensions.

Third, the contact with other peoples often leads to the introduction of new illnesses within the primal society. In 1918, a major influenza epidemic spread through many areas of West Africa causing thousands of deaths. Influenza was a white man's illness, and as such Europeans had developed a degree of immunity, but this was not so with the African. Among some of the smaller societies of the Amazonian basin, many have died through the introduction of such illnesses, and many have been left crippled as a result of polio. In such situations the traditional healer is unable to assist, and in many cases the white doctor also has no cure. Where can the people find hope in such a situation?

Frequently, contact with more powerful societies has led to the primal society being dominated and even exploited. The more developed technology of the outsiders allowed them to assert their influence so that during the nineteenth century much of the world became dominated by the European powers. The old leaders were subjugated to obey the new rulers who came from great distances. The old laws and traditions were often condemned by the new rulers who introduced their own laws. The young people often rebelled against the old authorities and disobeyed the elders.

Fifth, the new rulers took over the traditional lands for their own use. They dug mines and built railways to carry away the ore. They grew whole plantations of crops to be exported to Europe, and they used local workers to do this task. They paid the workers with money, which was usually a new concept to the people who were more used to barter. In the company store the new goods were placed on sale for those who had the money. The strong and healthy who could work for the white men were the ones who could earn the money and so acquire the new goods and the status that went along with ownership. Once again the old ways were seen to be changing.

Finally, the outsiders brought with them a new and different religion—a religion that like theirs had its own priests, but they were white men who wore their own strange garments. It was a religion that did not make sacrifices, but people came together to sing and listen to the white man speak from a book. For a people coming in contact with books and literacy for the first time, it seems like great magic. In this remarkable way these strangers were able to send messages to each other without speaking. Books and papers therefore took on a magical significance, and since this is used by the white priest, this book must have special magic powers. This book must contain the secrets of the white man's powers and the reason why he has these material possessions.

On the one hand the traditional ways seem to be discredited, and yet on the other hand the new ways seem beyond the reach of the people. Old values seem to be irrelevant, old beliefs are being challenged, and young people no longer listen to the elders. The young men start indulging in the white man's alcohol, which frequently leads to increasing crime and immorality. *Things Fall Apart* as Chinua Achebe so graphically describes it in his book.[3]

The Man with the Message

Out of this situation of confusion and stress within the society there may arise a person with a message that he has found resolves his own inner tensions. These new ideas form a new way of thinking that, in resolving the tensions, brings together the issues of the traditional culture and those of the new. It is in fact a new worldview that the person believes will give hope to his confused and disoriented society. One can identify several important features with regard to the man or woman who becomes a prophet and the message the person brings.

A Message from God

It may be as a result of a dream or a vision that the prophet first receives his revelation of god. One of the most notable prophet figures from among the Zulu people was Isaiah Shembe born in 1870, who died in 1935. Sundkler describes his call in the following words:

> His first revelation was imparted to him when as a young boy he was praying in the cattle-kraal. During a thunderstorm the Word was brought to him by lightning: "Cease from immorality (*ukuhlobonga*)!" Later, as a young man and husband of four wives, he had another vision, also brought by lightning: he saw a multitude of people, or angels, and they pointed to something lying on earth. He saw his own corpse, in a rotten state, evil-smelling. The Word reminded him of his first vision, and the command to cease from immorality. And that day, though he was an industrious man, he did not work, and he ceased working until Sunday, because he said: "I have seen Jehovah." In a third vision it was revealed to him that he should leave his four wives, and though this was so hard that he almost committed suicide, yet he finally followed the divine command. The decisive, final call to be a prophet was also conveyed by a terrifying storm when lightning killed his best ox and burned Shembe, leaving a scar above his thigh. . . . Shembe was cured, because Jehovah saw that he wished to obey Him.[4]

The experiences of Shembe are reminiscent of those of Moses and his call at the burning bush and of Isaiah in the temple (Isa. 6). The call was in most cases not deliberately sought but was definitely interpreted as coming from God. It was this sense of call that inspired the prophet with zeal and dedication.

The Message of Hope

For Shembe, the message was one of repentance and the hope for a new world, the city of Zion. For many prophets their message is initially only partly formed, and yet the central issues are clearly apparent. These usually consist of repentance from sinful ways, an outline for a new way of living, and the hope for a new future.

The prophet may foretell future events, such as a coming catastrophe, but essentially the message is more one of telling the message of God to the people. Although the message may contain elements both from the traditional religion and from the new religion, for the prophet and his followers this message is not merely new but is unique.

A prophet must not only have a message but be able to communicate that message. The messages of some prophets have been put in writing, some being put in a poetic form. As Harold Turner has said,

> Islam may be regarded as having emerged from the interaction between the religious traditions of the Bedouin tribes of Arabia and the Judaeo-Christian faith, under a creative indigenous leader. It was a new religious form, neither Bedouin nor biblical, born within its own tribal milieu under the influence of a universal religious tradition.[5]

For Islam the beautiful poetic form of the Qur'an is considered to be an important proof of its divine origin.

A Message of Power

Not only must the message carry intellectual credibility, but it must be seen to work in practice. Many prophets are therefore credited with miracles of one sort or another. For example, Simon Kimbangu (1889–1951) received his call in 1918. This was the year that the whole of Zaire was suffering from a terrible epidemic of Spanish flu. Lacking medical help, thousands of people were dying. In the midst of this crisis Kimbangu heard the voice of Christ. It was a heavenly tongue that reached his ears and that he took to mean: "I am Christ. My servants are unfaithful. I have chosen you to bear witness before your brethren and to convert them. Tend my flock."[6] Although Kimbangu initially resisted the call, he finally submitted. It was on the following morning while he was on his way to market that he passed a hut in which lay a young woman with fever. Believing that Christ wanted him to enter the hut and pray for the woman, he placed his hand upon her and healed in Christ's name. This was the first of Kimbangu's healings, and during the following days scores of people came to him and were healed.

Many of the African prophetic figures of this century have come with a ministry of healing. They have therefore provided an answer to the medical needs of the people by providing a substitute for the traditional healers and witch doctors. Unlike some missionaries, they considered issues such as witches, barrenness, and sorcery as being real problems to be addressed. Further, they came with the power of God to do the work.

A Man for the People

Usually the prophet reflects within himself the tensions within the community, and so his message comes as an answer to those needs. He knows the needs and frustrations of his own people and is able to empathize with them.

There are, however, those prophetic figures whose message receives a wider following. This is well illustrated in recent years by the attraction of various new sects within Western society. The Holy Spirit Foundation for the Unification of World Christianity, otherwise known as the Moonies, is an example. The movement was founded in 1954 by the Korean-born Sun Myung Moon. According to Unification theology, Jesus came as the second Adam to restore fallen mankind. It was not God's plan for Jesus to die on the cross, but to find a wife by whom He would have perfect children and so start a new stream of mankind. His failure meant that another Messiah had to come, this time born in Korea. It was to be this Messiah, Sun Myung Moon, who would father the new race in the perfect family.

The movement is claimed to have a following of more than 300,000 in Korea, 30,000 in the U.S., and some 350 in Britain (in 1985). The interesting question is why such a movement would find a following in Western society. This is considered to be because it is meeting a need among a particular group of people within Western society. These tend to be young people who are disillusioned by the accepted secular Western culture. Especially in the 1960s, many young people were looking for an alternative to war, and some found it in the love movement.

Those prophetic figures, such as Moon, who stressed this aspect naturally became a center of attraction for young people.

True and False Prophets

A major issue in Old Testament Israel related to the question of whether a man was a true prophet sent from God or a false prophet. A similar sort of situation has faced many Western missionaries in Africa during the last hundred years. A man suddenly appears on the scene claiming some supernatural call or vision and preaching a message that has many similarities to that proclaimed by the missionary and yet not quite the same. How does the missionary know if the man is one he should encourage or not?

Often the missionary has reacted to the personal appearance of the man or woman. Take, for example, the case of Prophet Harris who made his appearance in the Ivory Coast in 1913. The following description was made by Deaville Walker after talking to eyewitnesses and studying a photograph:

> The photograph represents him as a man well past middle age—probably at least 65 years old. He was of medium height, had a grey beard and moustache, and always dressed in a long white gown with sleeves, and a big white turban. Round his shoulders and hanging down in front, he had a broad red band, and upon his breast there hung a small cross. Like most Africans, he walked bare-foot, and carried a long bamboo walking staff, to the top of which he fastened a small cross-piece which gave his staff the form of a rude cross, and he used it as the symbol of his mission. He held it up before the people who crowded around him, and told them that on a cross God's Son died for them. When some of them mistook it for a fetish, he broke it before their eyes and threw it away, and then made another. He also carried a small Bible apparently well worn; he always seems to have had it with him, and often held it up for the crowds to see; he constantly told them that it was God's Book.[7]

How should a missionary regard such a person? Should conclusions be made on the basis of personal appearance?

Reference has already been made to the fact that the people of

Israel were forbidden to practice divination and magic. However, their religion did create an important role for a prophetic figure who would complement that of the priest: "The nations you will dispossess listen to those who practice sorcery or divination. But as for you, the LORD your God has not permitted you to do so. The LORD your God will raise up for you a prophet like me from among your own brothers" (Deut. 18:14–15).

The story of Jeremiah and Hananiah before King Zedekiah in Jeremiah 27 and 28 provides an interesting illustration of the problem of distinguishing between a true and a false prophet. Jeremiah comes before the king wearing a yoke strapped across his neck and proclaiming a message that the people of Israel will be taken captive and will be made to serve the Babylonians. Hananiah comes in the usual dress and, in reaction to Jeremiah's pronouncements, takes the yoke and breaks it in front of all, proclaiming that God will release the people from all bondage. Who is the true prophet? The one who behaves in the normally accepted way, or the other man? The story goes on to show that it was Jeremiah who was the true prophet. Throughout the Old Testament many of the true prophets behaved in ways that seemed to be unusual to the people. External appearance alone cannot be used as a criterion for the genuineness of a prophet.

There are three notable characteristics used in the Old Testament to distinguish a false prophet. The first is a negative test and relates to whether the prophecy comes to be fulfilled or not: "If what a prophet proclaims in the name of the LORD does not take place or come true, that is a message the LORD has not spoken. That prophet has spoken presumptuously. Do not be afraid of him" (Deut. 18:22). It needs to be stressed that the fact that a prophecy does come true does not automatically mean that the prophet is a true prophet. The test applies only in a negative sense.

A second characteristic is one that may be regarded as theological:

If a prophet, or one who foretells by dreams, appears among you and announces to you a miraculous sign or wonder, and if the sign or wonder of which he has spoken takes place, and he says, "Let us follow other gods . . . and let us worship them," you must not listen to the words of that prophet or dreamer (Deut. 13:1–3).

The Scriptures proclaim a historical continuity of revelation such that there will not be a contradiction between previous revelations, as recorded in the Bible, and contemporary prophecy.

The final characteristic relates to the moral character of the prophet himself. This is what God, through Jeremiah, indicates: " 'Both prophet and priest are godless; even in my temple I find their wickedness,' declares the LORD" (Jer. 23:11). The false prophet not only is immoral in his own life, but he does not seek to stem the immorality of the community. He prophesies a message of peace and well-being without any regard to morals, whereas a true prophet has a message of judgment upon sin.

It can be seen that the question of the discrimination of prophets is by no means academic but is thoroughly practical in missionary work today. The Western missionary must be careful not to condemn an African or Asian prophet just because his approach is not that normally accepted. The man may be presenting the same message as the missionary but in a way that is more in tune with the heart and character of the people themselves. On the other hand, prophets may arise who confuse the people and lead them away from the truth. The missionary must be equally discerning of these.

Notes

1. Elisabeth Elliot, *Through Gates of Splendour* (Hodder & Stoughton: London, 1957).
2. Rosemary Kingsland, *A Saint Among Savages* (Collins: London, 1980), p. 9.
3. Chinua Achebe, *Things Fall Apart* (Heinemann: London, 1978).
4. Bengt G. M. Sundkler, *Bantu Prophets in South Africa* (Oxford University Press: London, 1961), p. 110.
5. Harold W. Turner, "New Mission Task: Worldwide and Waiting," *Missiology* 13, no. 1 (1985): 5.
6. Marie-Louise Martin, *Kimbangu* (Basil Blackwell: Oxford,

1975), p. 44.

7. F. Deaville Walker, *The Story of the Ivory Coast* (Cargate Press: London, 1930), p. 14.

19

New Religious Movements

In the previous chapter we considered the place and role of the prophet within society. Such a person may quickly gather around himself a group of disciples, and these may become the focus for a wider movement among the population. Scholars have used a variety of expressions for such phenomena. Wallace has used the term *revitalization movements*,[1] while Turner has proposed the term *new religious movements*.[2] These terms are attempting to describe an important phenomenon that is occurring across the world.

The rise of many new movements within Western society has been well documented. Groups such as the Moonies, Scientology, Divine Light, and the Rajneesh Foundation have all gained newspaper headlines. The tragic case of the People's Temple with its disastrous climax at Jamestown in Guyana is yet another example.

However, within primal societies one can observe many more such movements that have emerged during this century. Among the Indians of North America there have been many such movements, including the Handsome Lake Religion, which was founded among the Iroquois in 1800 and is now one of the oldest prophetic movements. There have been a dozen such movements among the Maori of New Zealand, one of which has issued in the formation of the large Ratana Church. This church was founded by the prophet Wirenu Ratana during the epidemic of 1918. In Polynesia and Melanesia, there have been hundreds of such movements, popularly called "cargo cults."[3]

It has been in Africa that the greatest number of new religious movements have occurred. David Barrett listed some 6,000 in his book *Schism and Renewal in Africa*.[4] South Africa alone has

3,000 such movements with over 3 million adherents. The largest movement is the Kimbanguists of Zaire who now number over 3 millions followers. These have mainly occurred through the interaction with the European form of Christianity that was brought to Africa by the missionaries.

Understanding New Religious Movements

Out of the wide diversity of new religious movements, Harold Turner has proposed the need to distinguish between the general theme of New Religious Movements (for which he proposes the acronym NERMs) and those that have particularly emerged from primal societies (PRINERMs).[5] The term NERMs would include not only those covered by the term PRINERMs but also those cults that arise from within any religion to give it a new dynamic and formulation. The Japanese sect Nichiren Shoshu Soka Gakkai,[6] which has grown since the Second World War to over 8 million members, provides an example of a NERM that has emerged out of Japanese culture. Messianic cults have been common throughout the history of the Jews. Similarly, among Muslim peoples, one can identify various popular movements following a *mahdi*—a savior who has emerged to liberate his people from foreign domination. The NERMs within Christian societies have tended to emphasize the coming of a future millennium, as with the Jehovah's Witnesses.

In this text we are primarily concerned with primal societies, and so we shall focus attention particularly on those movements called by Turner PRINERMs. He has defined these in the following way:

> A historically new development arising from the interaction between a primal society and its religion, and another culture and its major religion, and involving some substantial departure from the classical religious tradition of both the cultures concerned in order to find renewal by reworking the rejected traditions into a different religious system.[7]

Because the major cultural impact upon primal societies in recent centuries has come from the interaction with Europeans who were at least nominally Christian, the new religion was

usually Christianity. The new religious movements have therefore come from an interaction between primal societies and
their religion and that of European culture and Christianity. This
often occurred as a direct result of the European missionary
endeavor but also out of a wider, more general contact with
Western society.

During the great missionary activities of the nineteenth and
twentieth centuries, many primal societies responded to
Christianity. Often they have done so as a result of a group
decision in which the whole or a section of the tribe have come
to the mutual decision to adopt the new religion proposed by
the white missionary. In some cases these people movements
have been remarkably sudden, as with the Dani of Irian Jaya,[8]
while for others it occurred over a period of years by what
Donald McGavran would call a "web movement."[9] Initially,
the converts adapted to the new teaching and the new ways of
worship. Missionary societies established a multitude of
churches, and although most of the missionaries recognized
the need to take into account the local culture, the general
pattern of the churches was based upon that of Western rather
than indigenous culture. The Western missionary working
from the context of the Western worldview was often unaware
of some of the major questions of the primal worldview.
Important issues such as those of ancestors and ghosts, witchcraft and sorcery, *mana* and taboo were classed as primitive
superstitions. Polygamy and other traditional customs were
condemned.

Even the issue of healing seemed to the people to be left out
of the new religion and limited to hospitals and clinics. Yet
even these new white "healers" were often unable to deal
with the major epidemics that spread through their people.
During the major influenza epidemics in Africa in 1918, the
colonial government prohibited the gathering of any number
of people. Even the churches were closed. What value is a
religion if it is unable to help you in your time of greatest
need? Thus there arose a growing dissatisfaction with the
new religion brought by the white man. This situation therefore provided the context for the emergence of a prophet to
bring hope to the people.

It was David Barrett who said that there is often "an

incubation period averaging sixty years'' before one can observe the second response, which is the reworking of the new religion with the old as a PRINERM.[10] These movements have taken on a variety of forms, depending upon the primal culture, the social issues of the time, and even the character of the prophet himself. However, Harold Turner has provided a useful classification of such movements into four types.[11] This is illustrated by Figure 19.1.[12]

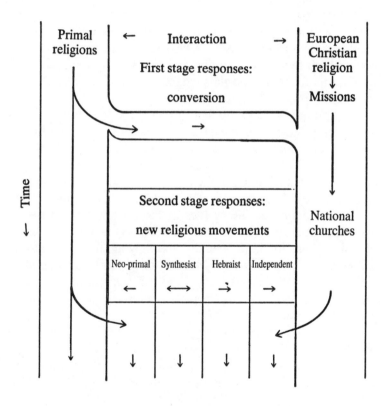

Figure 19.1. The various interactions between Western Christianity and primal religions, according to H. W. Turner

The first, Turner has called "neo-primal." These movements are closest to the traditional primal religion of the people and in fact constitute an attempt to revitalize the original religion in the light of Christian influence. Although they may borrow various aspects from the Christian faith, they are often strongly opposed to Christianity. The *Dina ya Msambwa* Religion of the Ancestors in Kenya is an example of such, as are the Godians in Nigeria. Both these groups have sought to replace the Christian God and also the gods of their traditional religion by a new "God of Africa" who allegedly first revealed himself in Egypt many centuries ago.

The second group of movements includes those in which a deliberate attempt has been made to mix the traditional religion with Christianity and so form something new. These movements are therefore called "synthesist." These movements look toward both the primal religion and Christianity for their inspiration, unlike the neo-primals whose intention is directed solely toward the primal culture.

Third, there is the group that Turner calls "Hebraist." These movements have made a radical break from their traditional religion and look solely to the Bible for their inspiration. However, their faith corresponds more to the prophetic religion of the Israelites recorded in the Old Testament than the teaching from the New Testament given by the mission church. Often such movements see themselves as the descendants of the ten lost tribes of Israel. The Bayudaya, whose name means "People of Judah," are found in Uganda, and they are now allied to the fellowship of world Jewry. Most of the Maori movements of New Zealand are of this class. Another example is the movement owing its origin to Prophet Shembe referred to in the previous chapter.

The fourth class is probably the most numerous and may properly be called "independent" churches. They aim to be Christian, they make use of the Bible, and they give a central place to the person of Jesus Christ. In Africa, where this form predominates, they may be defined as churches founded by Africans to worship God in an indigenous way.

This group may be further subdivided according to the observations of Sundkler concerning the independent churches in South Africa.[13] Sundkler distinguished between what he called "Ethiopian" and "Zionist." Ethiopian churches are those that left the established mission church primarily over a disagreement concerning the matter of leadership. They reacted against what appeared to them as a dominant white leadership and sought to establish an African-led church. These churches usually resemble the church or mission from which they divided but are African in leadership and more African in certain cultural matters. Often these churches have had Ethiopia in their name, but many call themselves "African Methodist Church" or "Native Baptist Church." An example is the African Christian Church and Schools (ACC&S), a Kikuyu organization that divided from the Africa Inland Mission Church in 1947 and now numbers 30,000 affiliated members.[14]

The second subtype of the independent churches was called "Zionist" by Sundkler because many were influenced by an American organization founded by John Dowie with its headquarters at Zion, Illinois. However, they may better be called "prophet-healing churches" because this description applies far wider than South Africa. These churches not only have an African leadership but also have a more African form of worship. Dance and drumming are common, and healing always takes an important place. The Church of the Lord Aladura is an important example of this form of independency movement that has occurred among the Yoruba of Nigeria.

The Ethiopian variety of church first emerged in Africa in the 1880s, primarily in South Africa and Nigeria. The Zionist churches came later, following the epidemics of 1918. However, the author has observed in Ghana and Nigeria the emergence of yet another group of churches in the 1980s. These are formed by Africans but have a Western style of worship. Some are consciously applying church growth methods to build large congregations. Although they are independent of the established mission churches, they do not want to be classed with the prophet-healer class of churches.

Characteristics of the Independent Churches

A study of the independent churches reveals a number of important issues that relate back to an understanding of primal religions. It also provides a valuable appreciation of the missionary task of the European church among primal societies and so important lessons for mission strategy today.

Revelatory

Common to all the new religious movements is the call of the prophet. This may have come through a dream or a vision, and as such this has provided a charter for the church as having come from God. Isaac Kwesi Prah was moved by a night vision to leave the Methodist Church of Ghana in 1958 to found a prayer movement: "One night in a vision it seemed the windows of heaven opened and a shaft of heavenly sunlight touched his lips and flooded his soul. He saw the Lord Jesus Christ, who baptized him with Holy Spirit and healing power." This account of the dream is now stamped on the sheet given to every new member of the Divine Healing and Miracle Church, which Prah founded.[15]

The comment was made in a previous chapter about the importance of dreams within primal societies. Dreams are considered to be potential revelations from the supernatural realm. The prophet Josiah Oshitelu not only had visions but later developed a complete sacred script. Others have made use of extrabiblical material such as the "Sixth and Seventh Books of Moses." These two books have been banned in some West African countries because they have a history of causing mental illness. They do illustrate, however, a feeling found among many primal societies that there was something missing from the Bible. At first, the people thought that the power of the white man somehow lay in the Bible, which he brought with him. But it became obvious with time that the white man still prospered, while the African did not. Then it was often believed that some important teaching was missing from the Bible that gave the white man his supremacy.

Relevant

The movements are also particularly relevant to the needs of the local people. The importance of healing has been mentioned on several occasions, and this is a characteristic of most of the new movements. When major epidemics have come to primal societies, both traditional healers and Western medicine have often failed. It is at these times the people have turned to the prophet healers. This happened in the major influenza epidemic in Africa in 1918, and it may well happen again with the AIDS epidemic. It is the poor, unable to afford the costly Western medicines, who are principally turning to the independent churches in Africa today.

The prophets of the independent churches, especially of the prophet-healing type, offer healing by means of prayer. This is usually made with great vigor and with the laying on of hands and possibly the use of fasting, holy water, and oil. People often come to the independent churches after they have been to the local clinics, which have been unable to help them. Barrenness among women is a major problem in Africa because the birth of children gives the parents both social status and provision for their old age. When the clinics cannot help, it is to the faith healers that the women turn with varying success. It is important to realize that these are areas of concern often neglected by the mainline missionary churches.

Biblicist

The two classes of movements called by Turner "Hebraist" and "independent" churches make great use of the Bible. This occurs even if the leader is illiterate, as is common among many of the Zionist-type churches. The leader will be able to quote quite long portions of the Scriptures, which will be frequently used in preaching, together with the appropriate chapter and verse. Discussions will always entail reference to the Bible as the provider of the norm of behavior.

Here is found one of the major differences in the use of the Bible from that found in the Western context. The independent churches apply a literalist interpretation of the Bible with little regard for the historical or cultural context. For example, the many laws given to the people of Israel in the first five books of the Bible take on great significance. The Bible here provides answers to questions not considered by the mission churches.

May a woman go to church when she is having her period? What foods may one eat in order to avoid pollution? The Old Testament especially gives clear rules and a set of taboos that satisfy the people that they are behaving in a way pleasing to the deity. This is probably one of the reasons why the Old Testament is favored, and the Hebraist movements have occurred.

In general the Western missionary movement condemned polygamous marriage, and polygamous men were excluded from the church. However, when the Africans were able to read the Bible, and especially the Old Testament, they saw that many of the important characters of the Bible had more than one wife. They felt, in fact, that the Old Testament had a greater cultural relevance than the form of Bible teaching provided by the white man. Some of the new movements therefore allowed polygamy, and often the prophet was accompanied by his wives as "spiritual attendants." Although such groups are more tolerant on the subject of polygamy, they are frequently stricter with regard to drinking and smoking. The many denominations and missions of the white man are perceived to have different teaching, even though all claim theirs is based wholly on the Bible. If this is the case, why cannot the African read the Bible and draw his own conclusions? This is, in fact, what has occurred with varying results.

Ritualistic

The Ethiopian churches tend to have a pattern similar to those of the mission churches. However, in the more numerous prophet-healing churches one finds a radically different form of worship. It is much livelier, longer, and more colorful. Drums, clapping, and dancing are an important feature of their meetings. The use of modern amplification systems has added to the vigor and life.

Long white flowing robes are commonly worn by the members in fulfillment of the promise, "They will walk with me, dressed in white" (Rev. 3:4). Often incense is burned as an offering to God, in accordance with Revelation 8:3. They may also have a seven-pronged candlestick on the altar because one reads of such a lamp in the first few chapters of the book of

Revelation. Shoes are also removed because, like Moses, they are standing on holy ground (Exod. 3:5). Each feature of the ritual is backed up by chapter and verse as they literally apply the word of the Lord.

Although one is at first struck by the distinctive patterns of worship, it soon becomes obvious that they still have retained many features of the mission churches. The Church of the Cherubim and Seraphim contains many Anglican aspects in its order of service. However, it is the dynamic African expression that comes through so clearly to the observer. The traditional mission church pattern of worship frequently seems foreign and inhibitive to the African scene. The Christian message was not contextualized within the African culture. Ritual, which made up such an important part of primal religion, was neglected, especially by Protestant missionaries. The Christianity introduced by the missionaries failed to provide relevant cultural substitutes. But these cultural substitutes are just what one can observe within the new religious movements. For some, however, this has led them beyond what would be considered as biblical tolerance.

Power

Many of these new movements believe that they are restoring what Western missionary Christianity has lost—the power of the Holy Spirit. They see Western Christianity as being academic and book-centered and lacking the power to deal with the real issues of life. As one Ghanaian prophet said to me, "Send us only those missionaries who have the power to deal with the fetish!"

One of the most important departures within the independent churches is the rejection of the use of traditional magic as a solution to everyday problems. This has been replaced by a new source of power, which is faith in an almighty God. The belief in the effectiveness of magic, sorcery, and witchcraft is still recognized, but the real answer is now seen to be in the greater power of the Holy Spirit, realized through faith and prayer. This is seen most clearly in the area of sickness. Some groups would even reject the use of all medicines, arguing that faith and prayer are sufficient.

This is illustrated in the following quotation from a leaflet produced by the Brotherhood of the Cross and Star:

> Many thousands of miracles are reported performed in the Brotherhood of the Cross and Star...those suffering from spiritual illnesses of all sorts, are merely spiritually X-rayed and the source of illness located and removed through the electronic-eye of the power of the Holy Spirit.... After brief prayer and within seconds, one could see the sick vomiting out into a bowl of water the actual source of his/her illness. Some of the patients end up vomiting out live crocodiles, snails, lizards, coins, pins, cowries, etc, and immediately the sick are relieved of their pains and completely healed.[16]

Communal

Another notable characteristic of the independent churches is the strong sense of community that they have. The leaders will visit the members almost every day and pray for their particular situations. Sins may be freely confessed within the context of what is a new family and tribe. Salvation is understood as a communal event, for man is not merely a solitary unity but a "family." This is the outworking of the African proverb: "I am, because I participate."[17]

The Attitude of Western Missions

The initial attitude of the missionaries was one of condemning these movements as heretical and divisive. They were regarded as being the churches of the uneducated and allowing sexual immorality. Most Western missionaries, therefore, did not take much interest in such movements until the 1960s. Since that time a growing number of missionaries have begun to realize the relevance of these independent churches and are beginning to work with them. The ministries of Edwin and Irene Weaver[18] and Stan Nussbaum[19] and David Shank[20] provide useful models. The Weavers have sought to work alongside an independent church in Nigeria in a supportive role. They have assisted the church as directed by the indigenous leadership in providing relevant biblical teaching.

To summarize, what lessons must the missionary movement

recognize? Although the message of the gospel has been accepted by multitudes of primal societies, it has been presented in a form that has failed to meet the basic felt-needs of the people. The gospel has come dressed in European secular culture and has failed to provide meaningful answers. Thus many primal societies have sought to rework the Christian message into a form that is relevant to their own particular needs.

In the past, missionaries have tended to reject the traditional customs of a people as being "pagan" and "primitive." We have seen that this wholesale condemnation of traditional culture is inadequate. On the other hand, the Christians cannot uncritically accept the old ways. What is required is critical analysis of the meaning and role of the beliefs and customs within the society and then an appropriate contextualization within the life of the church. This will be the topic of the final chapter.

Notes

1. Anthony F. C. Wallace, *Religion: An Anthropological Perspective* (Random House: New York, 1966), p. 157.
2. Harold W. Turner, "Religious Movements in Primal (or Tribal) Societies," *Mission Focus* 9, no. 3 (1981): 45–55.
3. Friedrich Steinbaur, *Melanesian Cargo Cults* (George Prior Publishers: London, 1979).
4. David B. Barrett, *Schism and Renewal in Africa* (Oxford University Press: Nairobi, 1968).
5. Harold W. Turner, "New Mission Task: Worldwide and Waiting," *Missiology* 13, no. 1 (1985): 8.
6. David J. Hesselgrave, "Nichiren Shoshu Soka Gakkai," in *Dynamic Religious Movements* (Baker: Grand Rapids, 1978), pp. 129–48.
7. Harold W. Turner, lecture material given at Missionary Orientation Centre, 1986, and see also "Tribal Religious Movements, New," in *Encyclopaedia Britannica* (Encyclopaedia Britannica: Chicago, 1981), 18:698.
8. Donald McGavran, *Understanding Church Growth* (Eerdmans: Grand Rapids, 1970), p. 304.

9. Ibid., pp. 320–25.
10. Barrett, op. cit., p. 139.
11. Turner, "Religious Movements," pp. 48–50.
12. Joel B. Kailing, "Inside, Outside, Upside Down: In Relationship with African Independent Churches," *International Review of Mission* 77, no. 305 (1988): 53.
13. Bengt G. M. Sundkler, *Bantu Prophets in South Africa* (Oxford University Press: London, 1961), pp. 168–79.
14. David B. Barrett, *World Christian Encyclopedia* (Oxford University Press: Nairobi, 1982), p. 435.
15. Personal comments from leaders of Divine Healing and Miracle Church, 1986.
16. Brotherhood of the Cross and Star leaflet, 1985.
17. John V. Taylor, *The Primal Vision* (SCM Press: London, 1977), p. 85.
18. Edwin and Irene Weaver, *The Uyo Story* (Mennonite Board of Missions: Elkhart, Indiana, 1970).
19. Stan W. Nussbaum, "Toward Theological Dialogue with Independent Churches" (University of South Africa, doctoral diss., 1985).
20. David A. Shank, "Mission Relations with the Independent Churches in Africa," *Missiology* 13, no. 1 (1985): 23–44.

20

Christian Worldviews

Throughout the previous chapters we have been comparing and contrasting two very different worldviews. The first was the secular worldview, common to the Western world, and the second was that group we have called primal. In this final chapter we will attempt to draw together the many implications that have been raised for Christian mission among primal and folk religionists.

Opening the "Closed Universe"

In comparing these two classes of worldviews we have seen the weaknesses of each. However, it is necessary to realize that there is another important option that was almost universally accepted among Europeans up to the end of the seventeenth century: the theistic worldview. Folk Christianity was evidently common among many European peoples, but few would have questioned the existence of a personal deity—the God of the Bible. Even evil men, who rejected Christianity with its moral standards, knew themselves to be "bad" because of basic theistic presuppositions.

James W. Sire has usefully summarized eight basic propositions that he considers essential with regard to the theistic worldview:[1]

1. God is infinite and personal (Triune), transcendent and immanent, omniscient, sovereign and good.

2. God created the cosmos *ex nihilo* to operate with a uniformity of cause and effect in an open system.

3. Man is created in the image and likeness of God and thus possesses personality, self-transcendence, intelligence, morality, gregariousness and creativity.

4. God can and does communicate with man.

5. Man was created good, but through the Fall the image of God became defaced, though not so ruined as not to be capable of restoration; through the work of Christ God redeemed man and began the process of restoring man to goodness, though any given man may choose to reject that redemption.

6. For man death is either the gate to life with God and his people or the gate to eternal separation from the only thing that will ultimately fulfill man's aspirations.

7. Ethics is transcendent and is based on the character of God as good (holy and loving).

8. History is linear, a meaningful sequence of events leading to the fulfillment of God's purposes for man.

The theistic worldview provides an alternative position to the secular and primal worldviews. It recognizes the reality of an unseen world and of a supreme Creator who is distinct and greater than His creation. It also recognizes clearly defined moral absolutes based upon the fact that there is an ultimate Creator. Further, it recognizes the presence of evil as well as good within the created order.

The advocation of theism is not a journey to a past rejected philosophy but the recognition that it provides a satisfying worldview. It has a realistic appreciation of the natural world and the place of human beings within creation. People are not conceived as being dominated by powers beyond their control but in the role of cultivators responsible to the Creator God for their dealings within nature. Humanity therefore is not merely a randomly created organism but has a significance and meaning born out of the possibility of a personal relationship with the Creator. However, during the last two centuries, Western society has been increasingly affected by the secular worldview to such an extent that Christians have felt that the final refuge of Christianity must be in making it relevant and modern by applying the secular worldview to their interpretation of Scripture. In so doing, Christians have failed to realize that in adopting a different worldview they have seriously affected the revelation presented in those Scriptures.

Human beings are incurably religious, as is seen from the fact that no society has been encountered that does not have a religious cosmology. No wonder many secularized Westerners are turning to exotic religions and magic. As mentioned in chapter 11, witchcraft has taken on a new acceptability, but what is currently practiced is ritual magic drawn from the primal religions of many ancient peoples. This is part of a widespread reaction against the secular established order in practicing what was once condemned. Some, such as Anton LaVey, have developed a religious system based on the anti-God of the Christians—Satan. They have a satanic Bible and a series of rituals based on a perversion of Christian worship. This is all part of a growing interest in the occult.

A growing number of Western Christians have in recent years been calling the Christian church to recognize the limitations of the secular worldview that they have in practice adopted.[2] As John Wimber has written, "If Christians have a worldview that is affected by Western materialism, they will probably deny that signs and wonders are for today. Though they may use a theological rationale, the real issue is that it upsets their worldview."[3] Christians of our generation must seek to open the "closed universe" in order to make the gospel message more relevant to the people of the world and also to make it more in line with the plain reading of the Bible.

If the missionary is working on the basis of a theistic worldview, how will this affect his mission strategy? There are several important themes that must be considered.

Theme 1: Reality of the Unseen

Throughout this book we have shown that primal societies are those in which the people are very conscious of the unseen powers that influence the world. People recognize the need for technical skills to grow crops and make articles, but they also realize that there are those powers beyond their control. As we have seen, they attempt to deal with these unseen powers by ritual and magic. The missionary must have a strategy that seriously recognizes the existence of the unseen and does not reject those ideas as being mere superstitions.

Most primal societies have a belief in the existence of some "alienated creator" but do not know how he can be known. Here lies an important bridge for the presentation of the gospel message. They need to discover that the all-powerful Creator God cares about them and has provided a way by which they may approach Him. Although there are always certain features concerning the nature of God that may be lacking in their religion, there are often many positive points of contact. These can provide redemptive analogies for the presentation of the Christian message.

One needs to build from what is known into what is unknown. The Old Testament has many stories that are closely related to the culture of primal societies. The Karimojong are a nomadic pastoral people who are quickly able to identify with many of the events that happened to the patriarchs of Genesis. When the Karimojong gather their cattle into makeshift kraals, often the herdsman will sleep across the entrance. Such a person has no difficulty in understanding what Jesus meant when He said, "I am the gate for the sheep" (John 10:7).

As we have seen, sacrifice is a common practice among traditional societies. This can provide a meaningful analogy of the concept of reconciliation:

> An example of this is the annual sacrifice of water buffalo by the Bentian of Indonesia. After being speared, the animal is killed and its blood applied to the foreheads of all adult males who represent their families. The analogy to the atonement of Christ can readily be made.[4]

However, there is also the issue of the lesser gods, spirits, and ghosts that are considered to inhabit the universe. Missionaries have frequently discounted the traditional cosmology of the people in their eagerness to focus their non-Christian hearers upon the salvation found in Christ alone. One cannot expect a people who for generations have feared their gods, spirits, and ghosts simply to regard them now as nonexistent. This is especially so when the Bible that the missionary brings with him actually speaks of other gods, angels, and evil spirits.

Theme 2: Concepts of Sin

We have already discussed the fact that all societies have some notion of sin, although it reveals itself in different ways in different cultures. In primal societies, sin is essentially regarded as ceremonial error or the violation of the honor of the community. Any antisocial person may be suspected of witchcraft or sorcery.

Turning to a biblical understanding of sin, one may identify four common Greek words.

Hamartia

This is the most common word for sin in the New Testament and means "to miss the mark." It refers to an inward twist in man that results in sin, whether or not one feels guilty. Most primal societies are conscious of this, as shown in an Akan proverb that says of man: "He thinks evil in his heart."

Paraptoma

Sin is here spoken of as "to trespass" or "to leave the path (way of God)." The fact of a broken relationship between man and the Creator was mentioned before in chapter 3 when the story of the pounding of the fufu was recounted. This concept of sin is quickly understood as a broken relationship.

Opheilemia

This word conveys the idea of debt. This is another concept that is understood in traditional society. When a man sins, he incurs a debt with respect to God. This must be paid with the offering of a sacrifice. The concept of Christ being the supreme sacrifice to God for all men's sins can readily be grasped. However, this can easily be taken further with the assumption that no further payment is necessary, and whatever sins are committed, the debt is canceled by Christ's death.

Anomia

Sin is also described as lawlessness. The emphasis here is upon man's rebellion against God and related to the moral absolute of the supreme Creator. This is often a perception of sin that is not realized even by Christian converts. It is understood that God is distant from man, but the reason for this is not seen as the result of a moral issue. This is one of the major differences between the myths of many societies and that of the Genesis account of the Fall.

The concept of sin that is presented by Westerners may be so different from that understood by the people that it appears totally alien. This has led some people in Africa to regard sin as being something that only Christians do! An alternative approach is to start with the awareness of sin that the people already possess, that is, their conscience (Rom. 2:15). In this way the sense of guilt that God desires to generate comes from the discrepancies between their own ideals and behavior, and not from the imposition of someone else's ideals. From this starting point can come the process of raising their ideals to approximate those of God.

Wayne Dye has suggested the following steps:[5]

1. Learn the ethical system of your potential hearer.
2. Compare your findings with your own culture and the Bible. . . .
3. Learn to live a loving life by their cultural standards. . . .
4. Preach repentance for areas in which the Holy Spirit is already convicting. . . .
5. Expect the Holy Spirit to be working. . . .
6. Teach the converts to obey and rely on the Holy Spirit.

Dye in his work among the Bahinemo people started where the people were in their own culture. He explained to them the expectations of God for them to live up to the standards of their own ideals. He then explained that the saving work of Christ had been performed so that they could live up to their own ideals with the purpose of uniting them with God.

Theme 3: A Holistic Message

An African proverb says, "Our world is like a drum; strike any part of it and the vibration is felt all over." In most traditional societies, life is not divided into distinct compartments but is perceived as an integrated whole. Hence, religion is not restricted to one area of life but permeates all. The Western distinction between the sacred and the secular is not understood, and religion performs many social and economic functions.

When a form of Christianity is introduced with narrow religious concerns, many functions met by primal societies are neglected by the new faith.

Healing

Can Christ deal with physical illness? Missionaries have rightly fulfilled a medical ministry to care for the physical needs of people, but so often what has been communicated is not the power of Christ but the power of Western medical technology. Western medical knowledge must be placed into the wider context of holistic healing of the whole man and his society. The traditional healers of Africa and Asia have lacked modern medical technology, but they have realized the importance of a holistic approach to healing. Family problems are exposed and dealt with, and for this reason confession and atonement are commonly part of the healing process. It is this very issue that many Christians are currently recognizing as being necessary within Western society.

Community

In many societies people are resistant to Christianity because they feel that a change of religion will weaken their social ties with their community. A person is both an individual and part of the community, which has not only a relevance now but one that passes back in time through a chain of ancestors. It is, therefore, difficult for a person to take an individualistic stand against the general feeling of the group. How will the traditional gods or ancestors react to the rebellion of one of their children? They may punish the person or the tribe as a whole with sickness, drought, or pests.

Primal societies often turn to Christ as communities rather than as individuals. The more tightly related the society, the more likely this is to occur. "People movements" should be encouraged because they express a natural way for primal societies to make decisions. This does not mean that personal discipleship is unimportant, but it recognizes the cultural significance of the community. It enables the effects of Christianity to penetrate to every area of community life as the people abandon idol worship, head-hunting, and sorcery.

It is therefore necessary for the missionary to observe the traditional religion and understand how it functions in the various areas of the people's lives. Christian mission should be planned to meet these needs, irrespective of whether they fall outside what are generally regarded as church activities.

Theme 4: Power Encounter

If one believes in a world of unseen powers, it is logical that one would want to see the reality of a greater power before changing allegiance to another god. Can this new god meet my basic needs? Or, more simply, does this new religion work? People may be convinced intellectually that Christ is Lord of creation, but often they are uncertain if He is able and willing to be all-powerful in their daily lives. Christians have rightly proclaimed the truth of the message of the gospel, but we have often failed to demonstrate its power. The sick are looking for healing, barren women are hoping to have children, and those fearful of evil spirits want the protection of a loving, almighty God.

The demonstration of the power of the gospel and the communication of its message must lead to a personal commitment to the gospel. Before this can be reached there is a struggle within those considering conversion as to whether or not they should take the risk of burning their fetishes and idols. Throughout the Bible one sees the necessity of making such a commitment to the Lord, and often this was accompanied by some form of visible demonstration of that allegiance. The book of Joshua ends with a notable challenge to the people of Israel: "Choose for yourselves this day whom you will serve, whether the gods your forefathers served beyond the River, or the gods of the Amorites, in whose land you are living. But as for me and my household, we will serve the LORD" (Josh. 24:15). After the public debate the decision is made, "We too will serve the LORD, because he is our God" (v. 18). However, Joshua requires them to make a demonstration of that decision: "Throw away the foreign gods that are among you and yield your hearts to the LORD, the God of Israel" (v. 23). Similarly, in the New Testament we read of a dramatic case: "A number who had practiced sorcery brought their scrolls together and burned them publicly. When they calculated the value of the scrolls, the total came to fifty thousand drachmas" (Acts 19:19). As Tippett has written, "Be it noted that this demonstration was both an act of commitment, and an act of rejection, a spiritual encounter."[6]

Today in many primal societies Christian converts must make a similar demonstration of their commitment to the Lord. Among the Fanti of Ghana, the totem animal is eaten; in India, an idol may be smashed; in other areas a fetish would be burned in the fire. These are not merely iconoclastic actions encouraged by Western missionaries but are symbolic demonstrations by the people in recognition of the greater power of Christ over that of their former gods and spirits. This is what van Gennep would call a "rite of separation" (see Figure 8.1) because it marks a precise point of removal from an old way of life.

Theme 5: Encounter by Challenge

The term *power encounter* has been broadened and is loosely used for any type of encounter between Christianity and non-Christian religions. It includes encounters such as those Elijah experienced on Mount Carmel (1 Kings 18:24). The important aspect of such an encounter is that the outcome is due not to the personal strengths of the contestants but to the power of the God or spirit on whom the contestants call. These encounters by challenge have played an important part in the spread of Christianity among primal societies. A notable case is that of

St. Boniface who Christianized the Saxons of eighth-century Germany. He heard about a great tree at Geismar known as Thor's oak. It may have been struck by lightning, which was believed to be a symbol of Thor's power. Boniface found people worshiping the tree, seized an axe, and started to cut it down. Willibald wrote that as soon as he had made a vee-shaped cut, a great wind dashed the old trunk to the ground, and it split into the shape of a cross. When the people saw that Thor did no harm to Boniface, they lost their faith in their old gods.[7]

As with this clan of the Saxons, such an encounter can lead to a whole society accepting Christianity. A more recent example of this is found among the Dagarti people of northwest Ghana. In 1932, the region was in the midst of a major drought, and the rituals of the rainmakers did nothing to rectify the situation. In desperation the people asked the Catholic missionaries to pray to their God, and they duly prayed for rain. The next day rain did fall on all the land except that of the traditional rainmakers. This made a tremendous impact upon the people, and they started coming to the Catholic missionaries in the hundreds to become Christians.[8]

Several points, however, need to be made in this discussion. First, other missionaries in Ghana have been in a similar situation and have prayed for rain, rain has come, but the people took no interest in the gospel. Perhaps the response of the Dagarti was partly due to the medical work that had been previously done among them and had made good social relations. The social factors that made the Dagarti responsive may have been missing among other groups, and this could have caused their subsequent lack of interest.

Second, in some cases, an apparent initial victory has even made rainmakers and religious leaders more hostile because they have seen their traditional authority challenged. Likewise, after Elijah had won on Mount Carmel and fled, Jezebel appointed 400 new prophets of Baal. One can see a similar response to Jesus who healed the sick and cast out demons, but this ultimately led the Pharisees and Sadducees to crucify Him.

Third, although the Dagarti were baptized into the church in large numbers, even after all these years only 10 percent attend church, and most have only a syncretistic form of Christianity. Biblical teaching is a necessary follow-up to any such change of religious allegiance.

It is too simplistic to suggest that all a missionary needs to do is to heal the sick and cast out demons. This is indeed part of the task, but it is only a preliminary part of the total battle.

Theme 6: Contextualization

How should Christians deal with traditions? The primal worldview remains deeply a part of most societies. The Christian is faced with two extremes. On the one hand, he may totally reject all aspects of the primal religion and its culture, as did many of the former missionaries. As we have already stated, to do this only causes a cultural vacuum that needs to be filled. The Western forms of Christianity fail to replace what is lost, and they so often lead to a foreign church that stands out with notable incongruity within the community. The church buildings are constructed to Western designs, and the music that is sung and played is European. The form of service, dress of pastor, and patterns of worship are all from a Western tradition. As Alan Tippett has said, "These churches have been misfits in their own worlds."[9]

On the other hand, one may uncritically accept all the rituals and customs of the primal society as being meaningful and significant. This approach answers many of the questions raised by the first option in making Christianity seem both relevant and meaningful to the people. However, it overlooks the essential sinfulness of humankind. Sin affects not only individuals but human cultures as well. As the Lausanne Covenant states, "Because man is God's creature, some of his culture is rich in beauty and goodness. Because he has fallen, all of it is tainted with sin and some of it is demonic."[10]

As the gospel enters a culture, it comes as both judge and redeemer. Many components of a culture will be brought almost unnoticed by people into their new Christian life. However, other aspects of their culture will need to be evaluated by the gospel according to its own criteria of truth and righteousness. There will even be those aspects that will be rejected as being incompatible with the revelation of God. Yet other aspects of the culture of a people will have to be modified and transformed in ways more in keeping with the Scriptures.[11]

Paul Hiebert has called this "critical contextualization." He argues that old beliefs and customs should be neither accepted nor rejected without examination: "They are first studied with regard to the meaning and place they have within their cultural setting and then evaluated in the light of biblical norms."[12] This will involve three stages:

1. The Christian needs to appreciate that the gospel relates to every aspect of human society. He needs therefore to be aware of all the customs and rituals of which his traditional culture is composed. The young church must realize the importance of the traditional rites of passage and other rituals within its Christian life. The missionary has often been so concerned with winning converts that he has neglected the need for these people to be built into meaningful communities of the people of God.

2. The church leaders must examine the many customs of their old traditions in the light of the Scriptures. It is important to stress that the missionary must not enforce his own cultural reading of the Bible upon the young church. This requires a great deal of humility and trust in the working of the Holy Spirit in the lives of the young believers. The young church among the Gonja of Ghana spent many days discussing if Christians should be involved in the local dances. The missionaries could detect little difference between the various dances because they all sounded foreign and quite similar in form to their undiscerning ears. The church leaders finally decided that there were certain classes of dances that would be "bad" for a Christian to attend while others would be acceptable. It was the Gonja church leaders who made the decision in the light of their reading of the Scriptures.

3. The church then needs to create new contextualized Christian practices that are relevant to them as a Christian people. The absence of rituals within the Protestant church has given the impression that the church is colorless compared with the traditional rituals and festivities of the primal society. The existence of this cultural void can cause a dissatisfaction with their faith among new Christians. It is important to recognize that most of the new religious movements place a strong emphasis upon ritual and symbolism.

Once again the choice concerning the rituals must lie with the people themselves. The missionary should play the role of a facilitator in helping them understand the Bible and give information on how other societies deal with similar issues. The church may adopt foreign symbols or rituals, which they borrow from other communities. On the other hand, they may create new rituals that are particularly relevant to them. The bread and wine of the Lord's Supper may be replaced by water and sweet potato, which is their own staple food. The important fact is that it is the Christian meaning of the symbol or ritual that is carried through into their culture. Their church music, ritual, and practice should express the life and feelings of the people in their worship in ways that are meaningful and relevant to them.

There is, nevertheless, a danger of syncretism, but as the young church reads the Scriptures, it will continue to reassess its own customs and beliefs. The members will find answers to their own problems and seek to manifest the life of Jesus Christ in their own society, not as a group who have left their own culture for one that is new, but a people who remain as part of their own culture and yet are totally Christian.

A further difficulty that is developing in many parts of Africa, Asia, and Latin America concerns those churches that have been in existence for decades. These well-established churches have accepted a Western form of liturgy and continue to hold firmly to that tradition. They are now perplexed at Western missionaries from Europe and America speaking of the need for their church practices to be made more indigenous. This seems to contradict the very issues that the first missionaries to their countries had stressed. What they have failed to realize is that Christianity is not a static set of religious practices but a living faith that must interact with the needs of society. It will therefore see a process of change with the movements of human history. Every generation of Christians in each culture will have to formulate their own patterns of worship to enable them to express the truth and reality of their own experience of Christ in their society.

This is not a matter of compromise or hypocrisy but a discerning application of basic Christian principles to social issues. It requires an understanding of the roles of various cultural forms and practices within a society. This has been the primary aim of this book: to show the essential questions asked within primal societies and how their traditional religions answered them. Then comes the process of analyzing the practices in the light of living out the life of Christ within that particular community. There will be no uniform answer in the sense of one unique way of life, but there will be a unity of expression as the Christian life is manifest in all societies through the work of the Holy Spirit and the revelation of the Scriptures.

What applies to the young church growing within a primal society should also apply to the church within a Western society. Christians need to appreciate the influence of their own secular Christianity and live a life that is in tune with the revelation of Scripture. Christ incarnate through every church in every culture should be the aim of mission.

Theme 7: The Role of the Missionary

In reaching primal and folk societies the role of the missionary is of great importance. The people will always interpret the missionaries' presence within the context of their own world-view. After Paul healed the lame man in Lystra, the people exclaimed, "The gods have come down to us in human form!" (Acts 14:11).

The ultimate model for Christian mission is found in the person of Jesus Christ who said: "As the Father has sent me, I am sending you" (John 20:21). The missionary is to be the very embodiment of Christ and the vehicle through whom Christ reveals Himself despite the human frailty of the person.

The Christian witness must humbly learn to understand the complex religious beliefs and practices of the people to whom he is sent. Premature judgment and attitudes are harmful and easily occur because of our own worldview assumptions. We must not discard notions of spirits, ghosts, vampires, and witch-craft as outmoded remnants of primitive people. We need to listen to the people as they describe their hopes, fears, and perceptions, and we will find that it is we who acquire a new awareness of reality. As we study the Bible together with our new Christian brethren, we will receive new insights as we appreciate the application of the gospel to a culture different from our own. As we pray with our new Christian brethren, we will know a greater depth of worship as we praise the living Lord together. There is an underlying bond that unites us with them and takes us further than mere identification.

Notes

1. James W. Sire, *The Universe Next Door* (IVP: Leicester, 1977), pp. 26–42.
2. Francis Schaeffer, *Escape from Reason* (IVP: London, 1968), p. 91; Os Guinness, *The Dust of Death* (IVP: London, 1973).
3. John Wimber, *Power Evangelism: Signs and Wonders Today* (Hodder & Stoughton: London, 1985), p. 95.
4. Lausanne Occasional Papers, no. 16: *Christian Witness to Traditional Religionists of Asia and Oceania* (LCWE: Illinois, 1980), p. 7.
5. T. Wayne Dye, "Toward a Cross-Cultural Definition of Sin," *Missiology* 4 (1976): 27–41.
6. Alan R. Tippett, "The Evangelisation of Animists," in *Let the Earth Hear His Voice* (World Wide Publications: Minneapolis, 1975), p. 848.
7. David Keep, *St. Boniface and His World* (Paternoster Press: Exeter, 1979), p.11.
8. Hans W. Debrunner, *A History of Christianity in Ghana* (Waterville Publishing House: Accra, 1967), p. 328.
9. Tippett, op. cit., p. 853.
10. J. D. Douglas, "The Lausanne Covenant," in *Let the Earth Hear His Voice* (World Wide Publications: Minneapolis, 1975), p. 6.
11. David Burnett, *God's Mission: Healing the Nations* (MARC Europe: Bromley, 1986), pp. 179–88.
12. Paul G. Hiebert, *Anthropological Insights for Missionaries* (Baker: Grand Rapids, 1985), p. 186.

Appendix: Ministering to the Spirit Possessed

Throughout this book the aim has been to give an understanding of those foundation ideas of societies that practice primal or folk religions. A fuller understanding of these religions will enable the outsider to communicate more effectively and relate more meaningfully to the people who hold these beliefs. In many cases the missionary will find the practical situations that he may face cause him a conflict of ideology as he attempts to understand them as seen by the local people and according to his own secularized worldview.

There is no cross-cultural situation more difficult for the Western Christian to comprehend than that of spirit possession. This requires discernment as well as a commonsense approach to the Bible. Is what he is faced with some bizarre act, or is it some psychological illness or a form of possession or even a mixture of all three? This Appendix is written to provide a few insights into the practical issues of dealing with spirit possession, which have been raised in the previous chapters.

The Counselor

The person and place of the counselor must be our starting point in any ministry to the spirit possessed. Several points should be noted.

A Serious Approach

Most Western people are much influenced by the secular worldview and have some doubt concerning the reality of the phenomenon of spirit possession. The novelty of this ministry is a danger of which Christians must be aware. This should never lead one to deal lightly with this matter. Fasting with prayer may be an essential part of the counselor's preparation.

Be Humble Before God

An overt confidence in one's own ability is not only unwise but dangerous (Acts 19:13–16). Never minister to the possessed on your own. Always have one or two people with you whom you know and with whom you have warm Christian fellowship.

Confession of Sins

We are not perfect, and it is necessary for the counselor to recognize this and be willing to confess any sins before he attempts such a ministry. Often spirits seem to have a knowledge of such sins and will seek to undermine the credibility of the Christian by exposing any such unholy actions or thoughts. The counselor must be aware of this and know the assurance that he has been cleansed from all unrighteousness.

Willingness to Suffer

In any war there are wounds and hurts, and the counselor must be prepared for these in the spiritual battle. After the ministry of deliverance the counselor may be assailed by evil thoughts, bad dreams, depression, fatigue, or even physical sickness. This may come as a surprise at first, until one realizes the need to continually put on the whole armor of God. The prayerful support of others can be of great help at such times.

Gift of Discernment

Some people have a gift of discernment and are quickly able to identify the situation. However, all Christians should have a biblically formed intellect that should enable them to perceive something of the matter.

Ministry

Because spirit possession takes many forms, it is not possible to give any set procedure for a ministry of deliverance. A careful study of various New Testament passages is of great help. (See Matt. 8:28–34; 15:22–28; 17:14–21; Mark 1:21–28; 5:1–20; 7:24–30; Luke 4:31–37; 9:37–45; Acts 16:16–21.) However, the following points may provide assistance.

Desire for Deliverance

In the chapter on possession the helpful/harmful distinction was made. If a person does not wish to be helped, there seems little possibility of the spirit being cast out. The person may feel weak, impotent, or even trapped, and if there is a desire to be free, the Holy Spirit is eager to deliver. Never let the demonstration of exorcism become a public spectacle. Ministry should be undertaken with a genuine compassion and a concern for the dignity and safety of the individual.

Identification of the Problem

From the discussion in the text of spirit/human relations it is clear that this is a complex subject (chapters 13, 14, and 15). Spirit possession may occur by membership in a possession cult, through dedication to a spirit in youth, attendance at a seance, drug taking, immorality, and so on. Without spending too much time with the objective details of the individual's history, it is useful to know what is the nature of the affliction. Often one finds a definite point that allowed the spirit to enter the person's life. This often relates to some particular sin in the past.

It is at times possible to command the spirits to identify themselves, as was the case with Jesus and "Legion." However, this is not usually necessary, and one should beware the danger of holding conversations with spirits. They should be silenced in most cases, as they were by Jesus.

Word of Authority

Spirits are expelled not by some Christian ritual but by the exercise of the authority that Christ has given to His disciples. This contrasts with the rituals and incantations used by the traditional exorcists and healers. Such a word of authority does not require undue shouting or demonstrative action. Calmness and control characterized the ministry of Jesus, and they should also characterize our own ministry as we use the name of Jesus Christ. Often spirits will challenge the authority we have been given by Christ and resist in the hope that we may give up. Once the spirit realizes that we are convinced in the authority of Christ, it may leave with a surprising suddenness.

The deliverance may or may not be accompanied by physical reaction. Some spirits may cause the person to shout out as if in acute pain, while in other cases a person will be violently convulsed and left prostrate upon the floor (Mark 1:25–26). Such demonstrations are always disconcerting, but they should not be allowed to unsettle the counselor or bring panic and confusion into the situation.

Frequently, the spirit may seek to bargain with the counselor, but this should be avoided if possible. Jesus did allow this with the case of the Gerasene demoniac (Mark 5) when the spirits were allowed to go into the pigs. However, it must be noted that the deaths of the pigs were not sacrifices to appease the spirits but the destruction of ritually unclean animals.

Absolution

Once the spirit has left the person, it is necessary for the counselor to assure the person of his acceptance by God and the reality of his forgiveness. Some will respond readily to the fact of sins forgiven, while others will be so conscious of their past sins they will find difficulty in believing that a holy God will accept them. Past sins must be confessed, and especially any willful sins that provided the initial bridgehead for the spirit to enter the person's life. This is especially important if a person has willingly yielded to a spirit in a possession cult or has made a pact with the devil.

Anointing

Finally, the counselor should pray with the person so that he may know the reality of the Holy Spirit in his life:

> When an evil spirit comes out of a man, it goes through arid places seeking rest and does not find it. Then it says, "I will return to the house I left." When it arrives, it finds the house swept clean and put in order. Then it goes and takes seven other spirits more wicked than itself, and they go in and live there. And the final condition of that man is worse than the first (Luke 11:24–26).

Follow-Up

The actual deliverance is not the end of the ministry, just as an act of commitment to Christ is not the end of conversion. Both are the beginning of a new life in Christ and require care and nurture. For the formerly possessed person the following points are important.

Fellowship

It is essential that the person knows the continuing warmth of Christian fellowship. Many things may need to be put right in a practical way, such as marriage problems, effects of crimes, and so on. The person may also suffer from bad memories resulting from the painful feeling of guilt for past behavior and thoughts. Depression may occur months after the actual deliverance, in a similar way that many widows suffer depression months after the death of a beloved husband. At these times supporting fellowship is essential.

Teaching

A love for the Scriptures usually develops spontaneously within the person, and this should be encouraged. There are, however, many passages in the Bible that can cause difficulty, and these must be patiently studied with the person. This must not be done in a "know-it-all" attitude but in a humble way as a fellow disciple and learner of Christ. The person may be struggling with problems or habits of a depth that other Christians cannot appreciate.

Separation from Unholy Rituals

Frequently, an important aspect of a person's change of allegiance is the destruction of a particular fetish, charm, or idol. This sort of practice is seen in Acts 19:19. It is important to note that it is the person concerned who destroys the fetish, and not the missionary or counselor. The person must realize that it is the power of Christ in his own life enabling him to overcome the powers that formerly held him in bondage. This stops any undue dependency upon the counselor and focuses the person's relationship upon the living Christ.

Mission

In the case of the Gerasene man in Mark 5:18 we see the man asking Jesus if he might go with Him, but this Jesus refused. The person was not being inducted into some new possession cult but being freed to become a witness to a new life in Christ. None can be more certain of the power of Christ than was this man, and his genuine testimony had an important influence on the community. Care should be taken not to glamorize the person's testimony because in some cases this has become a problem later in his or her Christian life.

Glossary

The translation of words from any language is always likely to introduce different connotations, and this is especially true in describing the abstract ideas of the cosmology of primal societies. This glossary consists of some of the common words referred to in the book and their meanings as widely used in anthropological texts.

ancestors: spiritual beings, ghosts, who are in some ways supposed to be related to the living family, and so concerned about their well-being.

ancestral cult: those activities involved in the worship of, or communication with, the dead forebears of the family or group.

animism: a term used by E. B. Tylor to describe belief in spirits and the supernatural.

anthropology: the study of the culture and way of life of the peoples of the world.

astrology: the means of assessing the influence of heavenly bodies upon earthly affairs of humankind.

baraka: the Arabic word for blessing, but in folk Islam it means the supernatural power with which people or objects may be endued.

brahman: the absolute, impersonal essence of the universe in Vedanta Hinduism.

clairvoyance: the psychic ability to see things or people, past, present, or future, which cannot be seen by less gifted individuals.

cult: a term widely used in anthropology for a collection of religious ideas and practices that are associated with a given divinity, ancestor, or social group.

culture: the learned and shared attitudes, values, and ways of behavior of a people.

dervish: a member of a Muslim mystical order; a Sufi.

divination: the art of reaching a judgment concerning the cause and solution of some event that may be past, present, or future. It is usually fairly standardized in each culture and is believed to depend upon revelation by spiritual beings.

divinities: a set of spiritual beings that rule over some area of the world or some special activity of human life. Often regarded as the lesser gods.

ecstasy: a short rapturous trance during which the person feels an intense sense of well-being and a dissociation from his surroundings.

evil eye: a staring look that suggests envy and desire of a particular person or object and causes harm.

exorcism: the expelling of spirits or ghosts from persons or places, usually by means of rituals or incantations.

fetish: the word was coined from the Portuguese *feitico*, which as an adjective means "artificial" and as a noun "charm" or "sorcery." It has come to be used in various ways but generally is used for an object that has supernatural power (usually resulting from an association with spirits and gods). Commonly used in West Africa.

folk religion: a general term used for popular religious practices and superstitions within a major world religion.

ghosts: supernatural beings who were once human or animal; the souls of dead people.

gods: spiritual beings of nonhuman origin who are regarded as being in command of a particular domain or area of human life.

guru: literally meaning "to lead from darkness to light." A spiritual guide in Hinduism who oversees another's spiritual progress.

indigenous: aboriginal or native, pertaining to the original inhabitants of a region.

initiation rites: religious rituals that mark the rite of passage from the status of youth to the status of an adult.

jinn: an Arabic term used for spirits, usually evil, which may harm people and cause disease.

juju: the word comes from the old French word *joujoy* meaning a toy or doll, and so has often been used to denote the image or symbol of a god.

karma: a term used in Hinduism and Buddhism for those actions in one life seen to bring inevitable results in future reincarnations

living dead: a term, coined by John Mbiti, that refers to the persistence of a person's individual soul for some time after death.

magic: the performance of certain rituals that are believed to compel the supernatural powers to act in particular ways.

mana: a Polynesian term for supernatural power that is generally regarded as nonpersonal and is possessed by certain objects or people.

mantra: a sacred word or group of words used in Hinduism as an aid to meditation and mystic experience.

marabout: an Islamic holy man to whom has been accredited supernatural powers. Used in West Africa.

medium: a person claiming to be able to communicate with the dead by occult means.

millenarian: pertaining to a prophesied millennium; commonly found belief within new religious movements.

monism: the philosophy expounding that there is only one absolute reality and everything else is merely an expression of that reality.

monotheism: the belief in or worship of a single god.

multiple self: the view of human personality as consisting of a set of distinct entities.

mystic: a person claiming that through trance or spiritual exercises he is able to enter into a unity with deity, e.g., Sufi.

myth: a traditional story passed from one generation to the next and claiming to explain various customs and beliefs.

New Religious Movement (NERM): a new religion resulting from the interaction of two cultures and religions, and although having features in common with both, it is in itself new and different. *See also* prophet and millenarian.

nirvana: the Buddhist state of absolute blessedness in which the individual is fully released from the cycle of reincarnations.

oath: the act of calling upon a supernatural being to bear witness to the truth of what is said.

occult: literally "hidden" or "secret." Generally applied to "secret knowledge" of the supernatural and magical rites.

oracle: a priest who serves a deity that has the power to see the future and to discern the spiritual meaning of the present.

ordeal: a means used to determine guilt or innocence by submitting the accused to dangerous or painful tests believed to be under supernatural control.

pantheism: the teaching that god is all and all is god.

pollution: the quality of impurity or contamination that may result either from accidental contact or from deliberate choice.

polygamy: plural marriage; marriage to more than one spouse simultaneously.

possession: the temporary or permanent domination of a person by a supernatural being.

prayer: a verbal petition made to any object, but usually to a supernatural being, often associated with sacrifice.

priest: in primal societies, a priest is a person who acts as an intermediary between human beings and god(s); a religious expert.

primal religion: the word *primal* denotes something basic, fundamental, and coming before. Primal religions are the nonuniversal religions of preliterate people, existing before the influence brought by the major world religions.

PRINERM: an acronym proposed by Harold Turner for the class of new religious movements (NERMs) that develop within primal societies.

prophet: a person claiming to speak on behalf of a particular deity and who usually becomes the central figure of a new religious cult.

propitiate: to make favorably inclined; to appease or conciliate.

redemptive analogy: a particular story or ritual of a society that provides an analogy with some aspect of the gospel message and so assists communication.

reincarnation: the condition of being reborn in another body.

religion: the shared beliefs and practices of a people that relate to their understanding of the supernatural.

revitalization movement: a new religious movement stimulated by a prophet, which aims to give new meaning to a society.

rites of passage: religious rituals that mark an individual's passage from one life stage to another.

ritual: an established ceremonial procedure, with religious meaning.

sacrifice: the propitiatory offering of plant, animal, or object to some supernatural being.

saint: literally "a holy man"; one who is regarded by a society to be particularly dedicated in the service of a deity and who may thus possess supernatural powers.

seance: a gathering of people to establish contact with the dead by means of a medium.

seer: a person who practices divination by concentration techniques, e.g., using a crystal ball.

shade: the ghost of a particular dead person, which persists in some form of lesser existence for a period after death.

shaman: a healer who seeks to cure people by means of supernatural powers.

sorcerer: an antisocial practitioner who causes evil by manipulating material objects and performing rituals.

soul: the immaterial part of a human being or, in some cases, an animal.

soul loss: the belief that sickness is caused by the loss of one's soul; associated with shamanism.

spell: special words that are regarded as having power. Usually spoken in some particular formula: a charm or incantation.

spirit: a supernatural being who is lower in prestige than gods but closer to the people; it may be helpful, mischievous, or evil in nature.

Sufi: a Muslim mystic usually attached to a society or brotherhood organized around a religious leader.

superstition: beliefs and practices that are believed in part by the people but continue to be held.

supreme being: the transcendent, all-powerful creator god who exists above all the other gods and spirits.

syncretism: the fusion of two distinct systems of belief and practice.

taboo: a prohibition excluding something from use because of its sacred nature.

totem: an animal or plant name associated with a clan that provides group identification and may have special ritual significance for a family, clan, or individual.

trance: an altered state of consciousness, which may result in visions and ecstasy.

transmigration: any consciousness in man that he is a separate being is considered to be illusory and is the cause of a constant cycle of rebirths or transmigrations of the soul.

tribe: a group of people who share a common language, culture, and territory and see themselves as an autonomous unit.

Umbanda: an Afro-Brazilian cult that originated in Rio de Janeiro in the 1920s but is more generally used for all such similar spiritualist cults in Latin America.

voodoo: the English vernacular for a system of religious belief and practices brought to Latin America by African slaves.

wicca: a modern form of witchcraft and related practices founded by Gerald Gardner at the end of the nineteenth century.

witch: an antisocial person who is believed to be able to harm others by means of an innate spiritual power.

witch doctor: a term used loosely by Europeans to refer to a diviner-healer. He is able to identify witches and protect his clients.

worldview: the basic ideas and values shared by the members of a particular society. These concepts provide a way by which the people normally order their life experiences. Because of the widespread acceptance of these concepts within the society, the ideas are usually regarded as being nonnegotiable and beyond dispute.

Yoga: a Sanskrit word meaning "yoke" or "union." Used in Hinduism for any means that assists the union with the absolute.

Selected Bibliography

Achebe, Chinua. *Things Fall Apart*. Heinemann: London, 1978.

Ade Adegbola, E. A. *Traditional Religion in West Africa*. Asempa Publishers: Accra, 1983.

Ahmen, Akbar S., and Hart, David M. *Islam in Tribal Societies*. Routledge & Kegan Paul: London, 1984.

Bacon, Betty. *Spiritism in Brazil*. Latin American Group of EMA: London, 1979.

Barker, Peter. *Peoples, Languages, and Religion in Northern Ghana*. GEC: Accra, 1986.

Barrett, David B. *Schism and Renewal in Africa*. Oxford University Press: Nairobi, 1968.

Bartels, F. L. *The Roots of Ghana Methodism*. Cambridge University Press: Nairobi, 1968.

Beattie, John H. M. "The Ghost Cult in Bunyoro." In John Middleton, *Gods and Ritual*. University of Texas: Austin, 1967.

Birket-Smith, Kaj. *The Eskimos*. Methuen: London, 1959.

Bloomfield, Frena. *The Book of Chinese Beliefs*. Arrow Books: London, 1983.

Budge, E. A. Wallis. *Egyptian Religion*. Routledge & Kegan Paul: London, 1979.

Burnett, David G. *God's Mission: Healing the Nations*. MARC Europe: Bromley, 1986.

Campbell, Joseph. *The Way of Animal Powers*. Times Books: London, 1984.

Carroll, Michael P. "One More Time: Leviticus Revisited." In Bernhard Lang, *Anthropological Approaches to the Old Testament*. Fortress Press: Philadelphia, 1985.

Clements, R. D. *Gods and the Gurus*. IVP: London, 1974.

Codrington, R. H. *The Melanesians: Studies in Their Anthropology and Folk-Lore*.Clarendon Press: Oxford, 1891.

Cook, Robert R. "Ghosts." *East Africa Journal of Evangelical Theology* 4, no. 1 (1985): 35–48.

Davis, Hassoldt. *Sorcerer's Village*. George G. Harrap: London, 1956.

Debrunner, Hans W. *A History of Christianity in Ghana*. Waterville Publishing House: Accra, 1967.

Douglas, Mary. *Purity and Danger*. Routledge & Kegan Paul: London, 1966.

Dye, T. Wayne. "Toward a Cultural Definition of Sin." *Missiology* 4, no. 1 (1976).

Eades, J. S. *The Yoruba Today*. Cambridge University Press: Cambridge, 1980.

Eliade, Mircea. *A History of Religious Ideas*. Vol. 3. University of Chicago Press: Chicago, 1985.

Elkin, A. P. "The Nature of Australian Totemism." In John Middleton, *Gods and Rituals*. University of Texas Press: Austin, 1967.

Endicott, Kirk M. *An Analysis of Malay Magic*. Clarendon Press: Oxford, 1970.

Evans-Pritchard, E. E. *Nuer Religion*. Oxford University Press: New York, 1977.

———. *Witchcraft, Oracles and Magic Among the Azande*. Clarendon Press: Oxford, 1976.

Field, M. J. *Religion and Medicine of the Ga People*. Oxford University Press: London, 1961.

Firth, Sir Raymond. *Human Types*. Abacus: London, 1975.

La Fontaine, Jean S. *Initiation*. Penguin Books: Harmondsworth, 1985.

Frazer, Sir James G. *The Golden Bough*. Macmillan: London, 1978.

Gasson, Raphael, *The Challenging Counterfeit*. Logos Books: New Jersey, 1970.

van Gennep, Arnold. *The Rites of Passage*. Routledge & Kegan Paul: London, 1977.

Gibb, H. A. R., and Kramers, J. H. *Shorter Encyclopaedia of Islam*. E. J. Brill: Leiden, 1974.

Goode, William J. *Religion Among the Primitives*. Free Press: Illinois, 1951.

Greinacher, Norbert, and Mette, Norbert. *Popular Religion*. T. & T. Clark: Edinburgh, 1986.

Guerber, H. A. *The Myths of Greece and Rome*. George G. Harrap: London, 1925.

Guerry, Vincent. *Life with the Baoule*. Three Continents Press: Washington, 1975.

Guinness, Os. *The Dust of Death*. IVP: London, 1973.

Hall, Marjorie, and Ismail, B. A. *Sisters Under the Sun*. Longman: London, 1981.

Hesselgrave, David. "Nichiren Shoshu Soka Gakkai." In *Dynamic Religious Movements*. Baker: Grand Rapids, 1978.

Hicks, David, *Tetum Ghosts and Kin*. Mayfield Publishing Company: Palo Alto, 1976.

Hiebert, Paul G. "Folk Religion in Andhra Pradesh." In Vinay Samuel and Chris Sugden, *Evangelism and the Poor*. Partnership in Mission—Asia: Bangalore, 1983.

———. *Anthropological Insights for Missionaries*. Baker: Grand Rapids, 1985.

———. "The Flaw of the Excluded Middle." *Missiology* 10, no. 1 (1982): 35–47.

Horton, Robin. "The Kalabari World-View: An Outline and Interpretation." *Africa* 32 (1962): 197–220.

Huber, Hugo. *The Krobo*. Anthropos Institute: Bonn, 1963.

Idowu, E. Bolaji. *African Traditional Religion*. SCM Press: London, 1974.

James, William. *The Varieties of Religious Experience*. Longmans, Green: London, 1910.

Jones, V. R. and L. Bevan. *Woman in Islam*. Lucknow Publishing House: Lucknow, 1941.

Juliusson, Per. *The Gonds and Their Religion*. University of Stockholm: Stockholm, 1974.

Keep, David. *St. Boniface and His World*. Paternoster Press: Exeter, 1979.

Kenyatta, Jomo. *Facing Mount Kenya*. Heinemann: Nairobi, 1982.

Kiev, Ari. *Magic, Faith and Healing*. Free Press: New York, 1974.

Kingsland, Rosemary. *A Saint Among Savages*. Collins: London, 1980.

Kluckhohn, Clyde, and Leighton, Dorothea. *The Navaho*. Doubleday: New York, 1962.

Kluckhohn, Clyde. *Navaho Witchcraft*. Beacon Press: Boston, 1967.

Krader, Lawrence. "Buryat Religion and Society." In John Middleton, *Gods and Rituals*. University of Texas Press: Austin, 1967.

Kraft, Charles H. *Christianity in Culture*. Orbis Books: Maryknoll, New York, 1981.

Lamphear, John. *The Traditional History of the Jie of Uganda*. Clarendon Press: Oxford, 1976.

Lang, Bernhard. *Anthropological Approaches to the Old Testament*. Fortress Press: Philadelphia, 1985.

Leach, Edmund. *Culture and Communication*. Cambridge University Press: Cambridge, 1976.

———. *Social Anthropology*. Fontana: London, 1982.

Leacock, Seth and Ruth. *Spirits of the Deep*. Anchor Press: New York, 1975.

Levi-Strauss, Claude. *Totemism*. Beacon Press: Boston, 1963.

Lewis, I. M. *Ecstatic Religion*. Penguin Books: Harmondsworth, 1971.

Martin, Marie-Louise. *Kimbangu*. Basil Blackwell: Oxford, 1975.

Mathur, K. S. *Caste and Ritual in a Malwa Village*. Asia Publishing House: London, 1964.

Mbiti, John S. *An Introduction to African Religion*. Heinemann: London, 1975.

———. *Concepts of God in Africa*. SPCK: London, 1971.

McGregor, Pedro. *The Moon and Two Mountains*. Souvenir Press: London, 1966.

Middleton, John. *Gods and Rituals*. University of Texas Press: Austin, 1967.

Miller, Elmer S. "The Christian Missionary: Agent of Secularisation." *Missiology* 1 (1973): 99–108.

Morris, Desmond. *The Soccer Tribe*. Jonathan Cape: London, 1981.

Musk, Bill A. "Popular Islam: The Hunger of the Heart." In Don McCurry, *The Gospel and Islam: a 1978 Compendium*. MARC: Monrovia, 1979.

Nussbaum, Stan W. "Toward Theological Dialogue with Independent Churches.'' University of South Africa, doctoral diss., 1985.

Parrinder, Geoffrey, *African Mythology*. Paul Hamlyn: London, 1967.

————. *West African Religion*. Epworth Press: London, 1949.

————. *Witchcraft: European and African*. Faber & Faber: London, 1970.

Pazzaglia, Augusto. *The Karimojong—Some Aspects*. EMI Books: Bologna, 1982.

P'Bitek, Okot. *Religion of the Central Luo*. Kenya Literature Bureau: Nairobi, 1978.

Prince, Raymond. ''Indigenous Yoruba Psychiatry.'' In Ari Kiev, *Magic, Faith and Healing*. Free Press: New York, 1974.

Radin, Paul. *Primitive Religion*. Dover Publications: New York, 1957.

Reid, Janice. *Sorcerers and Healing Spirits*. Australian National University Press: Canberra, 1983.

Richardson, Don. *Eternity in Their Hearts*. Regal Books: Ventura, 1981.

————. *Lords of the Earth*. Regal Books: Glendale, 1977.

Ro, Bong Rin. *Christian Alternatives to Ancestor Practices*. ATA: Taichung, Taiwan, 1985.

Robertson Smith, W. *Lectures on the Religion of the Semites*. A. & C. Black: London, 1927.

Royal Anthropological Institute. *Notes and Queries on Anthropology*. Routledge & Kegan Paul: London, 1951.

Savidge, Joyce. *This Is Hong Kong: Temples*. Hong Kong Government Publications: Hong Kong, 1977.

Schaeffer, Francis A. *Escape from Reason*. IVP: London, 1968.

Schwab, George. *Tribes of the Liberian Hinterland*. Peabody Museum: Cambridge, Mass., 1947.

Shank, David A. ''Mission Relations with the Independent Churches in Africa.'' *Missiology* 13, no. 1 (1985): 23–44.

Sire, James W. *The Universe Next Door*. IVP: Leicester, 1977.

Smalley, W. A. *Readings in Missionary Anthropology*. William Carey Library: Pasadena, 1974.

Smith, Margaret. *An Introduction to the History of Mysticism*. SPCK: London, 1930.

Steinbaur, Friedrich. *Melanesian Cargo Cults*. George Prior Publishers: London, 1979.

Sundkler, Bengt G. M. *Bantu Prophets in South Africa*. Oxford University Press: London, 1961.

Sutherland, Anne. *Face Values*. BBC Publications: London, 1978.

Taylor, John V. *The Primal Vision*. SCM Press: London, 1977.

Thomas, Keith. *Religion and the Decline of Magic*. Penguin Books: Harmondsworth, 1978.

Tippett, Alan R. *Solomon Islands Christianity*. William Carey Library: Pasadena, 1967.

————. *Introduction to Missiology*. William Carey Library: Pasadena, 1987.

————. "The Evangelisation of Animists." In *Let the Earth Hear His Voice*. World Wide Publications: Minneapolis, 1974.

Trigg, E. B. *Gypsy Demons and Divinities*. Sheldon Press: London, 1973.

Trimmingham, Spencer. *The Sufi Orders in Islam*. Oxford University Press: New York, 1973.

Turner, Harold W. *Living Tribal Religions*. Ward Lock Educational: London, 1974.

————. "New Mission Task: Worldwide and Waiting." *Missiology* 13, no 1. (1985): 5–21.

————. "Religious Movements in Primal (or Tribal) Societies." *Mission Focus* 9, no. 3 (1981): 45–55.

Turner, Victor W. *The Drums of Affliction*. Hutchinson: London, 1981.

Tylor. E. B. *Primitive Culture*. John Murray: London, 1871.

Underhill, Evelyn. *Mysticism: A Study in the Nature and Development of Man's Spiritual Consciousness*. Noonday Press: New York, 1955.

von Hagan, Victor Wolfgang. *The Ancient Sun Kingdoms of the Americas*. Granada Publishing: St. Albans, 1973.

Walker, F. Deaville. *The Story of the Ivory Coast*. Cargate Press: London, 1930.

Wallace, Anthony F. C. *Religion: An Anthropological View*. Random House: New York, 1966.

Warneck, Joh. *The Living Christ and Dying Heathenism*. Baker: Grand Rapids, 1954.

Weaver, Edwin and Irene. *The Uyo Story*. Mennonite Board of Missions: Elkhart, Indiana, 1970.

Weber, Max. *The Protestant Ethic and the Spirit of Capitalism.* Allen & Unwin: London, 1930.

Westermarck, W. *Pagan Survivals in Mohammedan Civilisation.* Macmillan; London, 1933.

Wimber, John. *Power Evangelism: Signs and Wonders Today.* Hodder & Stoughton: London, 1985.

Yutang, Lin. *My Country and My People.* Heinemann: London, 1962.

Zaehner, R. C. *Hinduism.* Oxford University Press: Oxford, 1966.

Subject Index

279

Author Index

Tribal Index